World Food

JAPAN

John Ashburne
Yoshi Abe

WORLD FOOD Japan
1st edition – February 2002

Published by Lonely Planet Publications Pty Ltd ABN 36 005 607 983

Lonely Planet Offices
Australia Locked Bag 1, Footscray, Victoria 3011
USA 150 Linden Street, Oakland CA 94607
UK 10a Spring Place, London NW5 3BH
France 1 rue du Dahomey, 75011 Paris

Publishing manager Peter D'Onghia
Series editor Lyndal Hall
Series design Brendan Dempsey
Layout Wendy Wright
Editor Joanne Newell
Mapping Natasha Velleley
Photography Oliver Strewe

Photography
Many images in this guide are available for licensing from
Lonely Planet Images. email: lpi@lonelyplanet.com.au

Front cover – Bukkake udon (cold thick wheat noodles) with condiments,
            Yamadaya udon shop, Kagawa Prefecture, Shikoku

Back cover – Waitresses behind the scenes at the Nadaman restaurant, in Tokyo's Imperial Hotel

ISBN 1 74059 010 4

text & maps © Lonely Planet Publications Pty Ltd, 2002
photos © photographers as indicated 2002

Printed by
The Bookmaker International Ltd
Printed in China

MAP KEY

○ Place to Eat & Drink	Freeway	✪	National Capital
Mall	Primary Road	◉	Prefecture Capital
Building	Secondary Road	○	Town
Campus	Tertiary Road	🏛	Museum
Park, Garden	Lane	卍	Buddhist Temple
Railway, Station	⛩	Shintō Shrine
International Border	Metro, Station	✝	Church
Prefecture Border	Tram, Station	▲	Mountain

About the Authors

John Ashburne lives in Kyoto where he lectures on Culture and Cuisine at the Friends' World Program East Asia Centre. He is currently growing soba (buckwheat) from seed, and aims to be the first Yorkshireman to open an outdoor rāmen stand. He is the author of several books on Japan, and a twice winner of the Mazda International Photo Contest. As well as *World Food Japan* he has authored Lonely Planet's *Japan, Tokyo,* and *Tokyo Condensed* guides.

John wishes to thank the countless people who helped this book come to fruition: First and foremost to Sasha, his copine de table and culinary co-explorer, without whose knowledge, support and encouragement it could never have happened. Thanks also to Akihiro Yamamoto, Akihiro 'Paki-chan' Yoshida, Barbara Stein, Claudia Marte, Fumihiro Izawa, Ginzo Kobayasi, Goemon, Gosuke Murai of the Miyako Hotel, Hiroe Izawa, Hiroshi Matsuda of Hamasaku, James Bampfield & Deepen, Jonas Borg, Kana Asafuji, Kiyoshi Yamada of Yamadaya, Luç & Lucy Briand, Maiko of Fujimamas, Mariko Tatsumi of JNTO, Masanosuke Tsuda, Masami 'Gambaru' Ito, Mas Izawa, Miyazaki-san of Kyō-ichi Rāmen, Michiko Yamamoto of Ichinomata Keikoku Onsen, Mitsugu Okuda, Mitsuru Narita of Sasagin, Morihiro Taniguchi of Furusato, Moriyasu Kishi, Muromachi Sunaba, Naoko Yamamoto, Oliver Strewe, Prof. Etsuro Ota, Rumi Ishikawa, Ryoko & Junko Tanaka, Sally McLaren & Kyoto Journal, Seiichi Hirata of Kyohei Rāmen, Shuji Tanaka, Stefano Bandini, Tadaomi Inoue, Takatomo Kawanishi, Tomio Motohashi, Ton-chan in Kochi, all in World Food at LP for their inimitable patience, Yoshihiro Konishi of Namaraya, Kyoto, Yuki Nakatsu, Yutaka Izawa, Yutaka Yoshida and the regulars of Jidaiya, and all the generous Japanese people who have invited me into their kitchens, restaurants and bars over the last 16 years. This book is dedicated to Joan, of the mighty dumplings, in whose kitchen I learned more than how to braise liver.

Yoshi Abe wrote the 'Eat Your Words' language section. He loves seafood and gets up before dawn to commute to Tsukiji fish market in Tokyo to catch the latest news from traders and look for seasonal ingredients. He is a maritime anthropologist and writer who specialises in the fishing industry and trade in gourmet items such as sea cucumber, shark fin and sea urchin. He is also a trained linguist, who has taught Japanese in universities in Australia, and edited and contributed to various Japanese language text-books. Yoshi is also author of Lonely Planet's *Japanese phrasebook* (3rd ed).

Yoshi wishes Japanese specialist Leonie Boxtel for her valuable advice and incisive observations.

About the Photographer

Oliver Strewe is a leading Australian food and travel photographer. His work in the area of wine and cuisine is featured worldwide in magazines and industry journals. He is based at Sydney's Bondi Beach with Tina and two surf crazed kids, Halley and Billy.

Oliver wishes to thank Shigeo Kimura, Hiroshi Kobayashi and Danielle Robertson of JNTO. A special thanks to Mike Lilly of JALPAK, Soren Bisgaard for the tea ceremony, Jonas Borg of Kyoto, John and Sasha, Deirdre Spahr, Mr and Mrs Izawa and Kana Asafuji for the use of their kitchen, Yoshikazu Masuda of the Shiba Park Hotel, Robert Harris and all the chefs, cooks and vendors – many thanks for their time and energy.

From the Publisher

This first edition of *World Food Japan* was edited by Joanne Newell and designed by Wendy Wright with assistance from Brendan Dempsey. Natasha Velleley mapped, Katharine Day proofed and Lyndal Hall oversaw the book's production, while Peter D'Onghia, manager, dealt with big picture issues. Many thanks to Yoshi Abe and Yukiyoshi Kamimura for their guidance on Japanese food and culture. Thanks to Lonely Planet Images for coordinating the supply of photographs, and for captioning, cataloguing and pre-press work. Thanks also to Andrew Tudor and the production services team.

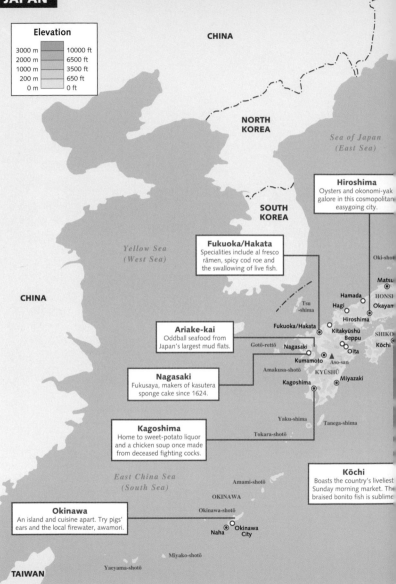

JAPAN

Elevation

3000 m	10000 ft
2000 m	6500 ft
1000 m	3500 ft
200 m	650 ft
0 m	0 ft

CHINA

NORTH KOREA

Sea of Japan (East Sea)

SOUTH KOREA

Yellow Sea (West Sea)

CHINA

Hiroshima
Oysters and okonomi-yaki galore in this cosmopolitan easygoing city.

Fukuoka/Hakata
Specialities include al fresco rämen, spicy cod roe and the swallowing of live fish.

Ariake-kai
Oddball seafood from Japan's largest mud flats.

Nagasaki
Fukusaya, makers of kasutera sponge cake since 1624.

Kagoshima
Home to sweet-potato liquor and a chicken soup once made from deceased fighting cocks.

Kōchi
Boasts the country's liveliest Sunday morning market. The braised bonito fish is sublime

Okinawa
An island and cuisine apart. Try pigs' ears and the local firewater, awamori.

Oki-sho

Matsu

HONSI

Hamada
Okayan

Hagi

Hiroshima

Tsu -shima

Fukuoka/Hakata

Kitakyūshū
Beppu

SHIKO

Kōchi

Gotō-rettō   Nagasaki

Ōita

Kumamoto   Aso-san

Amakusa-shotō   KYŪSHŪ

Miyazaki

Kagoshima

East China Sea (South Sea)

Yaku-shima

Tanega-shima

Tokara-shotō

Amami-shotō

OKINAWA

Okinawa-shotō

Naha   Okinawa City

Miyako-shotō

TAIWAN

Yaeyama-shotō

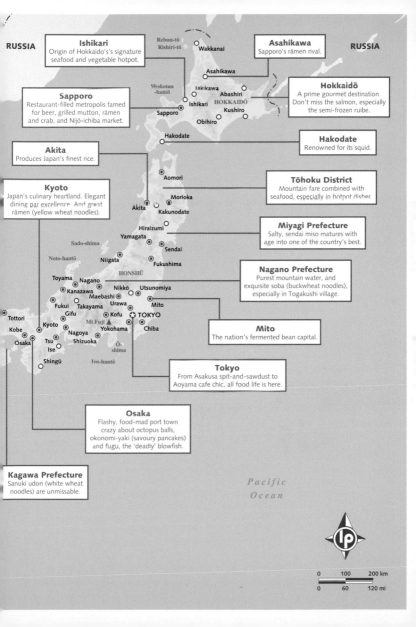

Yuki, a Japanese cook, sits slurping noodles in her favourite downtown Kyoto rāmen shop with a friend. As she noisily (and very appropriately) sucks up the yellow noodles, she nods in approval. "Nnn, koshi ga aru" – "They're just right, al dente, good texture." She turns a page of the magazine she's simultaneously reading (*Amakara Techō* – literally, the 'Sweet and Spicy Magazine'). "It's about, slurp, oysters – **kaki**. They're in season soon. The best are from Hiroshima. But Sendai's aren't bad."

She gestures towards the TV, which is showing a re-run of the immensely popular, no-expense-spared cooking contest *Ryōri no Tetsujin* ('The Iron Chef'). This show's theme is **ise-ebi** (lobster). "It's a fix," she opines, "the Chinese chef's best, but the Japanese guy always wins. Watch. He'll serve it raw, as sashimi, but on ice and in the shell. It'll look like it's still alive." And with that she turns back to 'How to Really Steam Oysters in Sake', and her favourite noodles … slurp.

She's not alone. The whole nation is obsessed with food, Japanese or otherwise. It permeates every walk of life, fills the airwaves and the bookshelves, and figures large in even the most casual of conversations. The seemingly casual, everyday phrase, "Gohan tabe ni ikō!" ("Let's go eat together!") is no mere suggestion akin to "Let's grab a burger". Rather, it's an invitation to commune over food, to bond in a primal act of mutual celebration, to reinforce group identities, or welcome outsiders into the fold. And, well, all the better if everyone gets blotto.

From **agedashi-nasu** (deep-fried eggplants) to **zōsui** (rice soup), from the succulent fresh salmon of Hokkaidō to the fiery, fermented bean curd of Okinawa, from the monosodium-glutamate-laden trucker's rāmen stand to the frostily elegant Kyoto **ryōtei** (high-class restaurant), Japanese cuisine offers something for everyone. There's variety, colour, texture, subtlety. There's the exquisite marriage of form and function, the immaculate presentation. There's … er, fermented soy beans.

Tomes have been written about Japanese food, not least on the delights of sushi, of the perils and pleasures of raw fish, and the health-inducing properties of everything from shiitake mushrooms to macrobiotics and miso soup. This book also covers these topics, but hopefully it goes beyond that, to reveal the areas of Japanese cuisine that generally go unheralded – its playfulness, its diversity, its quirky historical origins, its fascinating regional differences and specialisations, and above all, its role in defining and revealing Japanese culture. Let's eat, as they say – "itadakimashō!".

the culture of
japanese cuisine

To eat Japan is to understand Japan, from the discipline and rigour that epitomises Zen temples to the perfect centuries-old Kyoto **ryōtei** (high-class restaurants), to the humble farmhouse kitchen. Nothing in Japanese cuisine happens by accident – every last nuance, from the garnish to the wall hanging, carries meaning.

CULTURE

History

One can't help but feel the Japanese were predestined to be gourmands. Back in the early Jōmon period (see the historical periods boxed text, overleaf), early residents on the islands were living it up on shellfish sashimi. Not a bad diet for a group that had yet to discover the wheel. The remnants of their early feasts of **hamaguri** (Venus clams) have been found in many coastal areas.

Several centuries later, substantial villages had sprung up around freshwater springs, and the post-Paleolithic *plat du jour* swelled to include nuts, fruits, wild boar, fish and tubers. They were already eating the modern-day favourite **tai** (sea bream), and creating the sophisticated Jōmon cord-marked pottery that gives this period its name.

By 2000 BC they were hunting large fish, with their latest technical masterpiece, the toggle harpoon. Sea anemone became all the rage. Already, some 4000 years before the invention of the instant noodle, the basics of Japanese cuisine were beginning to take shape.

Rice was introduced from mainland north Asia, and towards the end of the Jōmon period the industrious folks of Kyūshū began to adopt a way of life markedly different from that of the northern islanders. They began wet rice farming.

Several hundred years later during the Yayoi period farming villages sprang up, united in the highly organised, closely cooperative work patterns that the new agricultural system demanded. Even the gods got in on the act, as tending the rice fields became regarded as a spiritual act, a worshipful invocation to, Ta no Kami, the god of the rice paddies.

The next sea change in Japanese cuisine came through contacts with China. By 239 AD, Japanese Queen Himiko of Yamatai was sending envoys to the kingdom of Wei in China, and soon wheat and barley were added to the list of culinary imports. Thes foods provided essential winter sustenance, and backup in case the rice harvest failed. Thus, some 300 years before they received Buddhism, they received the primitive versions of **udon** (wheat noodles) and **shōyu** (soy sauce).

A kimono-clad woman glides through the throng, Kyoto

It is not, however, until some 500 years later during the Nara period that we come across the first written record of a formal Japanese meal. This was the **daikyō**, the 'big feast'. It contained sea bream, carp, trout, octopus and pheasant, seasoned with shōyu, sake, vinegar and salt. The privilege of the ruling classes, daikyō was luxurious but simple, yet it gave rise to the **shiki shidai**, a highly ritualised way of serving food that came to characterise Japanese formal dining. It was at this time that the wonderful, aromatic **shiso** (beefsteak plant) started to be cultivated, and beef itself was expunged from the menu by decree of the Buddhist clergy.

Another Buddhist, the traveller monk Eisei, brought green tea and Zen from China at the beginning of the Kamakura period. At this time the nobility, despite their wealth, were in pretty poor physical shape, as their meals consisted of nothing but dried meat and dried fish. Ironically, the poor fared

rather better both gastronomically and nutritionally, as they soon came to eat **hishio** miso (possibly a type of grain miso), added to steamed and boiled fish, and **umeboshi** (pickled sour plums). Early in the period, the samurai (warrior class) still led a humble lifestyle, eating a meal called **ōhan**, consisting of plain rice with jellyfish, abalone and

Cherry blossom frames a decorative temple roof-line

umeboshi, seasoned plainly with vinegar and salt. As their political power and influence grew, their ōhan grew too, and within 200 years the Kamakura shōgunate (military rulers) was feasting on dishes that were once reserved for emperors. And although **shōjin-ryōri** (Buddhist vegetarian cuisine) had existed in some form since the 6th century, it was now that it became widespread with the popularisation of Zen, which demanded a spiritual practise even at the meal table.

The Muromachi period saw great cultural strides, as well as repeated political instability and bloodshed, as powerful rural daimyō (regional lords) successfully opposed central control. It was similarly a time of gastronomic rebellion. The increasingly wealthy samurai blended their own code of ethics and manners with those of the aristocratic class. Formal dining became more elaborate with **shikishō-ryōri**, which demanded specific cutting and serving techniques. This was the precursor to today's **honzen-ryōri** (celebration cuisine), a type of formal dining that consists of at least one soup dish and three side dishes. It is mainly found at weddings and funeral banquets.

CULTURE

A CULINARY INTERPRETATION OF JAPANESE HISTORY

Jōmon period *(ca 7500-ca 300 BC)*	Primitive coastal dwellers discover a liking for shellfish, starting a 9500-year trend.
Yayoi period *(ca 300 BC-300 AD)*	Rice becomes the food of the gods. And of a lot of humans, especially in Kyūshū.
Kofun period *(300-710 AD)*	The **kamado** (kiln-like oven) is invented.
Nara period *(710-94 AD)*	The Japanese begin to cultivate **shiso** (beef-steak plant), but stop eating beef. There are serious advances in tableware design.
Heian period *(794-1185 AD)*	A huge imperial court culture springs up in Kyoto. Moon-viewing parties are invented by nobility, who also start eating sweetfish ...
Kamakura period *(1185-1333 AD)*	Buddhist monk Eisei brings green tea and Zen from China
Muromachi period *(1333-1573 AD)*	Double cropping of rice and barley replaces the former, unpopular fad of crop-failure and starvation.
Azuchi-Momoyama period (1573-1600AD)	**Cha-kaiseki** (tea ceremony cuisine) becomes all the rage under star tea master Sen-no-Rikyū. Jealous Shōgun Toyotomi Hideyoshi promptly despatches him to the next life.
Edo period *(1600-1868 AD)*	Edo (later Tokyo) invents itself and its own cuisine, and starts slagging off Osaka and Kyoto, a rivalry that continues today.
Meiji period *(1868-1912 AD)*	All things western are groovy. Bovines ponder the temporal nature of the universe as Buddhists start bumping them off in droves, after a millennium or so of vegetarianism.
Taishō period *(1912-1926 AD)*	Between one and two million Japanese riot to protest against the price of rice. To no avail.
Shōwa period *(1926-1989 AD)*	Instant noodles fuel Japan's drive to become a world economic power. The **ichigo-sando** (strawberry sandwich) is invented.
Heisei period *(1989 AD-)*	Convenience stores and supermarkets wipe out the traditional mom-and-pop **yorozu-ya** (general stores). The nationwide **rāmen** (yellow wheat noodles) battle hots up with increased regional specialisation.

CULTURE

FOOD FOR THOUGHT

Before you study Zen, a bowl is a bowl and tea is tea. While you are studying Zen, a bowl is no longer a bowl and tea is no longer tea. After you've studied Zen, a bowl is again a bowl and tea is tea

Zen 'kōan' or riddle

Zen monks have long recognised the importance of food, and the act of eating, as part of their religious practise. The chief preparer of food in a Zen monastery, the **Tenzo**, was always an experienced monk, already firmly on the Zen path. Cooking and eating is a meditation and an opportunity for learning. When the great Zen master Dōgen-zenji wrote his *Tenzo Kyōkun* ('Instructions for the Zen Cook') in 1237, his observations went beyond "Take two eggs ...".

On the simple act of washing rice and cooking it, he wrote, "Keep your eyes open. Do not allow even one grain of rice to be lost. Wash the rice thoroughly, put it in the pot, light the fire and cook it. There is an old saying that goes, 'See the pot as your own head; see the water as your life-blood'". On whipping up a quick lunch, he wrote "Maintain an attitude that tries to build great temples from ordinary greens ... Handle even a single leaf of a green in such a way that it manifests the body of the Buddha". Remember *that* when you fix a pot of instant noodles.

Oh, and you gourmands, sorry but you've got it wrong. There's no good food and bad food, just food. **Kyō-ryōri** (the specialist cuisine of Kyoto) and KFC are equal, and we should be grateful to receive both.

To experience Zen cooking, and a taste of Zen discipline, join a four-day Sanrosha religious trainee retreat at Dōgen's Eihei-ji temple in rural Fukui Prefecture.

Towards the end of the Muromachi period and into the Azuchi-Momoyama period, **cha-kaiseki** (tea ceremony cuisine) was established under the patronage of tea master and culinary visionary Sen-no-Rikyū.

Rikyū's legacy is a remarkable one. His cha-kaiseki saw the popularisation of miso and mirin, and from this time **shun**, or seasonality, became a core consideration in Japanese cuisine. Director of tea ceremonies to the power elite of his age, including the tyrannical Oda Nobunaga and his scheming successor Toyotomi Hideyoshi, Rikyū transformed the **sarei** 'gathering to drink tea ceremonies' of the monks, begun by Dōgen at Eihei-ji temple in the 13th century, into a massively popular social custom. The **cha-no-yu** (tea ceremony) was formed. Rikyū replaced the refined and impossibly expensive Chinese tea utensils with common Japanese equivalents, putting the tea ceremony within reach of a much wider, although still privileged, audience. Rikyū also brought tea making into the tea ceremony room itself, creating a much more intimate and less formalised atmosphere.

By the time Rikyū, with another tea master, Tsuda Sōgyū, presided over Hideyoshi's legendary 10-day tea ceremony at Kitano-Tenmangū shrine in Kyoto in 1587 – invitation was by public edict! – the popularity of the tea ceremony was firmly established. Yet his association with the devious shōgun proved to be Rikyū's downfall. No one is quite sure why Hideyoshi forced him to commit suicide at Daitoku-ji temple, in 1591, but one suggested reason is that the aesthete Rikyū refused to bend to the ostentatious shōgun's taste in tea ceremony utensils. A less charitable theory says Rikyū overcharged him for a teapot.

A brief period of vigorous international exchange with the west took place during the Edo period, until shōgun Tokugawa Ieyasu grew wary of the growing influence of Christianity and stamped his policy of national seclusion on the nation. Chinese businessmen had been trading with Japan for centuries, and the Portuguese had come bearing their **kasutera** (yellow sponge cake), firearms, and legendary Basque Jesuit Francisco Xavier, but now Japan was closed. Limited trade was allowed through Nagasaki, where the Portuguese brought tempura and techniques for frying game, until 1639. After this time only the bachelors of the Dutch East India company were allowed to do business in the port enclave of Dejima off Nagasaki that was to be the sole opening to the west for about 200 years.

The new peace saw unrivalled prosperity, and the rise of a huge merchant class in the fast growing cities. A more laid-back variety of the tea ceremony

A tranquil tea moment

Kaiseki-ryōri (a multicourse meal originating from cha-kaiseki) became popular. Citizens flocked to the country's new capital, Edo (later called Tokyo), which, by the end of the 18th century, boasted a population of nearly a million people. A massive food industry sprang up to feed the newcomers and their august patrons, the residents of Edo-jō castle, with tempura and sushi leading the wave of culinary fashion. Many of modern-day Tokyo's finest restaurants date back to the Edo era.

It was around this time that the city's characteristic strong, salty **dashi** (broth) and its obsession with **soba** (buckwheat noodles) developed. The poor feasted on **shirauo** (icefish), which prompted the great wandering Haiku poet Matsuo Bashō to pen the following peian:

Frail fish, shirauo
You will splinter into nothingness
If you run into a rock

When Commodore Matthew Perry led four gunboats of the US East India Squadron into Edo Bay in 1853, Japan's isolation was over. Within four years, Izu had a reverbatory steel furnace. Within six Japan had British consul Rutherford Alcock, and his gun-toting countryman Thomas Blake Glover, who was only too happy to ply the pro-imperial forces of Satsuma and Chōshū with weaponry. Within a decade the nation had an emperor back in power.

During the Meiji period a modern industrial culture was born. Western fashions became all the rage, as did eating habits. Knives and forks appeared for the first time. The centuries-old Buddhist prohibition against eating beef was summarily ditched, as Japanese gentlemen in sebiro suits (from a Japanese pronunciation of 'Saville Row') tucked into all-the-rage beef, with gusto. Even the emperor succumbed to the fad, stating in 1873, "His Imperial Highness graciously considers the taboo [against meat eating] to be an unreasonable tradition". Favourite was the ubiquitous **sukiyaki** (beef, tōfu and vegetables cooked on a grill, served with a raw egg dip), which may have been introduced by Portuguese traders back in the Edo period. In his excellent *Taste of Japan*, Japan-scholar Donald Richie quotes food anthropologist Ishige Naomichi on the depth of meat addiction: "Beef became to food what, in a comparative sense, the orgy is to sex".

With the advent of the 20th century came militarism, grinding poverty, world war, Hiroshima and Nagasaki, and the non-punitive postwar reconstruction by the Americans. They left Hersheys, **meriken-ko** (American wheat flour), coffee, and a renewed penchant for things western, including western-style restaurants. These still survive today, with many unchanged from half a century ago.

The mixture of hard graft and invention that propelled Japan from devastation to the status of world economic power, in just decades, applied too to its domestic food industry. It was the age of the giants Kirin, Suntory and Asahi, but its undisputed champion was Nisshin Shokuhin, the company that in 1958 introduced Chikin Rāmen, and gave the world instant noodles. The company's success, and that of its competitors, was breathtaking. In the first year of sale, instant rāmen sold 13 million units.

Sushi, tempura and beans marinated in shōyu and tempura tsuyu
at Yamadaya udon restaurant, Kagawa Prefecture

A decade later it was shifting 4 billion packs a year. As writer Tanemura Suehiro points out, this "bastard offspring of emergency wartime conditions" resembled the freeze-dried sustenance that astronauts carry into space, but that did nothing to blunt its popularity among a workforce slaving through compulsory overtime in support of the Japanese economic miracle.

Today there are 53 thousand million cups of instant noodles consumed annually, 42 per head of the population. Twenty-four-hour convenience stores vend tasteless plastic dross to students working so hard in cram schools that they don't care what they eat. Yet Japan's fascination with food remains strong, with TV programs such as the *Ironman Chef* commanding audiences of millions, and the bookstore shelves groaning with food titles. Nearly 10,000 years after the Japanese ate their first Venus clam, they can't stop living, breathing, talking, and eating **washoku** – Japanese food.

Snow-covered Silverbirch, Hokkaidō

Geography

The Japanese may cling desperately to the edges of a mountain-packed, densely populated archipelago with a paucity of arable soil (at least relative to size), but it doesn't seem to have hindered the development of their cuisine. In fact, Japanese chefs have thrived in adversity, aided and abetted by some crafty agricultural techniques borrowed from their Korean and Chinese neighbours. Fish-filled oceans and rivers provide the natural source of staples (at least historically so), and the warm current from the south brings a regular influx of exotic species, and the yearly migration of the valuable, exquisite oceanic bonito. Rice is perfectly suited to the heavy rainfall of the rainy season, and even the thin alpine soils are at the perfect altitude for the cultivation of buckwheat. Hokkaidō's open pastureland provides dairy produce and vegetables.

The only fly in the geo-culinary ointment is the tendency for volcanoes to suddenly erupt, and for cataclysmic earthquakes to cruelly level farmland and cities alike. However, the Japanese are far too serious about their food to let a little seismic chaos spoil their dinner. They even harness it to cook **onsen-ryōri** (hot-spa cuisine). **Onsen-tamago**, eggs poached in thermal waters (especially alkaline waters), are simply exquisite.

How Japanese Eat

Japanese meals usually consist of many separate, small dishes. The individual offerings are all generally served at once, on a single lacquerware tray or table, with only miso soup and rice coming later. And there's *always* rice.

The absence of, say, rich French sauces, or intoxicating Indian spices, means that at first glance Japanese cuisine can appear rather bland. But the Japanese perceive food, and seasoning, in a different way. Most **nihon-ryōri** or washoku focus on the natural flavours of ingredients, which must be artfully 'drawn out' by the chef. Only at the last minute an addition of something like

Slurping down cup noodles

aromatic yuzu, or **sanshō** (prickly ash pepper) may occur, but this will always complement and enhance the natural flavours of the dish.

The Japanese food day starts with **asa-gohan**, literally 'the morning rice', or breakfast. In big cities this has become quite westernised, and you may find yoghurt and cereal, or at worst a slice of bleached, somewhat disappointing toast. The traditional Japanese breakfast, however, is savoury with lustrous rice, fried fish and that wonderfully aromatic miso soup. The minute you visit a rural community, expect a step back in culinary time, as chairs and kitchen counters once more give way to zabuton (cushions), tatami mats and low tables, and a more leisurely pace prevails. Eating a slow, simple breakfast of locally produced ingredients, in a minka (a rural, traditional farmhouse) is a great luxury, and one that is slowly disappearing. If you get the chance, take it. The traditional breakfast always followed a farmer's calendar (early, early) and still does. Another great joy of dining with a family in the countryside is that there's the strong possibility of the young hosts taking off to tend the rice paddies, while the grandad and grandma fuss around and spoil you outrageously. More often than not they'll bring out futon, or lay out more zabuton, and everyone will take a much needed post-prandial nap.

In the cities, women will prepare not only breakfast, but the **bentō** (lunchboxes) that their spouses and children take to the office and to school. Newlywed wives may prepare **aisai bentō** 'the loving wife lunchbox', complete with a heart-shaped pickle arrangement that is guaranteed to cause maximum embarrassment when discovered by fellow company workers.

CULTURE

Schoolkids dread the totally uncool poor man's **hinomaru-bentō**, plain rice with a single umeboshi at the centre, named after the Japanese flag. For **hiru-gohan** (lunch), rāmen, soba and udon shops, company or school canteens, or even the humble convenience store are all popular alternatives. Eating lunch at home is very rare.

Ban-gohan (the evening meal) is the one that the family is most likely to eat together. If families dine out together, it will mostly be at a **fami-resu**, the 'family restaurant' chains serving inexpensive, inexpressive, at times inedible *papier mâché* fare. They are at best fair, but are always handy. A popular twist of late are the sushi restaurants where each dish is a set price. A trip to a 'proper' sushi shop is reserved for special occasions. Couples without children, and young adults are most likely to head off to an **izakaya** (traditional restaurant-cum-bar).

Shun (Seasonality)

Take the **shun** out of Japanese cuisine, and it loses its soul. The Japanese are keenly aware of seasonality. It extends beyond your meal, to the choice of flowers in the tokonoma (recessed alcove), and, indeed, to the motifs at the bottom of your tea cup. Shun's importance grew from Sen-no-Rikyū's cha-kaiseki, but long before that, the poets and farmers of ancient Japan mapped out the year with reference to the harvests of field and sea. Concerned gourmets perceive today's obsession with convenience, including freezing food, as a serious threat to shun.

Using seasonal ingredients has long been a given in Japanese cuisine, and chefs will particularly concentrate on **suimono** (a clear soup), and **suikuchi** (its topping). When the customer opens the bowl of the suimono, they must be able to recognise the season. This has not always been as easy

as it sounds, as the only ingredient used in the clear soup garnish was **yuzu** (a type of citron). The chef would choose it according to season, when its colour would be yellow or green, or use the **yuzu no hana** (the flower of the yuzu), or even cut it to represent the shape of seasonal imagery. These days, leaves from the sanshō (prickly ash pepper), and **fuki** (Japanese butterbur) buds, are commonly used.

Beef and clear-seasoned soup

CULTURE

Presentation, Presents & Gift-wrapping

A glistening black lacquer rice cask set off in a dark corner is both beautiful to behold and a powerful stimulus to the appetite. Then the lid is briskly lifted, and this pure white freshly boiled food, heaped in its black container, each and every grain gleaming like a pearl sends forth billows of warm steam – here is a sight no Japanese can fail to be moved by. Our cooking depends upon shadows and is inseparable from darkness.

Tanizaki Junichirō, *In Praise of Shadows*

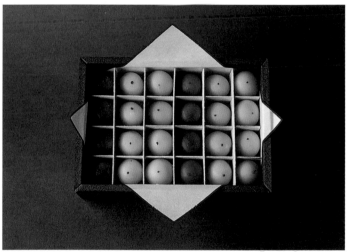

Exquisite Japanese sweets

Japanese cuisine is unashamedly visual. This applies to every meal, from humble **shokudō** (small, cheap eateries), to high-class **kaiseki-ryōtei** (restaurant serving tea ceremony cuisine). If something looks as though it has been plonked on a plate, you can guarantee it will taste poor. Yosou is the verb to 'dress up' or 'ornament' and is the formal word used to describe how food is arranged. Creating a harmony of colour, shape and texture is essential, and every element is considered from the food itself to the colour of the garnish to the shape of the dish. And in best Zen tradition, there must be **ma**, or space, that small element left forever to the imagination. Thus, **kaiseki** (a shortened form of 'kaiseki-ryōri' – Japanese formal cuisine) dishes are never completely full.

The Chinese-derived definition of a 'perfect meal', dating back to around the 3rd century BC, demands it contains the five colours – black (or purple), white, red (or orange), yellow and green; the five techniques – boiling, grilling, deep frying, steaming, and serving raw; and the five tastes – sweet, salty, sour, bitter and peppery hot. The Japanese embraced the concept, but replaced the peppery hot with their own – **umami**. An echo of the peppery hot taste is only found in **shichimi-tōgarashi** (seven spice mix) and sanshō.

Some sources, most notably the Japanese food giant Aji-no-moto, declare that umami is indeed a separate basic 'taste' with its own territory mapped out on the taste buds. International opinion remains divided, but Aji-no-moto's vested interest not-withstanding, it is undeniable that the 'tastiness factor' exists. It refers to the 'tastiness' of the amino acids of MSG (found not only in canteen kitchens, but naturally in **konbu** (kelp) and fresh tomatoes), and other amino acids and nucleotides in **niboshi** (dried anchovies) and **katsuobushi** (dried bonito flakes) and the sodium guyanilate of dried shiitake mushrooms. While food scientists duel over theory, the populace know what they have always known. These ingredients, at the heart of Japanese cuisine, taste absolutely marvellous.

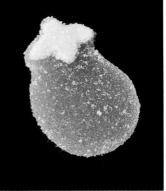

Jellied sweet shaped like an eggplant

The Japanese are proud of their cuisine, and the giving of food gifts is very common. These vary from souvenirs of trips in-country or overseas, to the mid-summer and year-end gift packages that companies present to cherished customers. If you are planning to visit Japan, a gift of your national or local speciality foodstuff or drink is wholly appropriate, though Aussies please note that a bottle of Hunter Valley semillon, or even a Darwin Stubbie, is universally preferred to Vegemite.

Accompanying the gift-giving is Japan's now legendary obsession with packaging. A cultural imperative that reaches an absurd pinnacle with Lipton teabags – each bag individually wrapped, then encased in paper, then clear plastic, then wrapped and put in your humble carrier bag. It might cause a small hiatus, but all you can do is say with a smile "sono mama de ii desu" or "sono mama de kekkō desu" – "I'll take it as it is".

Exquisitely elegant – the artistry of Japanese presentation

Etiquette

Much is made of Japanese 'politeness', although this may be a misconception. Japan observer Luc Briand has commented that "The Japanese are indeed a *formal* people, but mainly with their shoes off". He was referring to the social gatherings, where strict codes of behaviour must be followed. These include parties, formal dinners, weddings and funerals. Foreigners are rarely expected to observe every last detail. Indeed, if it becomes obvious that you are stressing about conforming to the detriment of enjoying your meal, the host will undoubtedly attempt to put you at ease by plying you with alcohol. Japanese parties often start with restrained formality, and end up with everyone three sheets to the wind, red-faced, and bellowing karaoke.

Getting in to a restaurant, or party hall, poses the first etiquette challenge. Who goes first? This will usually be the eldest person, or guest of honour. Most likely it will be you. Remember to bow as you're invited to go in first. The host will probably gesture with an open palm which direction you should follow. Bow slightly in thanks.

Negotiating the entranceway is the next hurdle. Taking your shoes off may require a small tightrope-walking balancing trick as you try to slip directly from your shoes into the slippers that are facing you. Once inside, walk to the tatami straw-matted room – and take your footwear off again. No slippers on the tatami, please.

The senior guest will be ushered to the low table, and invited to sit at the **kamiza**, the seat of honour, nearest the tokonoma. It probably has the best view of the garden, and the hanging scroll, or flower-arrangement in the tokonoma. At this stage there may be some debate among the guests over who the senior guest actually is, with hefty scientific calculations about age, status and seniority, along with lots of "please-you-sit-there"s and "oh-no-I-couldn't-possibly"s. If these leave you hanging around like a wet kikuna, a handy tip is to deftly admire the hanging scroll, until the chief guest is decided.

Things usually kick off with a toast, perhaps accompanied by a short speech, but more often than not just a quick "kampai!" ("cheers!"). Even if you don't drink, you're expected to pretend to take a sip. Someone (the host, or perhaps someone younger than you, or, especially if you're a man, a nearby female) will probably offer to fill your glass, in the drinking custom known as **henpai**. The done thing is to lift your glass from the table, tilt it towards the person offering you the beer, wait until the glass is filled, then put it down, and reciprocate. Then you drink together. This will continue through the meal, or party, often cwith several people coming to fill your glass. The polite way to signal you're in danger of keeling over is to cover your glass with your hand.

Trendy gals enjoying donburi (rice with shredded beef)

Before eating, you will be offered **oshibori** (hot towel, or cool in summer) with which to wipe your hands. It's considered rather boorish to use it to wipe your brow, but many people do that anyway.

At **kaiseki** meals, **sencha** (green tea) precedes the meal, and dishes arrive in a carefully prescribed order. A typical offering is **sakizuke** (hors d'oeuvre), **zensai** (appetiser), **suimono** (clear soup), **tsukuri** (slices of raw fish), **taki-awase** or **nimono** (stewed seafood and vegetables), **yakimono** (grilled fish), **aburamono** or **agemono** (deep-fried seafood and vegetables), **sunomono** (vinegared seafood and vegetables), **kōnomono** (pickles), **gohan** (cooked rice), **mizumono** or **mizugashi** (fruit) and **hōjicha** (roasted tea).

Then, of course, come the chopsticks. A little practise before you start never hurts. Depositing beans in a cup is the Japanese way. While there is a rather complex etiquette about how you hold the chopsticks, it's not worth losing sleep over. Many young Japanese adopt the casual, easiest way, and non-Japanese guests will be forgiven for doing the same thing.

There are a few no-nos, however. **Mayoi-bashi**, the 'lost and wandering' chopsticks, where you dab uncertainly at different dishes, is frowned upon.

Passing food from your chopsticks directly to someone else's is strictly taboo, as it mimics Japanese funerary practise. So is sticking chopsticks vertically into a bowl of white rice. Pointing at someone with chopsticks, despite the vehemence of your conviction, is not polite. In fact, it implies, "Do you wanna step outside?". Free-form jazz percussion using empty beer glasses is also frowned upon, though it is often hard to resist after the umpteenth bottle of Kirin. When you remove a food item to your plate from a communal bowl, it is proper to use the opposite, thick end of your chopsticks. This culinary back-hand is easy to forget, not least when you're ravenous. Should you inadvertently catapult a piece of raw squid across the banquet table, worry not. The Japanese themselves have been known to do this. Simply say "shitsurei shimashita" ("sorry"). Be careful too not to imitate the waiters and waitresses, who often say "shitsurei shimasu" ("excuse me") as they clear away empty dishes.

There are several more handy phrases to help you negotiate the behavioural minefield. Before you eat, say "itadakimasu", and after "gochisōsama deshita". The latter is a rather beautiful invocation, derived from Buddhist practise, which gives thanks to the cooks who ran around to gather all the ingredients. In informal situations it may be abbreviated to "gochisōsama".

A very common practise, and one that disgruntles many a non-Japanese visitor, is saying "oishii" ("that's delicious") after the first mouthful of any dish, *regardless of its quality*. This wee bit of gastronomic hypocrisy tends to drive some individualist, empirical-minded foreigners up the wall. It comes as second nature to the Japanese, though it makes their TV cooking shows somewhat repetitive. This 'false compliment' only applies to situations of some formality. Among friends, the Japanese are as quick as any to call a culinary spade a spade. If they're being nice they'll say "omoshiroi" or "omoshiroi-aji" – "an er, interesting taste", or if they're downright blunt, "mazui!" ("it's awful!").

If you think that someone is being overly complimentary, and you know they are teasable, there's a splendid food-related metaphor you can use to accuse them of brown-nosing. Pretend you are holding a bowl in your left hand, and make a circular clockwise movement with your right hand, as if grinding sesame, and say "goma-suri!". It literally means 'sesame grinder'. This was traditionally the position held by the youngest acolyte in a Buddhist monastery, the person who was always sucking up to the elder monks to try to get out of the horrible repetitive job. It always gets a laugh – unless, of course, it doesn't. Use with care.

staples
& specialities

Despite the mind-boggling variety of dishes throughout the island chain, the staples that make up Japanese cuisine remain the same nationwide – shōyu, miso, fish, vegetables and above all, the divine crop, rice. For starters, try beans that ferment to perfection, and raw fish as sublime as it is poisonous.

STAPLES

Rice (O-kome)

The Japanese don't just consume **kome** (rice) all day, every day. They venerate it. This may baffle visitors, not least the members of the US and Australian rice lobby who flock to Japan in droves to try and prize open Japan's lucrative rice market. Yet for the Japanese, foreign-produced rice just doesn't rate. It's Japanese-produced rice or nothing at all.

In its uncooked form it is called o-kome, with the o- denoting respect, and kome meaning rice. Cooked Japanese style, it is called **gohan** (the go- prefix here the highest indicator of respect), denoting rice or meal. Blue-collar workers,

> **Japanese Proverb**
> Who could ever weary of moonlit nights and well-cooked rice?

however, may use the more informal **meshi,** something akin to 'grub'. When it is included in the primitive fusion cuisine and fast-food favourite, **yōshoku,** (Japanese versions of western dishes) it is termed **raisu**.

Japanese-produced rice possesses amylopectin, an element that gives it its wonderful texture and slightly glutinous quality that the Japanese adore, to the extent that they each wolf down, on average, 70kg of it per year. Culturally, most Japanese feel a meal is simply incomplete without the inclusion of kome. It is the building block on which a Japanese meal is based, the heart of the Japanese culinary DNA.

Topped with prickly ash seed, a bowl of rice is the traditional Japanese staple

Yet rice's omnipresence is not merely a dietary or culinary convention. Rice cultivation was traditionally regarded as a religious act (see the History section of the Culture chapter), and even in ultra-modern Tokyo a child will often be taught to scoop a small amount of white rice from the suihanki (electric rice cooker) to offer to the spirits of deceased ancestors in the butsudan (the family's home altar).

Hakumai, or **jūbuzuki,** is plain, white rice (yet no Japanese writer would ever describe it as 'plain' – lucent, perhaps? Delicately scented? Robust even, but never plain) that is used in every dish from the humble **eki-ben** (station lunchbox) to the finest **kaiseki** (Japanese formal cuisine). A meal will consist of, for example, a bowl of hakumai topped with **tsukudani** (fish and vegetables simmered in shōyu and mirin), served with a bowl of miso soup, accompanied by a side dish of **tsuke-**

Sakura-mochi, a rice sweet, covered with a cherry blossom leaf

STAPLES

mono (pickles). **Genmai,** unpolished, unrefined, brown rice, is rarely spotted outside organic restaurants (with the notable exception of **shōjin-ryōri;** Buddhist vegetarian cuisine) as it lacks that fragrance and glow so desired of simple hakumai. Rice is used in **zōsui** (rice soup), in **ochazuke** (where green tea is poured onto white rice), in **o-nigiri** (the ubiquitous rice balls), and vinegared in sushi.

Mochi-gome is a glutinous version of regular rice that is used to make the sticky **mochi** (rice cakes), which are especially served at New Year (not always to best effect – 'choked on mochi' is an unfortunately common cause of death among the elderly). Mochi are extremely popular, and are served toasted as **yaki-mochi,** or wrapped in salted cherry leaves as **sakura-mochi,** a spring speciality of Kyoto.

Traditionally, rice was steamed in a large cauldron that was set over an earthenware hearth fuelled with wood choppings, in a **kamado** (the heart of a farmhouse kitchen). Today, style has succumbed to convenience, and nearly every restaurant and private home relies on the suihanki. Rice grains are rinsed thoroughly in cold water, swished by hand in a circular scooping motion until the mix loses its cloudy appearance. The grains are then placed in the suihanki with, in the case of hakumai, an equal amount of water (with genmai, 50% as much again). After cooking, it sits (in Japanese – **murasu,** which originally means steam) for 10 minutes, and the rice is then ready.

STAPLES

Mame (Beans)

Given the country's Buddhist history, it's no surprise that Japanese cuisine has long been dependent on this protein-rich food source.

Top of the Japanese beanpile is the indispensable soy bean, the **daizu** (literally, 'big bean'), which provides the raw material for miso, **shōyu** (soy sauce), **tōfu**, **yuba** (soy milk skin), and the infamous **nattō** (fermented soy beans; see the boxed text in this chapter). It also wends its way into such dishes as **hijiki-mame**, where black spiky seaweed is sauteed in oil, with soy and sugar, and **daizu no nimono**, soy beans cooked with **konbu** (kelp) and dried **shiitake** mushrooms.

Next is **azuki** the adzuki bean, (written with the characters for 'little bean') used extensively in preparation of **wagashi** (Japanese sweets), often for the tea ceremony, and in the preparation of **seki-han** (red-bean rice) used at times of celebration and to commemorate a teenage girl's first menstruation. **Kintoki** is a large red variety of azuki, often cooked in sugar, which is named for its resemblance to the red-faced legendary child Kintarō.

The broad bean, **sora-mame**, is used as a vegetable, as a savoury garnish, and in sweets. Other less-common varieties of bean are the **tora-mame** (tiger beans, named for its stripes) and **hana-mame** (the flower bean, named after the beautiful flower it produces).

An extremely popular variation on plain white rice is **mame-gohan**, dried (usually canned) peas cooked in rice.

Plastic-wrapped dried beans for sale, including tiger beans, red beans, white flower beans and small green adzuki from an asa-ichi (morning market) in Kōchi

Nattō (Fermented black soy beans)

There are plenty of cuisines that produce stinky, oddly textured delicacies. Japan's is nattō (fermented soy beans), marrying a stringy-gloopy texture with the smell of long-discarded sports socks. Kansai dwellers hate it, but Tokyoites lap the stuff up. We have to confess to being total converts, and even mix it with sliced spring onion and a raw quail egg (see the recipe below). The egg and onion bind the beans together, and slightly lessen the stink. Try it. When you qualify as a certifiable nattō-nut, you'll crave that gorgonzola-in-the-car-boot effect, for sure.

Ingredients

50g	**nattō** (fermented black soy beans)
1	raw quail egg
1	small spring or welsh onion, or leek
1 Tbs	shōyu-based **dashi** (stock)
1¼ tsp	Japanese mustard (optional)

Place the nattō into a small, deep bowl. If you can arrange them into a 'peaked' mountain shape, all the better. Slice the spring onion as thinly as possible, and add it to the nattō. If you prefer a less acidic taste, soak the spring onion in water for 5 minutes first, then drain. Break the quail egg onto the nattō and spring onion, trying to keep the yolk intact. If quail eggs are not available, a regular egg, but only its yolk, will do fine. Add the mustard. If Japanese mustard is not available, English mustard (not French) is an acceptable substitute. Gently pour the shōyu-based dashi on the top. Take chopsticks and, in a rapid circular motion, whisk all the ingredients into a froth, and eat. This recipe works for any type of nattō, but the black bean variety is the most visually arresting.

When the strings connecting the nattō and chopsticks refuse to break, rotate the chopsticks, mid-air, in a circular motion, as that will be sure to liberate the beans.

Serves 1

Miso

A precursor of miso arrived on the Japanese mainland from China sometime around 600 AD, not long after Buddhism. Its inhabitants have been gargling it down as misoshiru ever since, at breakfast, lunch and dinner. Made by mixing steamed soy beans with **kōji** (a fermenting agent) and salt, miso is integral to any Japanese meal, where it is likely to be present as **misoshiru** (miso soup) or as a flavouring. It is also used in **dengaku**, where it is spread on vegetables such as eggplant and **konnyaku** (devil's tongue – see Root Vegetables later in this chapter).

There are three types of miso: the most common **kome-miso** made from rice; **mame-miso** made from soy beans, most common along the Tokai coastline of Honshū; and **mugi-miso** a barley miso popular throughout Kyūshū (except in Fukuoka, where they too make **kome-miso**).

Misoshiru is made of a mixture of **dashi** (stock) and miso, and shellfish such as **shijimi** (freshwater clams) or **asari** (short-necked clams); vegetables such as **daikon** (giant white radish), carrot or burdock (especially good for the digestion); pork; or simply tōfu. In preparation it should never boil, and is most often served with a topping of sliced spring (or welsh) onion, or **mitsuba** (Japanese wild chervil). Good **shijimi misoshiru** combined with the aromatic pepper **sanshō** is a heavenly combination, and good for your liver.

Some would argue that you can recognise a person's birthplace by their choice of miso. The dizzyingly salty **sendai-miso** of rural Miyagi Prefecture is a countryman's creation. A gorgeous ruddy brown, it can be kept, and indeed matures with age. **Shinshū-miso** from Nagano Prefecture in the Central Alps is less wild, less salty, with a much-praised slightly tart quality. **Edo-miso** is dark, fiery red, slightly sweet, and is as forthright and resolutely unpretentious as the Edokko (Tokyo-ites) who are its chief consumers.

Hatchō-miso has its own much-told history. It was initially made in the Hat-chō area of Okazaki, Aichi Prefecture, where it continues to be produced. It was shipped to Tokyo (then Edo) by the ruling elite family, the Tokugawa, who came from the Okazaki area and, naturally, were proud of their home-grown product. The Edokko were hugely underwhelmed, shipped it back, and developed their own.

Kyoto shiro-miso is a delicate, sweet and aristocratic white miso that inhabits the rarefied world of **kyō-ryōri** (Kyoto specialist cuisine). In particular, it is used in making **o-zōni** (see the Celebrating with Food chapter), a miso soup containing **mochi** (rice cakes).

When miso is not used in a soup, it is often used as dressing for **aemono** (cooked leafy vegetables, poultry or fish blended with the dressing) and **nimono** (simmered dishes). Combined with rice vinegar, white miso becomes **su-miso**. Both can accompany mountain vegetables and river fish.

Slurping down a hearty dish of miso-rāmen, Kōchi

Miso is an essential source of protein, calorie free, Buddhist-friendly and packed with salt. It has also proven effective in treating radiation victims. One cannot help but wonder what thousands of Ukrainians thought on receiving hundreds of tons of the stuff from the Japanese government in the wake of the Chernobyl disaster.

Agedashi-dōfu (Deep-fried tōfu)

Ingredients

2	blocks **momen-dōfu** (firm tōfu)
20	**ao-jiso** (green beefsteak plant) leaves
2 Tbs	sesame oil
	wheat flour

Sauce

½ cup	**dashi** (broth)
3 Tbs	shōyu
3 Tbs	mirin
1 Tbs	grated **daikon** (giant white radish)
1 tsp	grated ginger

Drain the water from the tōfu. The best method is to press it between two chopping boards tilted towards the sink. Leave it like this for half an hour, or until all the water has drained away. Then cut each block of tōfu into four cubes. Slice the ao-jiso quite finely, and fry it in the sesame oil over a low-to-medium heat for 3 to 5 minutes (make sure the oil is not so hot as to make the leaves crispy). Pat the tōfu with kitchen paper to remove the surface water, and dust it with flour. Fry the cubes in the oil over a medium-high heat until the tōfu becomes golden brown. Heat the dashi, shōyu and mirin in a separate pan, and place the tōfu in a deep-sided bowl. Top the tōfu with the daikon, ao-jiso and grated ginger, and add the dashi mixture slowly (from the side), so as not to disturb the presentation.
    Serves 4

Tōfu

Tōfu is oft-maligned in western countries, largely as a result of the plastic-wrapped, porridge-like goo that was passed off in its name in health-food stores in the 70s. Yet tōfu is one of Japan's most sublime creations. Best of all is to get up with the larks, and head down to your local tōfu maker for post-dawn, freshly made, creamy tōfu that is still warm.

Kōya-dofu, burdock root, yam and carrot served in lotus-shaped bowls

Tōfu is sold as the soft 'silk' **kinugoshi** and the firm **momen (or momengoshi)**. The former is mainly used in soups, especially misoshiru. The latter is eaten by itself, deep-fried in **agedashi-dōfu** (see the recipe in this chapter) or used in the Kyoto classic **yudōfu**, a hotpot dish. Both momen and kinugoshi take their names from the technique when the hot soy milk is strained – if the material used is cotton, the resulting firm tōfu is momen; when silk ('kinu') is used, it's kinugoshi.

A classic way to eat tōfu is as **hiyayakko**, cold blocks of tōfu covered with soy, grated ginger and finely sliced spring onion. This is a favourite on the menus of **izakaya** (traditional restaurants-cum-bars).

Abura-age is thinly sliced, especially thick tōfu traditionally fried in sesame oil (more recently, however, producers use salad oil or soy bean oil). It is a key ingredient in the celebratory **chirashi-zushi**, and in **inari-zushi** (where vinegared rice is stuffed into a fried tōfu pouch), named after the fox-deity and rice-god that protects shrines throughout the country, the most notable being Fushimi-Inari Taisha in Kyoto. Kyoto is indeed tōfu heaven, with the temple areas of Nanzen-ji and Sagano particularly famous.

The monks of Kōya-san in Nara make their own distinctive greyish, thick **kōya-dōfu**, (sometimes called **kōri-dōfu** – freeze-dried tōfu), always served cold. It was reputedly first made by Buddhist patriarch Kūkai, in the 9th century, who freeze dried the tōfu outdoors on a clear winter night.

Yuba (soy milk skin) is a staple of **shōjin-ryōri** (Buddhist vegetarian cuisine) and a speciality of Kyoto. It is a marvellous accompaniment to sake, when it is served fresh with grated wasabi and shōyu **tsuyu** (dipping sauce). Its creation is a time and labour intensive process, in which soy milk is allowed to curdle over a low heat, and then is plucked from the surface using either chopsticks, or equipment especially designed for the process. Lazy types can buy it pre-packed, and dried it is added to soups.

Shōyu (Soy Sauce)

Surprisingly, shōyu is a relatively new addition to Japanese cuisine. Although a primitive form of, **hishio** was made in the Yayoi period (see the historical boxed text in the Culture chapter for period dates) by mixing salt and fish. Shōyu in its current form dates back to the more-recent Muromachi era. It only achieved widespread popularity somewhere between 1603 and 1867 when it was first exported to Europe. Unsubstantiated rumour has it that Louis XV was one of the west's first avid shōyu fans.

Twentieth century mass production made a household name out of Kikkōman, but shōyu is still made, using traditional methods, at small companies throughout the country. It comes in two forms: the dark brown 'thicker taste' **koikuchi-shōyu**, and the chestnut-coloured 'thinner', much saltier **usukuchi-shōyu** (sweetened and lightened by the addition of mirin). Koikuchi is used for a variety of applications, especially in the Kantō region around Tokyo, and is perfect for **teriyaki**, where meat or fish is brushed with shōyu, mirin and sugar, and grilled. The aromatic usukuchi-shōyu, a favourite of the Kansai region, is best suited to clear soups and white fish. It is especially important in enhancing the colour of a dish's ingredients.

Regional variations include the thick, wheat-free **tamari-jōyu**, which contains only soy beans and salt. It was once the shōyu made in rural homes, but is now comparatively rare. It is generally made in Central Honshū, particularly in Fukushima Prefecture, and is used mostly with **sashimi** (raw fish), and in making the sauce for **unagi no kabayaki** (grilled eel) and **shottsuru**, a striking shōyu made from fish in Akita Prefecture.

The importance of shōyu lies not merely in its use as a condiment – it is integral to many cooking and pickling processes, and tsuyu, the linchpin of Japanese noodle cuisine.

Mirin

Mirin is used extensively in Japanese cuisine, and is most often referred to as 'sweetened sake' (although as Professor Richard Hosking, the author of *A Dictionary of Japanese Food*, most accurately points out, it isn't – it is the liquid formed from a mash of glutinous rice mixed with malted rice and **shōchū**, a distilled spirit). It is primarily used as a sweetening agent and is preferred over sugar. This is because the inclusion of mirin adds depth to **dashi** (stock) and sauces. It contains around 13% to 14% alcohol, though this is often largely burned off prior to use, especially in **sunomono** (vinegared food) and **aemono** (cooked leafy vegetables, poultry or fish blended with a dressing), whereupon it is called **nikiri-mirin**. Mirin was once served as an alternative to sake, and the good stuff, usually called **hon-mirin**, is still sold in sake shops today. If you fancy a swig, Japan's classiest, smoothest mirin is rural Aichi Prefecture's Mukashijikomi.

Men/Menrui (Noodles)

Japan must be the only country in the world where museums dedicated to noodles reach into double figures. The phrase "menrui wa amari suki ja nai" ("I'm not too keen on noodles") is heard about as often as a crooked politician's admission of guilt. Everyone has a favourite restaurant (preferably unknown to anyone else), a favourite dish, a favourite stock, even a favourite convenience store variety, and the endless discussion fuels a huge media industry. Noodle TV? Only a matter of time. And the hype is justified. Japan's noodles may not match Italy's in variety and scale, but in quality, subtlety, presentation, and sheer style, they know no equal.

Soba (Buckwheat Noodles)

The aristocratic star in the Japanese noodle firmament, **soba** (buckwheat, or buckwheat noodles) was long thought to be a relative newcomer to the archipelago. But the buckwheat plant has recently been discovered in spore form, in burial tombs dating back to the Jōmon period. No doubt this has caused high excitement, academic outrage and possibly even a bit of scientific skullduggery in the closeted world of Japanese noodle archaeology. Until the discovery there was popular debate over whether the noodle was really invented at Seiun-dera in Yamanashi Prefecture, or 60km or so up the road in Kiso, Nagano Prefecture, sometime around 1596. Or was it 1614? Or ...

Oblivious to academe, the general populace slurps on, equating soba with Nagano in general, and Togakushi village in particular, both famed nationally for **shinshū-soba.** Other major soba areas include Izushi, renowned for **sara-soba**, which is soba served on many individual plates, and Iwate Prefecture, with its all-you-can-eat **wanko-soba**, where noodles are served in small bowls with **tsuyu** (dipping sauce) and accompaniments.

Buckwheat's popularity arose not with its delicate aroma or distinctive, subtle, elegant-but-earthy taste, but with its ability to deter starvation. It grows in thin mountain soils where nothing else will, and, with its rapid 75-day passage from seed to grain, it made an excellent backup whenever the rice crop failed. It is also packed with nutrients, protein, and heaps of vitamins such as C, B and E.

Soba noodles are traditionally sliced by hand, to make **teuchi-soba**, but as the dough breaks easily when stretched after kneading, a binding agent (usually wheat) is added, or the soba is sliced by machine. A ratio of 20% wheat flour to 80% buckwheat is said to produce the finest results, though some purists swear by the dark 100% buckwheat.

Soba can be eaten hot or cold. Seasonal preferences apply, but cold soba always carries a slightly snooty air: if you order pricey **tenzaru** – **zaru-soba** (plain, cold soba with dried **nori** seaweed) with tempura, usually prawn, with its own separate tempura tsuyu – it implies you mean business.

Hot soba comes in a bowl of shōyu, mirin, sugar and **dashi** (stock). Cold soba comes on a bamboo grid to be dipped in separate cold, stronger tsuyu. You add ingredients such as grated **daikon** (giant white radish), sliced spring onion, pounded yam, bonito flakes, **yuzu** (the wonderfully fragrant Japanese citron), and, ubiquitously, wasabi.

Popular cold dishes include zaru-soba and **mori-soba** (like zaru-soba but without dried nori). Hot favourites are **tempura-soba,** and **kamo-nanban** and **tori-nanban,** featuring duck and chicken respectively, with sliced spring onion. Another is the exquisite **sansai-soba,** whose mountain vegetables perfectly complement a delicate broth and the subtle buckwheat flavour.

Adding a final touch to the proceedings are condiments, generally **sanshō** (the gorgeously aromatic, aniseed-like Japanese pepper), and also **shichimi-tōgarashi** (seven spice mix).

Udon (Thick White Wheat Noodles)

Udon, or o-udon to give it its Sunday name, is made from strong wheat flour that is mixed with salt and water, kneaded well, and stretched and sliced. Another arrival from China (in the Nara period), it was long a staple before soba appeared.

Today the white wheat noodles are found nationwide, in forms either fat, thin, round, or flat. One popular regional variation is Nagoya's flat **kishimen** served in a miso broth. On Shikoku island, Tokushima's famed **sanuki-udon** is often sold at self-service restaurants, where the customer steams their own noodles and dips them in the tsuyu, along with ingredients of their own choosing.

As with soba, udon is served hot with tsuyu or cold without, but a popular option is **kama-age-udon,** where hot noodles are dipped into a cold tsuyu. Other favourites are the cold, simple **hiyashi-udon; bukkake-udon,** with its cold tsuyu on the udon itself; **nabeyaki-udon,** a hotpot-style mix of vegetables and shrimp; and **misonikomi-udon,** which is like nabeyaki but has a miso broth.

Kama-age-udon, in traditional lacquer ware, with a dipping sauce

Sōmen (Thin White Wheat Noodles)

A close relative of udon is the wonderful summer noodle **sōmen**. Also made from wheat mixed with salt and water, it contains sesame or cottonseed oils (depending on the region), thus, despite its 'lightweight' refreshing image, it is quite high in calories. It is always hung to dry in sunlight, one of the Japanese winter's most evocative late-afternoon sights. Miwa village in Nara is the sōmen mecca, producing a very thin noodle called **miwa-sōmen**. There are similar regional variations in Kawachi, south Osaka and the island of Shōdoshima in the Inland Sea. The thinnest noodles are called **ito sōmen**, while Tochigi Prefecture's Nikkō produces a fat version, **nikkō-sōmen**.

While udon dough rarely has other ingredients added to it, sōmen often has additions, including green tea in **cha-sōmen**, egg yolk in **kimi-sōmen**, shrimp in **ebi-sōmen** and kudzu (where starch is extracted from the kudzu vine) in **kuzu-sōmen**.

Rāmen (Yellow Wheat Noodles)

Rāmen is Japan's national-dish-in-hiding. Unless you've seen the late, great Itami Jūzo's rāmen-western – and peian to the noodle – *Tampopo*, you probably still toil under the mis-assumption that Japan's favourite meal is sushi. Well, partner-san, get on your horse, drink your soup, and think again ...

OK, OK, it came from China. But so did green tea and just about everything else in this book. Rāmen's proletarian image is probably the reason its massive impact is not so well-publicised, though the reality is that rāmen shops are no longer solely the haunt of truckers and gangsters on the lam. These days, you're just as likely to rub shoulders with a bank manager or a student of a private girls' college.

'Rāmen' is an amalgam of the Chinese word meaning 'to stretch' and the Japanese suffix for noodles, '-men'. The stuff's popularity is enormous, with rāmen shops galore, instant rāmen noodles a multibillion yen business, and rāmen yatai (itinerant street vendors), a picturesque and welcome nocturnal stop-off in all major cities. Fukuoka in Kyūshū is especially famous for these, which run into the thousands.

At the heart of good (and bad) rāmen is the dashi, made from chicken bones or pork bones, with the addition of vegetables, shōyu or miso. Stocks range from a light, less greasy stock, to a thick, garlicky version. A chef wishing to create a subtle, delicate stock may use the expensive dried fish, such as the Japanese sardine, which is used in udon stock preparation. Occasionally the rāmen world throws up its culinary Magellans and Columbuses who explore radically new directions – one massively successful Yokohama chef currently employs tuna in his stock.

Rāmen types fit into four basic categories, each with a distinctive origin: **shōyu-rāmen** (soy rāmen), from Tokyo; **shio-rāmen** (salt rāmen) and

A bowl of nishin-soba (buckwheat noodles topped with herring)

miso-rāmen (rāmen in a miso broth), both from Sapporo; and **tonkotsu-rāmen** (rāmen in a white pork broth) from Kyūshū.

The noodles are made from wheat flour mixed with egg, and, present in most rāmen, is kansui, an alkaline mixture. The noodles are kneaded, left to sit, then stretched with both hands.

The noodles are cooked, then served in a hot soup, with toppings such as sliced pork, bean sprouts, pickled Chinese bean sprouts, spring onion, **naruto-maki** (thinly sliced white fish-cake with a pink, whirlpool-shaped inset) and nori. With tonkotsu expect cloud-ear fungus, boiled egg and **beni-shōga** (red pickled ginger). Curly noodles, in a Taiwanese style are called **chijire-men**, and should you like your rāmen 'al dente', make sure to specify you'd like **katame**.

Rāmen doesn't pretend to be a health food. If you live in mortal fear of MSG, avoid rāmen like the plague.

Dashi (Basic Stock)

A great **dashi** (stock) is essential, as it is the crucial element in soups, dipping sauces, **nimono** (simmered dishes) and **nabemono** (hotpot dishes), and for cooking fish and vegetables. Typically it is made from either **katsuobushi** (dried bonito) or **konbu** (kelp). Its role in enhancing the flavour of food is paramount, and good chefs guard the precise details of their dashi ingredients with a zest bordering on paranoia. Stocks may also be made with **shiitake** mushrooms, shellfish, or small fish such as sardines. Often these are added to a basic katsuobushi or konbu dashi.

Katsuobushi is easy to spot in a Japanese market. It is the thing that looks least like fish – it is more like a piece of driftwood. The Japanese have been drying bonito since ancient times, when the summer fish was dried to preserve it for the winter season. Today's katsuobushi, however, most probably dates back to 16th century Tosa (now Kōchi), when it was used as troop rations for itinerant samurai during the Warring States period (1477–1573). Superstitious warriors also enjoyed the play on words that makes 'katsuobushi' sound like 'katsu-bushi' or 'victorious samurai'.

Superstition attaches itself to the humble bonito in several other ways. It is still a common gift at New Year and is given to teething babies so that they will develop perfect teeth. More often, though, it is grated either by hand, for dashi, using a plane (the same as a carpenter's plane), or by machine in the marketplace. Ready-shaved katsuobushi is convenient, but less tasty.

Konbu was first harvested in Japan around the 6th or 7th century, and was an early export to China. But it was not until 1000 years later that the black, shiny **ma-konbu** ('true' or 'proper' konbu) began to be collected in earnest on the southern and eastern shores of Hokkaidō. Its dashi became instantly successful in the Kansai region, and in particular in Kyoto, where it appealed to the Buddhist chefs preparing strictly vegetarian temple cuisine (**shōjin-ryōri**). It was especially liked for its health-giving properties and its suitability for use with tōfu.

Katsuo and konbu stocks are both prepared in the same way. The water containing the ingredients is brought to the boil, after which the heat is immediately turned off. The flakes slowly sink to the bottom of the pan, and the liquid is filtered through a muslin sieve. It is important not to squeeze the katsuo or else the stock will become bitter. When making a soba dipping sauce, however, a slight amount of bitterness is considered desirable.

Traditionally, there's a two-step process in dashi making. **Ichiban-dashi**, the first stock, is created out of fresh materials, and is used in clear soups, to impart an aromatic element. **Niban-dashi** is a second use of the initial ingredient – it is much lighter tasting and is used with miso soup, and in nimono and vegetable preparation.

Uminomono (Seafood)

Japan's historical dependency on the sea is best illustrated in its use of fish, and shellfish. Alas, seafood catches are dropping alarmingly through overfishing and poor management. Recently, in a supermarket on the western coastline of Ishikawa's Noto-hantō peninsula the shelves were packed with imported Norwegian cod. Local communities, though, are aware of the need to preserve what resources remain.

Sushi

It may be the country's most successful culinary export in terms of fame, but sushi is, despite the hype, rarely done well outside its homeland. Corners are cut in terms of rice authenticity, shōyu quality and freshness. And somehow the great Tokyo chefs resist the lure of big bucks and west-coast climates, in favour of cramped grubby apartments with a sort-of view of the Sumida River. OK, we exaggerate, but the exceptionally great sushi is found in Japan – certainly the really great *affordable* sushi – and the greatest of the great is in Tokyo.

Sushi is not raw fish. It refers to anything served on, or within, vinegared rice. The most likely ingredients are fish or shellfish (mostly raw, but not exclusively so), raw vegetables or cooked egg.

There are differing views on sushi's origins. Some say it came from South-East Asia, others say it came from China. Either way, it was, essentially, a pickling technique, where fish was salted and encased in rice and left to mature (some would infer 'rot') for up to a year. This original method, which is recorded as reaching Japan in the mid-Heian period, remains the basis for such dishes as Shiga Prefecture's strong, some would say stinky, **funa-zushi** (carp sushi). However, sushi as we know it today originated in the early 19th century sushiville itself: Edo (later called Tokyo). Contemporary sushi falls into four broad categories: **nigiri-zushi** (hand-pressed sushi), **maki-zushi** (rolled sushi), **chirashi-zushi** ('scattered sushi') and **oshi-zushi** ('pushed sushi'), a Kansai speciality.

Nigiri-zushi, where toppings are pressed onto rice dabbed with wasabi, originated in Tokyo. Typically it is placed directly on the white wooden counter, accompanied by **gari** (pickled, pinkish-red ginger), whereupon you dip it in shōyu, the classic way to eat sushi. It is the most elegant, visually appealing, and expensive part of a sushi menu, and the one you order first. Toppings such as raw squid and octopus; shrimp (raw as sweet shrimp, or cooked); cod roe (raw, surrounded by nori) or sliced egg-omelette are favourites. Luxuries include conger-eel brushed over with teriyaki sauce, an exquisite crunchy-soft combination; sea urchin; and the sake-lover's favourite accompaniment, **kani-miso,** that is, er, crab reproductive organs.

Nigiri-zushi, slices of fresh, raw fish pressed onto rice, and maki-zushi, served in a seaweed roll, accompanied by pickled ginger

The latter loses something in translation, but it is really rather magnificent. Imagine a kind of dark olive-green caviar-without-the-crunch, tinged with the scent of a diver's antique respirator ... just try it.

Maki-zushi, the familiar nori-wrapped torpedo (or triangular cornet-shaped concoction), is always the sushi shop's cheaper-end offering, but price shouldn't be confused with quality. **Shiso-ume-maki** (sour plum with beefsteak leaf) is a fabulous aromatic-meets-sour, nori-meets-succulent-rice delight. Kappa-maki with cucumber is equally humble and delicious. Maki-zushi is rolled in the makisu, a bamboo mat. It is eaten, facing a propitious direction, at the Setsubun demon-exorcising festival in February (see the Food Calendar section of the Celebrating with Food chapter).

Chirashi-zushi, sometimes called **bara-zushi**, is traditionally eaten at celebrations. Vinegared rice is topped with **shiitake** mushrooms marinated in shōyu, sliced omlette, **beni-shōga** (red pickled ginger), and other ingredients, designed to be especially pleasing to the eye.

Oshi-zushi is sushi pressed into a wooden mould, then sliced. It's best known form is **battera-zushi**, a strong, deliberately 'fishy' mackerel dish.

Sashimi from the Miyako Hotel, Kyoto

STAPLES

Sashimi (Raw Fish)

Sashimi, or **tsukuri**, as it's called in Kansai, is a key component in Japanese formal cuisine, not least in **kaiseki-ryōri** (a multicourse meal). It is also a regular on sushi-shop menus, and eaten at home as a small luxury. Freshness is paramount, and in the best restaurants expect to have the fish, squid or octopus fished from a tank and sliced before your eyes. **Ikizukuri** is a common way of offering sea bream. It is laid out between the head and tail, and skewered in its death throes on an elegant porcelain dish.

More often, sashimi is simply arranged, with garnishes typical of the season, on a dish. Sea bream, cod, yellowtail, octopus and squid are commonly used. You dip the fish, perhaps wrapped in an **ao-jiso** (green beefsteak plant) leaf, into strong shōyu (often **tamari-jōyu**, a wheat-free shōyu) containing wasabi and **benitade** (water pepper), a dark red peppery garnish. Even ordinary fish deserves the best shōyu, and freshly grated wasabi. Sashimi is not solely used to refer to fish. It also refers to thinly sliced raw meat (a la carpaccio), as in Kumamoto's speciality **basashi**, an abbreviation of **basashimi** (raw horse meat).

Yaki-zakana (Grilled Fish)

The classic Japanese way to serve fish is **shio-yaki** (grilled with salt), which is simple but endlessly satisfying and gives full reign to the flavours of the fish itself. The grilled fish is served with shōyu, perhaps containing grated daikon and citrus, perhaps **sudachi** or **yuzu** (citrons). **Sakamushi** is an interesting variation for which the fish is steamed with sake.

One of Japan's most marvellous fish dishes is **katsuo-tataki**, which is a speciality of Kōchi Prefecture. Tataki refers to the process for which fresh bonito fillets are briefly grilled over charcoal, while the inside is left raw with pink, fleshy meat. The bonito is then thinly sliced and served with sliced onions, garlic (lots of it), grated ginger, spring onion and ao-jiso.

Hokke-yaki (grilled atka mackerel) with grated daikon (giant radish) and lemon, served on a bamboo grass leaf

Saltwater Fish

As a cheap source of protein, the **hokke** (atka mackerel) became popular during WWII. This grey fish with light brown stripe, caught off Hokkaidō and Northern Honshū, winter to spring, has a high fat content. It is best grilled, especially with a teriyaki sauce, deep fried, or served as nimono (simmered). Hokke is also made into fish paste and as bait for tropical fish.

Hirame (flounder or flatfish with eyes usually on the left of its head) and **karei** (flounder or flatfish with eyes usually on the right) are easily confused. Hirame is best from autumn to winter, with **kan-birame** (coldest season hirame) considered the very finest. Its light white meat is expensive. Generally, flounder is used in nimono, sashimi, **mushimono** (steamed dishes), **furai** (dishes where fish, prawns or meat are crumbed and deep-fried) and **itamemono** (stirfried dishes). In both Kōchi and Ōita Prefecture it's called **oya-nirami**, 'the fish that gave its parents a dirty look' and was thus cursed to have its eyes on the same side of its body.

Of the 11 Japanese species, the **ma-garei** taken on the Hokkaidō and Japan Sea coast is the most common karei. Another is the **mako-garei**, caught from southern Hokkaidō to southern Japan. When caught in the Beppu Bay off Ōita Prefecture, this fleshy, especially tasty variety is called the **shiroshita-garei** 'the flounder from beneath the castle', as it is rumoured to have once fed in the fresh waters beneath the Kinoshita fiefdom castle.

As the eye-placing distinction is unreliable, the best way to tell a karei from a hirame is to look for a smaller mouth. The smaller the fish body, the better the taste. It is served as **kara-age** (dusted in flour and deep-fried), **nitsuke** (a dish where fish or vegetables are simmered, leaving little liquid), shio-yaki, and also as sashimi if the fish is fresh enough.

Buri (the yellowtail or amberjack) weighs up to 15kg and is especially good as sashimi, grilled, or served as teriyaki (brushed with mirin, shōyu and sugar, then grilled).

Best in autumn and winter, it is eaten at New Year in western Japan, first as sashimi, then added to **o-zōni** (a soup with rice cake in it).

There are over 100 varieties worldwide of **tai** (sea bream), long regarded as Japan's finest, most auspicious fish. Its high rank in the fish stakes is reinforced by the play on words of 'o-medetai' meaning, loosely, the 'wish-to-congratulate fish' and is present, symbolically or actually,

Sashimi served in a lacquer ware box

at wedding ceremonies. **Madai** is considered the best type of sea bream. Peach-red in colour, plentiful in the Sea of Japan and Inland Sea (but scarce on the Pacific side), it reaches up to 1m in length. It is best in early spring, and is used in sashimi and yakimono (grilled dishes) and also in clear soup.

Saba (the Pacific mackerel) is a beautiful, mother-of-pearl hued fish. Along its back is a silvery black stripe, which turns pale blue to silver along the side of the body, then changes again to a delicate pink underbelly. It is the key ingredient in Osaka's **battera-zushi**, Kyoto's purposely 'ripe' **ki-zushi** (also called **shimesaba**), and in Kōchi's **saba-no-sugata-zushi**, where the fish retains its original, multi-hued shape. Found throughout Japan, and best in autumn, saba is also used in misoni (fish simmered in miso stock) and as shio-yaki.

Chidai, literally, 'blood tai', is bright pink, and smaller than the madai. The slightly yellowish **kidai**, is inferior to the above, but cheap. It is served as shio-yaki not sashimi. Another poor man's sea bream is the **kurodai**, the black bream or porgy. Best in April, it is somewhat 'fishy' so is served as shio-yaki. This is the same fish served in Italy as **orata**, with olives or salt.

The spectacular-looking **matōdai** (John Dory) is found in central and southern seas of Japan, and is easily recognised by the big black spot on its side, hence its Japanese name 'target' – the 'mato' is the target in traditional longbow archery. Best in winter, it is good as teriyaki and **miso-zuke** (pickles in miso).

The **amadai** (tilefish) is in season from October to March. Red amadai and white amadai are the best quality, yellow amadai being less tasty. Wrapped with ao-jiso leaf and deep-fried as **kushi-katsu**, amadai is simple and exquisite.

The **nishin** (herring) is not as widely used as in Europe, though it is found most famously in Kyoto with buckwheat noodles, in **nishin-soba**. Its female roe is dried to make the delicacy **kazunoko**, while the herring itself is mostly served as shio-yaki.

If nishin's associations with Kyoto lend it a faded nouveau riche dignity, pity the poor unheralded sardine. In Japanese its name, **iwashi**, means 'weak fish', from its tendency to get scoffed by bigger, nastier fish. However, its ability to proliferate in huge numbers has long made the sardine a cheap staple in Japanese cuisine. Small and good in June, larger from August to October, sardines make good, cheap sashimi. Traditionally, street vendors filleted it in front of customers' houses, though these days the custom is very rare. It is also used in tempura, and as **dango** (round balls made from rice and flour). Boiled and sometimes dried, anchovies or small sardines are served with shōyu as **chirimenjako**, an **izakaya** (traditional restaurant-cum-bar) staple.

Yet the sardine is not just a cheap lunch. Its true nature is revealed in its role as a key ingredient in that most fundamental item of Japanese food – **dashi** (stock). Discover a great, clear, deep, light stock, and the chances are that it's a humble sardine at work.

The Japanese characters for **aji** (horse mackerel or jack), combines 'sakana' (fish) and 'san' (the word for 'three'), indicating that it was traditionally caught in the third month, March. As 'aji' is also a homonym for 'taste', it has long been held in high esteem. Now taken all year, it is most prolific in west Japan from spring to June, in east Japan from May to July, and is used as sashimi, shio-yaki, **sunomono** (vinegared food), and nitsuke.

The Japanese love **katsuo**, the oceanic bonito (or skipjack). Bonito grow to 2.5m in length, though those caught in Japanese waters rarely reach half that. The real giants are bought from Australia.

Katsuo appear in January and February in the warm Ogasawara islands, riding the warm current up to the Sanriku-oki islands (Aomori) from August to September. In autumn they finally reach Southern Hokkaidō, and then turn back south towards the mainland of Honshū. These big **kudari-gatsuo** (descending bonito) have the finest tasting meat, best of all in May. Katsuo are especially famed in the waters off Shikoku, especially in Kōchi Prefecture. Katsuo is served as **tataki** (charcoal-grilled on the outside), and as teriyaki and sashimi. Most of the catch, however, goes into making **katsuobushi** (dried bonito flakes), for use in dashi.

The greasy biker of the fish world, the **kawa-hagi** (leatherjacket), with its tough outer skin, is used in nabemono, soups, and furai. The liver is especially prized. In Wakayama Prefecture it is called **tsuno-hage** ('bald horn'), in Niigata Prefecture **kōmori** ('the bat'). Famed for its expense, and

deadly propensities (see the Are You a Culinary Devil? boxed text in this chapter), the **fugu** (pufferfish or blowfish) comes in several varieties, and is most famously caught in Western Honshū's Shimonoseki, or in Kita-Kyūshū, from late autumn to February. When the rapeseed blooms, it is called **natane-fugu**, indicating the end of the season, when it is tastiest and most poisonous. **Tora-fugu**, the 'tiger fugu', is preferred, and is used as sashimi and in the **nabemono** (hotpot dish) known as **chiri-nabe**. **Tessa** (fugu sashimi) is sliced so thinly that you can see the design on the porcelain dish beneath. Just enough of the poison is left in the fish to slightly numb your tongue. **Fugu-shirako** (fugu milt) is also a sake accompaniment, and in **hire-zake** the pufferfish's toasted fins are served in hot sake.

S(h)ake (dog salmon) is usually termed **shiro-zake** ('white sake'), because of its white meat, although in Hokkaidō it is called **aki-aji**. Most Japanese people assume this comes from the phrase for 'autumn taste'. However, it really originates from the indigenous Ainu name, **akiachip**. This large, handsome fish reaches a length of up to 1m, has a silvery dark blue back, and silvery white belly. River salmon is best in October, with high seas' salmon best for eating from early May to late June. Sake is served a number of ways, and most sake is salted as **shio-zake**, and grilled, made into **namasu** (steeped in vinegar), used in nabemono, or steamed with sake (the rice wine) as **sakamushi**. It is also used fresh, in sushi. The roe is also salted, creating a boozer's delicacy.

The grotesque deep-sea **ankō** (angler fish) is mostly used in nabemono. It is not cut on a cutting board, but while hanging. Caught in the cold season, and tastiest from November to February, it is especially famous in Mito, Ibaraki Prefecture, which has its own ankō cuisine. Oddly, its skin and guts are tastier than its flesh.

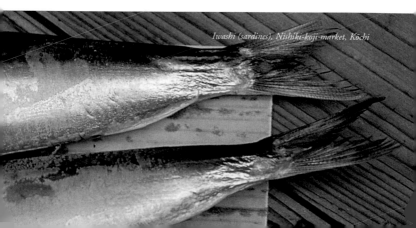

Iwashi (sardines), Nishiki-koji-market, Kōchi

STAPLES

ARE YOU A CULINARY DAREDEVIL?

There are few cuisines that actively threaten to dispatch you into the next life. Japan's famed, poisonous blowfish or pufferfish, fugu, will happily do so. Its ancient nickname is the teppō, 'the pistol', from its ability to bump off careless eaters. Its active ingredient is tetrodoxin, a clear, tasteless, odourless poison 13 times stronger than arsenic. One species of fugu contains enough to kill 33 people. Specially trained chefs remove most of the poison, leaving just enough to numb your lips. No one ever pisses off fugu chefs.

Yet some consumers actively choose to poison themselves. How's this for bold? A good friend's grandfather, a man of somewhat decadent sensibilities, would eat fugu liver (a practice now outlawed), and slip into a state of semi-paralysis for three days! The near-death sensation was, it seems, rather agreeable, and he was always somewhat disappointed when he regained full control of his limbs. Lonely Planet Publications wishes to remind the reader – DO NOT TRY THIS AT HOME.

Fugu, life-threatening as it may be, at least has the saving grace of having shuffled off its own mortal. No such luck with 'dancing-eating' or odorigui, however, the practice of wilfully consuming live animals. It originated in Fukuoka and the chosen Fukuoka victim is usually shirouo, a small transparent fish, which at least wriggles to its suffocating oesophagal doom half-drunk, washed down with sake.

Really bold diners can try the same thing with an octopus. In a Gunma sushi shop I once fatally left the ordering to 'friends', who grinned malevolently and asked the chef for the 'special'. He promptly lifted a poor cephalopod from a large tank on the counter, sliced up one tentacle, put it on a plate with soy sauce, and passed the still twisting and writhing limb to yours truly. The sensation, as the suckers attach to the roof of your mouth, is impossible to convey. Equally difficult to put into words is how it feels to try to murder an octopus leg by chewing it to death.

Same sushi shop. Same evening. It got worse. Dismayed by my refusal to pass out, the said friends brought out the big guns in the shape of shirako. Staring at the frothy, white objects shaped like pasta-spirals but exuding an unmistakable deep-sea odour, I feebly requested a translation. Poker-faced Mr Suto offered the deadpan "cod sperm". I ate. I turned green. I drank large quantities of cold beer.

That was 15 years ago. Since then I have consumed many strange dishes, and survived. But it's only now that I can recognise Mr Suto's translation error. Shirako is not "cod sperm" at all. It is the "sperm-filled reproductive gland of the male cod". Enjoy!

John Ashburne

The **tobiuo** (flying fish) is a warm-sea fish found in southern Japan, famed for its prodigious leaps and constant year-round flavour. Also called **tsubame-uo** (the swallow fish) or **tombo-uo** (dragonfly fish), its light, low-fat meat is good as teriyaki and shio-yaki. It is an ingredient in **kamaboko** (blocks of minced, steamed white fish meat).

Famed for its ability to predict earthquakes – not kidding, the nation's top seismology labs all keep 'em – the freshwater **namazu** (catfish) is at its best in winter, when it is used in nabemono. It is bewhiskered and rather jovial looking.

The tasty **hamo** (pike-conger) is scary-looking, with its sharp mouth, and teeth like a hacksaw blade. Caught in Kansai, especially in Kyoto and Osaka, hamo is a summer delight, but one that is best eaten in a restaurant because it's a murder to debone. Especially good is **hamo no bainiku-ae**, where the boiled fish is immediately plunged into ice water. It is also used in sushi, **suimono** (clear soup), sunomono, and **sanshō-yaki** (where the hamo is grilled then dusted with powdered prickly ash pepper). Specimens reach up to 2m, but the 60cm to 80cm varieties are tastiest.

Anago is the conger-eel, and literally means 'The Child of the Hole', referring to its nocturnal underwater habitat. Ma-anago, caught throughout Japan, is the best tasting. **Kuro-anago**, a black-bodied eel, the largest of the species, growing up to 1m in length, is mainly used in kamaboko and is found in southern waters. The **gin-anago** is a short, overweight version.

Kantō dwellers shun **bera** (wrasse), but this fish is a Kansai favourite, especially the **kyūsen** or **sasanoha-bera**, good for shio-yaki and nitsuke. It is best from early summer to autumn.

Taken in the southern part of Chūbu, **hata** (grouper), another early summer to autumn fish, is used in sashimi, and is also good for nitsuke.

In Akita and Hokkaidō if they don't eat **hatahata** (sandfish) it's not yet winter. Its name incorporates 'sakana' (fish) and 'kaminari' (thunder), so in Akita is called **kaminari-uo** (lightning fish) as thunderstorms regularly appear during the spawning season. It is the main ingredient in **shottsuru** (fermented fish sauce), and is eaten as tempura and shio-yaki.

It is taboo for pregnant women to eat **bora** (grey mullet), due to its dirty estuarine image. However, if you're not expecting, it makes excellent **miso-yaki**, or **saikyō-yaki** (grilled, topped with a sweet miso paste), and is at its best in winter, when it's called the **kanbora**. It is too smelly for sashimi.

A recent addition to the world's endangered species list, **tara** (cod) is literally 'the snow fish', after its white belly. Renowned for greedy behaviour, it gives rise to the Japanese epicurean phrase 'tarafuku'- loosely, 'to be as stuffed as a cod'. For sashimi it must be extremely fresh, otherwise it is good in nabemono and as shio-yaki. Particularly delicate is the clear, low-salt soup **tara-no-ushio-jiru**.

STAPLES

Kairui (Shellfish)

Sazae (whelk) is a strong-tasting gastropod, served as **tsubo-yaki** (in its shell grilled over a direct heat), from which you extract the muscle with a toothpick. It's a common accompaniment to sake. Be warned that the intestines and reproductive bits at the end of the muscle are also eaten, and are extremely bitter. The tradition has long been forgotten, but sazae used to be ceremonially offered, and eaten, at the **Hina Matsuri** (Girls' Festival) on 3 March each year.

The **awabi** (abalone) is a transgendered shellfish, (both male and female), best eaten as sashimi. It is a typical summer delicacy in high-class ryōtei or sushi shops. The **asari** (short-necked or baby clam) sports beautiful patterns and is yellow, red or purple. It is best from winter to early spring and is commonly used in miso soup, nabemono and **tsukudani** (fish and vegetables simmered in shōyu and mirin). **Bai(gai)** is a type of whelk, 7cm in height, especially good from Toyama Bay. It comes in sunomono, **aemono** (cooked leafy vegetables, poultry or fish blended with a dressing), tsukudani and yakimono.

In everyday Japanese, **ebi** (prawn or shrimp) refers to any number of sea- or river-dwelling edible 10-legged crustaceans. **Ama-ebi** (literally, the 'sweet prawn') is another Toyama speciality, where it is always on any sashimi menu. Best raw, it can't be found in Kantō. Its sweetness and soft texture doesn't appeal to all tastes. The **botan-ebi** is a good winter prawn, the colour of peony flowers ('botan' means peony), taken south of Hokkaidō's Uchiura Bay and down into Tōhoku from October to May. Born male, it later turns female, and is best, regardless of gender, as sashimi.

Sakura-ebi (small, dried shrimp)

To find the large **kuruma-ebi** (tiger prawn) in nature, hunt carefully on the Pacific coast, or on the Japan Sea coast south of Aomori, though few remain in the wild. Larger specimens (up to 20cm) are grilled, and fried in the popular **ebi-furai**, but smaller ones (**maki**) are used in tempura and as sashimi. **Ise-ebi** (Japanese spiny lobster, or crawfish) is taken in Ise Bay, and eaten at New Year as it has a long beard and curved back, symbolising long life. A tasty, expensive treat, ise-ebi is good as sashimi, yakimono, nimono, furai, and in salads. **Shibaebi** is a greyish white shrimp, caught in Tokyo bay's Shibaura, hence the name. It is excellent for tempura, sushi topping and sunomono. The cutey **sakura-ebi** (cherry shrimp), just 3cm to 4cm long, is best from mid-spring to late spring when it is used as sashimi, or dried. Once caught by the boatload in Suruga Bay off Shizuoka, pollution has all but killed it off. The enormous **taishō-ebi** ('Taishō prawn') or '**kōrai-ebi**' ('Korean prawn') is now caught in the East China Sea and imported frozen. It is not as good as kuruma-ebi, but it is large (up to 27cm), and cheap, often featuring in lunchtime **teishoku** (set menus). It was first eaten in the Taishō period, which must make it the world's only crustacean named after a historical timespan.

The **hamaguri** (Venus clam) was the first shellfish ever eaten in Japan. This spring speciality is caught in clean sea water, on the northern coast west of Hokuriku, and in Tokyo Bay, Ise Bay, the Seto Inland Sea, and the Ariake sea. Chestnut-shaped (its name means 'beach chestnut'), it features large in Hina Matsuri cuisine to suggest chastity (never opened) and also fidelity (its two halves perfectly matched). Hamaguri need to be washed well, then are often grilled in the shell with yuzu (citrus). The flesh is used in nabemono, and furai.

Hotate-gai (scallop) literally means 'the shellfish with the standing sail', referring to its style of crossing the seabed by opening and closing its shell. This large bivalve is taken mainly in Hokkaidō and Tōhoku where it is sometimes called **akita-gai** or **ōgi-gai**, the fan-shaped shellfish. It is served grilled or as sashimi.

The **i-gai** or **mūru-gai** (mussel), taken mainly in Hokkaidō and the Inland Sea, from winter to early spring, has a venerable history. It gets a mention in the Heian-period diary *Tosa Nikki*, where it is described as 'sushi', although it is not eaten that way today. It is mainly included in misoshiru (a soup made from miso paste and fish stock), sunomono and as **shōyu-yaki** (grilled with shōyu).

The **taira-gai** (fan shell or sea pen) is more correctly called the **tairagi**. It is famed for its resemblance to a piece of Heian-era headgear, the **eboshi** (a sort of single, spiked dunce's hat). In season from autumn to early spring, it is taken in Tokyo Bay, Ise Bay, and the Seto Inland Sea. It is eaten as sashimi, sunomono, shio-yaki, teriyaki, furai and sauteed in butter.

The **baka-gai** (surf clam or hen clam) is known as **aoyagi**, as it was often harvested in Tokyo's Aoyagi-mura village. The original name – used in Kansai and elsewhere – means 'idiot mollusc'. The flesh is said to resemble a face, with a red mark signifying a lolling tongue. Often it is simply boiled very lightly, or served as sashimi or sunomono.

STAPLES

Kani (Crabs)

Crab is a winter favourite, especially in Hokkaidō (see the Regional Variations chapter). It is usually cooked in nabemono with boiled or steamed vegetables. As **kani-zu**, crab is boiled and eaten with a vinegar dipping sauce, such as ginger vinegar or **ponzu** (a mix of dashi, shōyu, vinegar and citrus juice). When the flesh from below the claws is dipped into hot soup, or boiling water (as in **kani-shabu**), this is referred to as **hanasaki-gani** – the 'flower opening' crab, from the way the crab meat slowly expands and opens (just to confuse matters, hanasaki-gani is also a variety of king crab, a spiky-haired specimen found off of Nemuro, in Hokkaidō). There are many regional varieties, including **ke-gani** (horsehair crab), which is the common nickname for the **ōkuri-gani** (literally, 'giant chestnut crab'), which is famous in Hokkaidō.

One of the tastiest crabs is the **zuwai-gani**, which is taken on the Japan Sea coast, especially off Fukui and Ishikawa Prefectures (it is also called the **echizen-gani** after the Echizen coastline). In Kansai it is called **matsuba-gani**, the 'pine-leaf' crab. It is exquisite when steamed very fresh, and dipped in ponzu. Tottori's matsuba-gani cuisine and Fukui's echizen-gani cuisine are well known. Crab aficionados go for the legs.

Freshwater crab are found in pure waters throughout the archipelago. Most common are **sawa-gani**, which are often deep-fried – still wriggling – as kara-age. It's long armed cousin, the **Nihon tenaga-ebi**, is found in Kōchi where it is served with sansai cuisine.

Ke-gani (horsehair crab) for sale at a street stall in Sapporo

Ika (Squid)

Squid comes in around 100 edible varieties. The most popular is **surume-ika** used to make **surume** (dried squid). Surume is available from winter to spring, and all varieties of squid are served as sashimi, in **nigiri-zushi** (hand-pressed sushi), as yakimono, furai and tempura. **Shio-kara** (whole squid , entrails and all, pickled with salt and allowed to mature) is considered a sake-lover's delight.

Hotaru-ika are tiny squid often served as **ika-meshi** – stuffed with steamed sticky rice and simmered in shōyu, dashi, sake and sugar (found in **eki-ben** – station bentō boxes).

Tako (Octopus)

Varieties include the Seto Inland Sea's **ma-dako**, best in January and February, the large **mizu-dako**, most often taken in Hokkaidō and the small **ii-dako**. The latter 'rice octopus' gets its name for the cross-section of a sliced, mature specimen, where the ovarian tissue resembles rice grains. Superstition has it that octopus tastes better if you beat it into submission (it's already dead actually) with a **daikon** (giant white radish). Specimens from near Akashi in the Seto Inland Sea are especially prized. Octopus is rarely served raw in sushi restaurants. It is usually grilled or steamed, where it is often cooked in, or served with, a shōyu- and sake-based sauce. In Osaka, it appears as **tako-yaki** (flour balls with octopus filling – see Osaka in the Honshū section of the Regional Variations chapter). You can even eat it live (see *odorigui* in the Are You a Culinary Daredevil? boxed text earlier in this chapter).

Tako-yaki (flour balls with octopus filling)

STAPLES

Kawa-zakana (Freshwater Fish)

The origin of the word **unagi** (eel) is delightfully improbable. It could come from a combination of the 'u' of ushō, meaning cormorant fisherman, and 'nangi' meaning difficult, in the sense of difficult to catch, ie, slippery. But Tsukiji fish market dealers provide a more plausible explanation, believing it comes from 'muna-gi', meaning 'chest-yellow' (the fish has a yellow belly during the mating season).

Frequently the main subject of Rakugo (comic storytelling), eel is most auspiciously eaten during the dog days of summer, especially on a day corresponding to the bull in the Chinese zodiac, when it is believed to convey vigour and vitality. Eels are sliced down the back in Kantō, and down the belly in Kansai, further proof that these regions belong to very different culinary universes.

Long ago, eel was grilled on a skewer. More popular now, however, is the charcoal-grilled **kabayaki**, which takes its name from its colour, reminiscent of the kaba (birch tree), and is served in a teriyaki sauce. It is also often served as a donburi-dish, **una-don** (grilled eel on rice).

The eel-like **dojō** (loach) is actually related to carp. Found in rivers and lakes in Honshū, Shikoku, and Kyūshū, especially the latter's Yanagawa, its numbers are declining. Popular in Tokyo, it is usually served as nabemono **yanagawa-nabe**, as **dojō-jiru** (loach soup), as nimono or yakimono.

Local fishermen fix their nets at Yasuda Gyokō, a port in Kōchi Prefecture

The **shishamo** (Japanese capelin, or smelt) is an **izakaya** (traditional restaurant-cum-bar) favourite, not least in south-eastern Hokkaidō, where it spawns in estuarine waters in October. The female fish are prized for their tasty roe. Usually sold salt-dried, they make excellent inexpensive shio-yaki, tempura and furai.

Japanese anglers' best-loved river fish are the **iwana** (char), **yamame** (freshwater salmon) and **ayu** (sweetfish). The iwana inhabits the narrow, upper reaches of mountainous clear rivers, followed by yamame where the river widens, and the deepest-water dwelling ayu.

The iwana is found only in Hokkaidō, Honshū and Shikoku (not in Kyūshū). It is called 'rock-fish' after the boulder-strewn riverscapes it inhabits. As tasty as yamame, it is best in late spring and early summer. It is fantastic as shio-yaki, served with sanshō. It can also be served as **kara-age** (dusted in flour and deep-fried) and **kanro-ni**, a sweetened simmered dish similar to tsukudani, using glutinous starch syrup.

Yamame means 'mountain girl'. It is a beautifully marked freshwater version of both the saltwater **sakura-masu** (cherry salmon) or the **biwa-masu** (identified by two red spots on its body). Around 30cm in length, it is in season from early summer to autumn. Often it is just plainly grilled without salt and dipped in shōyu.

The Japanese character for **ayu** (sweetfish) consists of two elements, 'sakana' (fish) and 'uranai' (meaning 'fortune telling'). This bizarre nomenclature originates in Japan's distant past when the mythical Empress Jingū, en route for Korea, caught an ayu on Tamashima, in Matsu'ura. The empress decided this was auspicious, and that Korea would be defeated. History doesn't record whether the fortune-telling fish was right. Interestingly, the non-gutted fish are cheaper than the gutted variety. This is because the ayu feed on a freshwater algae that retains its smell in the entrails of the fish. Country folk distinguish natural ayu from cultivated ayu by their longer, more pointy chins (needed to root out riverbed algae). The domesticated, hand-fed variety are a bunch of fat-chinned softies. Ayu is usually served salted and grilled (shio-yaki), especially with water pepper vinegar, furai and **ayu no sugata-zushi.**

Masu (pink salmon) is a favourite of Hokkaidō, where the largest specimens reach up to 60cm. Its freshwater variety, **kawa-masu** (brook trout), is also called **hime-masu** ('princess trout') or **niji-masu** ('rainbow trout'). Usually it is served as shio-yaki, teriyaki or furai.

An import from China but now found in rivers and lakes countrywide, **funa** (crucian carp) is best known as the ingredient in **funa-zushi** (carp sushi). The Lake Biwa variety, **gengorō-buna**, reaches up to 30cm in length and is preferred. It is best from March to April.

Yasai (Vegetables)
Sansai (Mountain Vegetables)

'Mountain vegetables' would imply that **sansai** are gathered from the wild, as opposed to **yasai**, which are cultivated. However, some sansai are grown, and some yasai grow wild, so the terms are not strictly exclusive. Sansai are most commonly served as tempura, **aemono** (cooked and blended with a dressing), **nimono** (simmered dishes), **tsukemono** (pickles) and **sunomono** (vinegared food), or they are made into **tsukudani** (simmered with fish in shōyu and mirin). They are a part of the soba-shop standard: **sansai-soba**.

An important part of rural cuisine, their often outlandish appearance may be off-putting for first-time eaters. Some sansai even *sound* peculiar when translated into English.

Fuki-no-tō, the unopened butterbur bud, is a spring addition to miso soup. **Seri** (water dropwort) is most often used in soups and with **sukiyaki** (where beef, tōfu and vegetables are cooked in an iron pan and served with a raw egg dip). **Zenmai** (royal fern) and **warabi** (bracken) are tasty staples of sansai cuisine.

Yomogi (mugwort) is combined with **mochi** (rice cakes) or udon, imparting a dark green colour to both. **Junsai** (water shield) is another once-tasted-never-forgotten experience. Its leafy shoots, gathered from the surface of rivers in spring and early summer, are encased in a gelatinous cover reminiscent of frog spawn. Junsai, added to **suimono** (clear soups), is expensive – you pay for the weird sensation as it slips down your throat.

Na/Nappa (Leaf Vegetables)

All cultivated leaf vegetables are used in **o-hitashi** (vegetables are parboiled, then dipped in cold water to retain colour, and then covered with **dashi** (stock) and shōyu) or **nabemono** (hotpot dishes), or both.

The edible chrysanthemum leaf **shungiku** originated in Europe. A spring vegetable commonly used with sukiyaki, it is strong tasting and should be boiled once and soaked in cold water before use, except in nabemono. **Kyōna, mizuna, mibuna** and **itona** are all furry-leafed greens used in soups, aemono, and nabemono. They lose their taste if overheated. Strictly speaking a sansai plant, but most commonly cultivated, **mitsuba** (Japanese wild chervil) is found in Japan and China. It grows in damp places in early spring, and is often used as a topping for misoshiru (miso soup), or in the steamed savoury-custard dish, **chawan-mushi**. **Komatsuna** (mustard spinach) used in nabemono, o-hitashi, even in fried **itamemono**, gets its name from Komatsu-gawa, Tokyo, where it was originally harvested in early Edo. Mostly picked in winter, it is used in **o-zōni** at Kantō's New Year celebrations.

Aona no nibitashi (Green vegetable soup-salad)

Ingredients

1	medium-sized bunch mustard spinach
1	medium-sized head broccoli
50g	snow peas

Sauce

2½ cups	**katsuo-dashi** (bonito-fish broth)
1 tsp	salt
	shōyu to taste

Boil the mustard spinach (with a little salt added) for approximately 3 minutes. Rinse the spinach in cold water until it is cool, then cut it into 5cm strips. Cut and discard the stem. Cut and discard the stem of the broccoli, and boil the florets with a little salt for 3 minutes. De-string the snow peas and boil in lightly salted water for 1 minute. Heat the sauce ingredients, and add the green vegetables. When the liquid begins to simmer, turn off the heat. Allow everything to sit for a short while, then serve in either individual dishes or in a shared, slightly deep dish.
    Serves 4

STAPLES

Konsai (Root Vegetables)

Konsai feature large in rural cooking, in nabemono, and in **shōjin-ryōri** (Buddhist vegetarian cuisine). They also have much older folkloric associations with sexuality, the 'kon' element of the phrase implying 'root' of life, and by extension, genitalia, however, in the cities you'll find this reference is long forgotten.

Daikon (giant white radish)

The giant white radish, **daikon** is an important daily vegetable. It is grated finely as an addition to noodle dishes (it is said to help with digestion), or mixed with baby sardines to produce the splendid dish **jako-oroshi**, an **izakaya** or **shokudō** (small, cheap eateries) favourite. Daikon grated with **taka-no-tsume** (red-hot peppers) turns pink and is known as **momiji-oroshi**, ('maple-leaf grated daikon'). It is served as an accompaniment to nabemono. Daikon is boiled with other ingredients in nimono, and is pickled, most notably in the Kyoto speciality called **takuan**, a crunchy yellow nuka-pickle (for more on **nuka**, refer to Pickles under Condiments, Garnishes & Flavourings later in this chapter).

Apprentice chefs must learn how to peel daikon in a single unbroken strip, so as to master knife technique – and patience. Once the daikon is peeled, the outer skin is finely sliced to serve as the white, background mount for raw fish.

Konnyaku (devil's tongue, or elephant foot), is a tuber and is made into cakes and used in blocks (as in the **oden** hotpot of tōfu, fish cakes and potatoes), or coated with miso as **dengaku**. Thinly sliced it is called **shirataki**, and is a gelatinous bootlace lookalike used in sukiyaki. In slightly fatter bootlace form it is called **ito-konnyaku**, a common addition to nabemono. It is chewy, largely tasteless and devoid of calories.

Renkon (lotus root) is best from winter to spring and has connections with Buddhist cuisine by way of its webbed, wheel-like cross-section that is reminiscent of the 'wheel of reincarnation'. In season from winter to early spring, it has to be boiled with vinegar to remove its strong iron content that otherwise turns it black. It is served in sunomono, nimono, and tempura, also as **karashi-renkon**, in which it is steamed and the gaps between the 'spokes' are filled with Japanese mustard. **Gobō** (burdock root) must be immediately placed in vinegar water after cutting, to remove bitterness. It is then boiled in vinegar water or the water left over from rinsing rice. It is used in **yanagawa-nabe** with loach, and as **kinpira-gobō** (see the recipe in the Banquet chapter) where it is boiled in a shallow pan and served with whisked egg on top. Gobō is also fantastic in soups as it produces an excellent, deep, natural dashi.

Yama-imo (yam) grows wild in the mountains, its roots running long and deep. Yama-imo needs careful preparation. In order not to let it turn brown when grating, the key is to peel it thickly, and soak it in vinegar water for half an hour. Then one must pound it into a thick and sticky consistency. Mainly it is used in **tororo-jiru** (grated yam soup) and **yamakake-udon**, and added to plain white rice or deep-fried. Sliced in long square strips and eaten with a shōyu and wasabi dressing, topped with nori, it is **yama-imo no tanzaku**, an izakaya staple, notorious for its 'beneficial' effect on the male libido. Varieties include the less sticky, slightly watery **naga-imo**, and the bizarrely shaped **yamato-imo**, which looks like a koala's hairy claw.

Yer common spud (**jaga-imo**) is much appreciated in Japan, not least in Hokkaidō where the splendidly titled **danshaku** ('the Baron') is preferred. It originally arrived at the other end of the archipelago in Kyūshū, in the early 17th century, when the Dutch brought it to Nagasaki. Sometimes called the **bareisho** ('horse-bell potato'), it is used in sunomono, aemono, nimono, oden and **furai** (deep-fried; at McDonald's termed **furenchi-furai**). A favourite with foreigners is **niku-jaga** – stewed beef and potatoes with onion and carrot, in shōyu with mirin and dashi. Not only is this izakaya staple tasty, it is easy to order – just ask for a rubber-lipped Rolling Stones vocalist. Works every time.

Satsuma-imo (sweet potatoes) also arrived in Kyūshū around 1605, where they proved more popular than the non-sweet variety. Today the island still produces 50% of Japan's total.

A common sight and sound in even small Japanese cities is the roast sweet-potato vendor. The vendor usually does the rounds in a small, open-backed truck, on which a charcoal stove is roasting the potatoes. The smell is irresistible. A pre-recorded tape sings "oishiiiiii, yaki-iiiiiiiiiiiiiiiii-mo!" ("tasty sweet potatoes ...").

A sweet-potato vendor on the streets of Kōchi city

Kinoko (Mushrooms)

Japan's humid climate makes it a mycologist's dream, with over 4000 species of mushroom and fungus (as many as there are in all of Europe). Many are edible, and they are all generally used in the same way, in miso soup, as tempura, mixed with rice as **kinoko-gohan**, or in nabemono.

Best known are **shiitake**. Strong tasting, and easily cultivated, they are also used to make vegetarian-friendly dashi. Ōita, Shizuoka and Miyazaki Prefectures are renowned for producers, where they are harvested in spring and autumn. A mushroom pioneer at the International Mushroom Research Institute in Kiryū, Gunma Prefecture, even turns them into 'mushroom wine'.

Shiitake mushrooms

The grey autumn fungus **maitake** (literally, 'dancing mushrooms', from the waving, arm-like shape of their branches) are earthy and one of Japan's great tastes. It goes well with both creamy sauces and with shōyu- or miso-based soups. A white version is known as **shiro-maitake**. They are mostly grown in Hokkaidō and Tōhoku.

Shimeji are small, white-stemmed mushrooms most commonly served in miso soup. Their larger cousins **hon-shimeji**, are considered a delicacy. **Buna-shimeji** are a smaller yellowish variety. **Nameko** are vividly yellowy-orange, and have a gelatinous quality that fans adore. They especially suit thick, strong **inaka-miso** ('rural miso'). **Kabu-nameko** are larger and slightly less sticky.

Enoki-dake have long, thin, white fungal stems topped with a creamy-white cap. They're great lightly blanched in salads, sauteed in butter, or in miso soup. They are best from November to March.

Matsutake, sometimes called **mat'take**, are monumentally expensive. They are classified by the extent that their cap has opened, from the young, fully closed **koro**, via **tsubomi**, **naka-tsubomi**, to the fully open **hiraki**. The best and priciest are tsubomi and naka-tsubomi. Check to see that the edge of the semi-opened cap is still firm.

Matsutake are prized for their fragrance even more than their delicate taste. A common saying is 'Nioi matsutake, aji shimeji' meaning 'matsutake for the smell, shimeji for the taste'. Matsutake are most often served steamed in a small 'teapot', a dobin, hence the dish's name, **dobinmushi**. You savour the aroma from the pot, and from a small porcelain cup drink the juice in which the matsutake has been steamed. After which you then eat the mushrooms themselves. Matsutake can be grilled in foil, or steamed with rice to make **matsutake-gohan**. All are an autumn feature of rural ryokan (traditional inns).

Part of the reason for their expense is that matsutake are pretty much impossible to rear artificially. Imports from Korea, Australia, New Zealand and the USA are cheaper, but are considered pale versions of the real thing.

Charcoal-grilled vegetables: green capsicum, and shimeji and shiitake mushrooms

Other Vegetables

Japan's most visible green beans are **eda-mame** (young soy beans), literally meaning 'branch beans'. They are served in the pod, as an izakaya accompaniment to beer, especially in the summer. The pods are dusted in salt, which transfers to the beans as you pop them in your mouth between swigs of foamy ale (don't eat the pods!). These should not be confused with the thinner, edible mangetout **saya-endō** (sugar or snow peas), or the larger **oranda** (literally, 'Holland's). Both make excellent crunchy aemono, o-hitashi and suimono, and are often served in salads. Saya-endō are also called **kinusaya**, from the sound made when rubbing the fresh pods together, which is likened to rubbing kinu (silk). **Saya-ingen** (string beans) are mainly served as tempura, or **goma-ae** (mixed with a sauce of sesame, salt and vinegar). To keep their vivid green colour, they are washed, sprinkled in salt, left for five minutes, boiled briefly, then soaked in water again.

Take-no-ko (bamboo shoots) arrived in the 16th century from China, and are extensively used in nimono, soups, or as **take-no-ko-gohan**, where they are added to rice. They are also cooked with and wrapped in **wakame** (a type of seaweed) to make **wakatake-ni**, and are especially grown in Rakusai on the western outskirts of Kyoto, where a whole specialist cuisine has evolved around the vegetable. They are at their best in spring.

Negi (spring onion) is very widely used, primarily as a nabemono or soup ingredient, or as **sarashi-negi** (an addition to dipping sauces for noodles). In Kantō only the white part of the **shiro-negi** or **naga-negi** is used. Negi from Tokyo's Nerima ward is particularly popular. In Kansai only the green section of the softer variety (**ao-negi**) is used, and Kyoto's **kujō-negi** is preferred. Somewhat similar, **nira** (Chinese chives) are quite pungent, almost garlicky, and are added mainly to o-hitashi and itamemono.

Tama-negi (onions) don't feature largely in Japanese cuisine. One reason for this may be a nice balance of spirituality and pragmatics. Vegetables that were considered strongly yang in nature (such as garlic) – that is, positive, male and powerful – were discouraged in Buddhist monasteries, which were dedicated to peaceful meditation and quiet introspection. A relatively recent arrival, onions are known to increase blood circulation, cause sweating and alleviate insomnia.

Japan boasts a veritable plethora of **nasu** (eggplants). The **maru-nasu** and Kyoto-speciality **kamo-nasu** are roundish. The **kuro-nasu** is egg-shaped, and Osaka and Hakata/Fukuoka claim an elongated variety. A popular nimono, **agemono** (deep-fried) and tempura dish, it is perfect with miso, most notably in **nasu-dengaku**, where it is grilled with tōfu and fish, and topped with a miso sauce. Because they are naturally sweet, Japanese eggplants do not need to be salted prior to cooking. You can tell an eggplant is fresh by the lush purple colour of its skin.

A basket full of pickled miniature eggplants at Nishiki-koji market, Kōchi

Condiments, Garnishes & Flavourings
Wasabi (Japanese Horseradish)

Fresh wasabi, especially the naturally cultivated variety from the pure streams of alpine Nagano Prefecture, is sublime. The bright-green reconstituted stuff barely deserves the name. It is horrendously synthetic and filled out with cheap mustard. Its only saving grace is that nine times out of 10 it goes straight to your nasal passage, so you don't have to endure the chemicals, only a mucous-fest.

The real stuff, however, suffuses gently through your mouth. It is pungent and smooth. In combination with good shōyu or noodle dipping sauce, it is truly memorable. Recognise it by its very pale green, almost white colour, and slightly rough texture. The best soba shops will bring the wasabi itself, and a shark-skin topped wasabi grater, and you prepare your own.

A member of the cabbage family, it is extremely difficult to cultivate because it needs a constant source of flowing pure water. As a result, much is still taken from the wild.

Fresh wasabi (Japanese horseradish)

A bowl of sanshō, one of the few spices used in Japanese cooking

STAPLES

Sanshō (Prickly Ash Pod, Szechwan Pepper)

Zanthoxylum sanshō is its Sunday name, and the leaves or the pod (rather than the seed) are used for aromatic flavouring. Sanshō has a splendid taste, something akin to lemony aniseed. It also has the odd quality of numbing the tongue. It goes perfectly with white fish, eel (it balances out the eel's fatty oiliness), udon, **nabemono** stock, and is even used as a condiment for **kushikatsu** (breaded and deep-fried vegetables, meat or fish, served on skewers), which one dips in powdered dried sanshō. Its pods are made into **tsukudani** (fish and vegetables simmered in shōyu and mirin), whereupon they become the perfect accompaniment to cold sake. The leaves are used as a garnish, especially with **aemono** of **take-no-ko** (bamboo shoots).

Shiso (Perilla, Beefsteak Plant)

A member of the mint family, but with a certain pungency and hint of basil, this aromatic, nettle-shaped leaf is found across the globe from the Himalayas to Missouri, Arkansas and the Blue Ridge Mountains. It was introduced to the USA by immigrants from Japan and Korea in the 1800s, though it has long been a key ingredient in Asian cuisine.

In Japan both **ao-jiso** (green shiso) and **aka-jiso** (red shiso) are used. Ao-jiso is a perennial accompaniment to sashimi and sushi, and is used in soups and in tempura. It is a good accompaniment to beef, and in fusion dishes often joins or replaces sweet basil. **Aka-jiso**, which is only available fresh in July, is used in pickling. It is also made into a refreshing summer juice, and dried is used as a season for white rice.

Shichimi-Tōgarashi (Seven Spice Mix)

This popular condiment for noodle dishes and **nabemono** (hotpot dishes) literally means the 'seven-taste pepper'. It is traditionally composed of tōgarashi (hot red peppers), sanshō, citrus zest – usually of yuzu (citron) or **mikan** (tangerine) – and smaller amounts of black and white sesame seeds (counted as one), poppy seed, hemp seed and **ao-nori** (a type of seaweed). Some adepts demand it includes safflower seeds. All components are ground together to a coarse texture, and at traditional shichimi-tōgarashi dealers, you can choose the amount of ingredients that suits. Tōgarashi selling has long been the domain of tekiya, the small-time gangsters who ply their wares at festivals, even today.

Yuzu (Japanese Citron)

Yuzu is an aromatic citrus fruit, usually whitish-yellow or green. It is added to **ponzu** (a mixture of dashi, shōyu, vinegar and citrus juice) dipping sauces and to **suimono** (clear soups), and is squeezed or grated onto fish. Its zest is often added to soups and to soba **tsuyu** (dipping sauce). The yuzu ripens from autumn to early winter, turning from green (**aoyu**) to yellow (**kiyuzu**). The kiyuzu skin can be hollowed out, filled,

Citrus fruit for sale in Kōchi's market

and steamed, with, for example, crab meat, spring onions, **mitsuba** (Japanese wild chervil) and **shiitake** mushrooms in **yuzu-no-kamayaki**. The **sudachi**, a relative of the yuzu, is a small, sharply flavoured citrus, and is often used for its juice. **Kabosu** is another sharp citrus, which is normally used in **sunomono** (vinegared food).

Shōga (Ginger)

Although not used as widely as in other parts of Asia, ginger is often used grated to flavour dipping sauces or to put on tōfu. It is pickled as **beni-shōga** and added to or used as an accompaniment to sushi dishes, especially **chirashi-zushi** (vinegared rice topped with raw fish and vegetables), and **tonkotsu-rāmen** (pork-broth rāmen). It is also added to soups and stocks, and is the main flavouring in thick soba and udon dishes. **Shōga-yu**, made by mixing ginger and hot water, is the traditional cold cure and winter body-warmer.

Myōga is a ginger relative, but only buds and stems are eaten, not the root. Smaller and not as strong as western ginger, it goes wonderfully with vinegar, and is highly fragrant.

Su (Vinegar)

Japan's first vinegar, **ume-zu**, came as a result of salt-pickling plums. Its impact on the cuisine is reflected in the word anbai, literally 'salt-plum', which means spot-on, or well-balanced, especially in the phrase 'anbai ga ii', 'this is just right'.

Japanese vinegar is almost wholly made from rice. This rice vinegar is called **kome-su** (or, more properly, **yone-zu**). **Kasu-su**, made from sake lees, also exists but is hardly used. Kome-su is used like western-style vinegars, and especially in sunomono and as a purifier in cooking root vegetables

Tsukemono (Pickles)

As an accompaniment to boiled rice, pickles are present in most Japanese meals. They are also important **sake-ate** (accompaniments to sake and beer). Pickles are named for the ingredient – mostly vegetables, but also fish – the length of time pickled, and the pickling base, usually either miso, salt, vinegar or **nuka**, a paste made of rice bran. Nuka was once considered such an important part of household life that daughters would include it in their wedding dowry. **Nuka-miso zuke** (nuka pickles), which have been kneaded into a mixture of miso and nuka, and left to mature (sometimes through an entire winter), are unique to Japan.

Shio-zuke is the process of pickling in salt, which happens overnight for **asa zuke** (lightly pickled vegetables), or for much longer, as for **umeboshi** (pickled sour plums).

Regional varieties and specialities abound. Kyoto is particularly renowned for its pickles, notably the dramatic and gorgeously purple-hued **shiba-zuke**, which is a combinatoin of cucumber, eggplant and Japanese ginger pickled with **aka-jiso** (red beefsteak plant). (See Kyoto in the Regional Variations chapter.)

Our favourite sake-ate is undoubtably **tsukudani**, which is created with vegetables, (including **sansai** – mountain vegetables), mushrooms, fish, shellfish, seaweed, or even, er, locusts simmered in a broth of shōyu, mirin and sake until the liquid has been reduced to what can only be described as a treacle-like paste. Katsushika-Shibamata in Tokyo is a tsukudani mecca (see Tokyo in the Honshū section of the Regional Variations chapter). It was near here that the process originated, on the island of Tsukudajima in the Sumida River – tsukudani means Tsukuda-simmered – during the Edo period. The small settlement of Kurama, just to the north of Kyoto, is also well known for tsukudani, most famously at Watanabe Ki-no-me Ünpo, which has been in the pickling trade for years. It specialises in **shiitake** mushrooms, **fuki** (butterbur), **konbu** (kelp), and the magnificent **sanshō** (prickly ash pepper).

STAPLES

Yudōfu (Boiled tōfu hotpot)

Ingredients

2 blocks	tōfu (kinugoshi or momen)
4	shiitake mushrooms
1 bunch	**mitsuba** (Japanese wild chervil)
20cm-long	strip **konbu** (kelp)

Sauce

100ml	**dashi** (stock)
100ml	shōyu
3 Tbs	mirin
1 tsp	grated **daikon** (giant white radish)
1 tsp	grated ginger

Lightly wipe down the konbu with a wet cloth, to remove impurities. Soak it in a big pan half-filled with water for 30 minutes. Do not discard the water. Cut each block of tōfu into 4 pieces. Halve the mitsuba after removing the root end. Remove and discard the stems from the mushrooms, and cut a crisscross incision in the mushroom caps. Put the tōfu, mitsuba, mushrooms and konbu into an iron or clay **nabe** (hotpot) with the water left over from soaking the konbu, and heat over a moderate flame. For the dipping sauce, mix all the sauce ingredients in a pan and gently heat until almost boiling. Serve in small bowls. When the tōfu begins to wobble, scoop it from the nabe using a tōfu spoon or small ladle, and place all the ingredients (except the konbu) into the dipping-sauce bowls.
    Serves 4

Nabemono (Hotpot Cuisine)

This must surely be the most convivial way of eating ever invented. The guests gather around a heavy metal pot suspended over a hearth, the beer and sake flow, the conversation never slows, and as the mixture begins to bubble and simmer, the room heats up, the host brings more beer, and an irresistible smell of slowly cooking stew begins to fill the room ...

Nabemono, the great winter warmer, is an age-old rustic style of cuisine that took cities by storm – today in tiny Tokyo apartment blocks families will huddle around an earthenware pot set on a calor-gas single ring stove straight out of a 1950s Boy Scout catalogue, to re-enact (on a minor scale) the great country feasts of their forebears. Nabemono never loses its primitive campfire feel, even when it is served up as yudōfu (tōfu boiled in a delicate konbu broth) in a posh Kyoto restaurant. Its also refreshingly uncomplicated, requires little preparation, and little washing up, there's almost no waste, the natural tastes of the ingredients are allowed to come through, and, as every impoverished Japanese student knows, the room gets heated as appetites get satisfied.

Nabemono – hearty and fuss free

Cooking couldn't be any simpler. A basic stock, or in some cases just hot water, is placed in the nabe, then whatever ingredients are to hand are added and brought to a simmer. Guests then fish out the vegetables, shellfish, fish or meat of their choice, dip them in a sauce (**tsukejiru**) and ... eat! The tsukejiru will most likely be **ponzu**, a mixture of **dashi** (stock), shōyu, vinegar and citrus juices, most likely yuzu, sudachi or kabosu. Kōchi Prefecture's Umajimura is renowned for the excellence of its ponzu. When the main ingredients or the 'gu' (good bits) have all disappeared, the host will often add either rice to the stock to create a **zōsui** (rice soup), or **udon**.

Common nabemono dishes include **chiri-nabe** (fish), **kani-suki** (crab), **dote-nabe** (miso and oyster), **udon-suki** (udon, vegetables and shellfish), **botan-nabe** (wild boar), **ishikari-nabe** (Hokkaidō salmon and vegetables), and **chanko-nabe** (the sumō wrestlers' miso or shōyu calorie-fest containing just about everything). Regional variations and specialities abound, and one of the great joys of rural winter **onsen** (hot spring) hopping is to see how they prepare their nabemono. **Ishikari-nabe** *is* Hokkaidō. The Japan Sea coast of northern Hyōgo Prefecture proudly boasts of its **kani-suki**. Osaka scoffs at both, lauding its own **udon-suki** ... and so the nabemono wars go on.

Niku (Meat)
Gyūniku (Beef)

Since the Meiji-period emperor's 1873 'repealing' of the Buddhist prohibition against the killing of creatures, the Japanese have been scoffing bovines and fowl with distinctly non-Buddhist zeal, for everything from **shabu-shabu** (dipped into a boiling hotpot, then into various sauces) to **teriyaki** burgers (where meat is brushed with shōyu, mirin and sugar, and grilled).

However, logic asserts that if the priests of the Nara period under Emperor Shōmu felt the need to forbid the practice, 8th century Japanese must have already been chowing down on plenty of four-legged fodder.

We suspect that the pre-modern Japanese equivalent of the tractor, the water buffalo, was high on the menu. And not all believers were necessarily as devout as they should have been (see the mountain 'whale' reference under Venison & Wild Boar later in this section). By the Heian period, beef was eaten by Koreans and Chinese living in Kansai, the origin of Shiga Prefecture's **ōmi-gyū**, and there's a good chance neighbouring communities were lured by the smell of the odd steak.

The Japanese beef of choice has long been produced in Kansai: **kōbe-gyū**, famously massaged with sake and beer-fed (now mostly reared in the Tajima region of northern Hyōgo). **Matsuzaka-gyū**, is the slightly less well-known, but equally expensive Mie Prefecture counterpart, **ōmi-gyū**is Shiga's. The Tajima region is famed for its **tajima-gyū** veal. A slice of top-class Japanese beef has a marbled, delta-like network of fine, white strands, set against a luscious deep red flesh.

Freshly prepared Kōbe beef, a legendary Japanese delicacy and one of the most expensive types of beef in the world

Pumpkin with thick chicken-mince sauce

STAPLES

Toriniku (Chicken)

Long accepted by Buddhists working on the 'two legs good, four legs bad' principle, chicken was already being eaten in the Nara period. The first squawkers were probably arrivals from China, examples of the **kashiwa** (yellow chicken). Chicken still goes by that name in Kansai, whereas in Kantō it was, until recently, called **shamo**. The bird makes up 30% of Japan's meat consumption, of which more than two-thirds is, unfortunately, battery farmed.

Wakabina (chicks) are used in **kara-age** (dusted in flour and deep-fried), and are grilled as **amiyaki** (cooked on a griddle). The 60-day-old **hinadori** are used in **furai** (crumbed and deep-fried), and stuffed-chicken dishes. The tender meat of the 80-day-old **wakadori** is roasted, sauteed or used in stews. Japanese chefs make extensive use of the thigh, the area beneath the wings, the wing tips, the breast, the giblets and the skin. The bones are used in stock making, especially for rāmen.

Chicken is roasted whole, steamed, fried as kara-age and minced (which is often made into chicken balls). It can be served raw, or thinly sliced as **sashimi** (excellent with a **ponzu** dipping sauce of dashi, shōyu, vinegar and citrus juice), and is also made into **tori-wasa** (blanched in boiling water and served with a shōyu and wasabi sauce). Finally, it also features as **aemono** (a mixed dressing of tōfu, sesame or miso paste) with grated wasabi. An **izakaya** and streetfood staple is **yakitori** (skewered, grilled and served with tare or salt).

Skewered chicken pieces cooking on an open flame

Butaniku (Pork)

Eaten in Japan since the Edo period, the Yorkshire, Berkshire and Hampshire breeds of pig are preferred. In Okinawa the ears are served as a delicacy while in Kyūshū the carcass is prized for **tonkotsu** (pork broth). More generally, however, it is eaten as pork cutlets, in pork shabu-shabu, stewed, or served on rice as **katsudon**.

Shika & Inoshishi (Venison & Wild Boar)

There is a long-standing taboo against consuming venison because the deer is traditionally considered a messenger of the gods. That is why Nara's Kasuga shrine is famously surrounded by the wandering beasts. That said, non-believer rural hunters have long taken deer (the male of the species only), and its best season is autumn, when the light, subtle tasting red meat is served as sashimi or in **nabemono** (hotpot dishes).

The meat-hungry Buddhists of the Nara period were in a quandary. With the recent prohibition against eating four-legged creatures, they came up with the novel idea of turning a ferocious but now sacrosanct, mountain-dwelling boar into an edible, Buddhist-Kosher sea mammal. Thus, the wild boar became the mountain 'whale'. Astonishingly, nobody battered an eyelid at this blatant, bald-faced piece of linguistic jiggery-pokery. Today, wild boar is most often used in **botan-nabe** (wild-boar hotpot) its strong smell lessened by being stewed in miso. Kumogahata in Kyoto, Sasayama in Hyōgo, Asakuma-yama in Ehime, and Izu's Amagi-yama are famed for their boar cuisine. It is at its best from November to March.

Uma (Horse)

Hardly eaten outside Yamanashi, Nagano and Kumamoto Prefectures uma is most often found raw as **basashi**, or in nabemono, when it is generally called **sakura-niku** 'cherry meat' or **ketobashi**. Mare's meat is said to be best.

Kaisō (Seaweed)

Found throughout the country, although Tokushima's is considered the best, **wakame** (a type of seaweed) is harvested from May to June. Since the Nara period, its anti-ageing properties have been recognised. Fresh, it is used in **sunomono** (vinegared food), **suimono** (clear soup), and in **dashi** (stock). Dried wakame is also commonly used, including **ran-boshi**, dried unpretentiously on the nearest beach; **shio-boshi-wakame**, washed in salt water and dried; or **shio-nuki-wakame**, washed only in plain water (with no salt) and dried.

Nori (sea laver) is best known in its dried and toasted form as the outer layer of **nori-maki** (sushi wrapped in nori). Small sheets are used to scoop up rice mixed with raw egg in a typical ryokan breakfast. It is often added to soba and rāmen dishes (mainly in Kantō), mixed with salt and sesame for use in **furikake** (a savoury topping sprinkled on plain white rice), and is an ingredient in **shichimi-tōgarashi** (seven spice mix).

The role of **konbu/kobu** (kelp) in Japanese cooking cannot be underestimated, as it is a key ingredient in dashi. **Ma-konbu**, growing to almost 2m in length is harvested from Hokkaidō's Uchiura Bay, where it is also known as **yamadashi-konbu**.
From the northern island of Rebun, **rishiri-konbu** is excellent for dashi, while that from Shakotan peninsula is not as aromatic so is used mainly in **tsuku-dani** (fish and vegetables simmered in shōyu and mirin).

Hijiki is a black, spiky looking, but soft, seaweed. It is good sauteed in shōyu with soy beans, a dish called **hijiki-mame**. Taken from Japan's Pacific coast, it has proven to prevent hardening of the arteries. What's more, it strengthens teeth, is nutritionally good for in-utero babies' bones, and is economical. Famously, hijiki turns your hair a shiny black, however, as one anxious grandmother in rural Gunma Prefecture told us, "it may not work with foreigners".

Shredded nori (sea laver) with grated daikon (giant radish) and sliced negi (spring onion)

STAPLES

Kudamono (Fruit)

The Japanese consume lots of fruit imported from the west. They hold a particular fondness for watermelon. The summertime beach game of smash-the-watermelon, a kind of blind-man's-buff meets martial art, has irrevocably entered the nation's collective consciousness. Strawberries, bananas, pineapples, melons, apples, oranges and even figs, an early 17th century introduction, are common. Indigenous fruits are, however, relatively thin on the, er, tree. **Mikan** (mandarines or tangerines), and the related but larger, **ponkan**, are commonly eaten in the winter.

Sweet Snacks & Desserts

It may seem as if much **wagashi**, Japanese confectionery, is designed to be looked at rather than eaten, such is its visual attractiveness. Traditional Japanese sweets are not of the Sunday-treat, cavity-inducing variety, but rather are designed for offsetting the bitter taste of the **ocha** (Japanese green tea) used in the tea ceremony. The craft of making wagashi reaches its pinnacle in Kyoto, most famously with **higashi** (see later in this section).

Namagashi are uncooked sweet paste confections filled with red **an** (sweet bean paste). **Han-namagashi** are less-moist sweets, including Okayama favourite **kibi-dango**, made with proso millet, and the delicacy **mitarashi-dango** (rice flour dumplings), a speciality of Kyoto's Shimogamo shrine. **Higashi**, an all-

Kuri mushi yōkan, a steamed chestnut sweet

encompassing category of dried sweets and **senbei** (rice crackers), usually refers to the moulded rice-paste and sugar confections made especially for the tea ceremony. While these are delicately coloured, and crafted to reflect imagery appropriate to the season, Nagoya's favourite wagashi, **uirō**, is a plain, gelatinous brick, filled with powdered tea or red beans.

No summer festival is complete without **kakigōri**. Simply a mountain of shaved ice, doused in a violently vivid syrup of shamelessly synthetic vulgarity, it is, of course, hugely popular, with both adults and kids slurping it down. Equally odd-sounding is the green tea and ice cream combination called **matcha-aisu**, although actually it is rather palatable.

drinks
of japan

Alcohol is the 'social lubricant' that dissolves the strictures of rule-bound Japanese society. Whether you're drinking the locally brewed beer of Hokkaidō, the fine sake of Kyoto and Hyōgo, or the grain liquor **awamori** of Okinawa, the party will be hopping. The famed non-alcoholic tipple is Japanese tea. Try Uji's thick, caffeine-laced green tea, or the beautiful smoky **bancha**.

Non-Alcoholic Drinks
Ocha (Green Tea)

For many, tea conjures up images of Typhoo and Lipton, a British stiff upper lip and a Boston punch-up that got nicely euphemised into a 'party'. But Japan's love affair with tea, the green variety, that is, dates back to its introduction from China, although no one can really agree when that was. Some suggest the Nara period, while another source credits the introduction to Buddhist saint Saichō in 805.

The Chinese Buddhists had long appreciated the role of a good cuppa in preventing one from nodding off during prayers. Indeed, its very origin is shrouded in Buddhist myth. Basil Hall Chamberlain, the 19th century British humorist and Japan scholar, tells the story in his excellent *Things Japanese*: 'Daruma [dharma], an Indian saint of the sixth century, had spent many long years in ceaseless prayer and watching. At last, one night, his eyelids, unable to bear the fatigue any longer, closed, and he slept soundly until morning. When the saint awoke, he was so angry with his lazy eyelids that he cut them off and flung them on the ground. But lo! Each lid was suddenly transformed into a shrub, whose efficacious leaves, infused in water, minister to the vigils of holy men'.

> The tea ceremony is nothing more than boiling water, steeping tea, and drinking it.
>
> *Sen-no-Rikyū*
> *16th Century Tea Master*

But it was not until the 12th century, when Eisai brought back from China not only tea seeds, but the Chinese tea ceremony, that it really took off. Tea became as popular as Zen. At the end of the 12th century, green tea was sowed at Uji, near Kyoto (even today a centre of tea production) and the Japanese court and aristocracy took wholeheartedly to tea, and its formalised ritual drinking, known as **cha-no-yu**. It took another half a millennium or so for the rank and file to pick up the habit. Its popularity was spurred on by the invention of a convenient, newfangled form – **sencha** (leaf tea). Since then, from exquisite teahouses purpose-built for the job, to factory canteens, to convenience stores, the Japanese have become well and truly tea-struck. (See the Fit & Healthy chapter for information on the health benefits of ocha.)

The expensive powdered form used in the tea ceremony is called **matcha**, sometimes called **hiki-cha**. However, the common tea of choice is **bancha**, a coarse tea, always drunk hot, and often served free of charge in restaurants. It is drunk to quench thirst, is cheap, and is made from larger, older tea leaves someimes including stems. When it is roasted (creating the

DRINKS

Matcha (powdered tea), used in the Japanese tea ceremony

magnificent smell that pervades every Japanese shopping arcade) it becomes **hōjicha**, roasted tea, which possesses a deep, wonderfully smoky taste, and is good hot or cold. When roasted and popped rice is added to bancha, it becomes **genmai-cha**, which possesses a nutty, less-smoky quality.

The leafy green sencha, literally, 'infused tea', is enjoyed in its own right. It is made from leaves that are reasonably tender and young, and tends to be served on more special occasions. When the real top brass stop by, however, out comes the **gyokuro**. This is a fragrant, comparatively rare tea that is grown in specially constructed bamboo cages that shut out much of the early spring light, resulting in extremely tender leaves that are picked in a single harvest.

Mugi-cha (wheat tea), **konbu-cha** (kelp tea) and **soba-cha** (buckwheat tea) are not strictly teas at all, but infusions made with their respective ingredients. Mugi-cha is served in the humid Japanese summers; konbu-cha tastes more like a seaweed soup, and often contains an **umeboshi** (dried and pickled Japanese plum). It is found on sale at temples, such as Kyoto's famed Ryōan-ji. Soba-cha, which, as the name suggests, has a flavour reminiscent of noodles, is often served following a soba meal, and its powdered form can be bought at the more upmarket soba restaurants.

Sadō/Cha-no-yu (The Tea Ceremony)

No one can dispute the influence of **sadō**, the ('way of tea'), or **cha-no-yu** ('tea's hot water') on Japan's spiritual, artistic, and cultural heritage.

Born from Zen Buddhist meditative precepts, and popularised among a warrior class that used its silent private spaces as a momentary antidote to the ever-present terror of violent, death, tea has created some of Japan's most spectacular works of art. The gardens and teahouses of Kyoto, that city's incomparable raku ceramic teaware, its calligraphy, its poetry, indeed, even Japan's most refined cuisine itself, **kaiseki** (see cha-kaiseki later in this chapter) – all owe their existence to, and are informed by, the 'way of tea'.

Sadō incorporates the delicately rigorous aesthetic of wabi-sabi, the unadorned purity of natural imperfection fused with a relaxed and peaceful satisfaction in being solitary. It demands awareness of (and sensitivity to) nature and the changing of the seasons; a spiritual, meditative, reflective quality; and a socialising role of equanimous meeting, symbolised by the teahouse design with its low entrances that require each participant to lower their head in humility upon entering.

There is an amalgam of complexity and simplicity to a tea ceremony, and an understated but very real discipline. The mechanics, overtly at least, are none too complex, though difficult for the beginner to master. And even more difficult for the experienced practitioner to refine. A tea ceremony *can*, in fact, be an informal affair among friends.

The rarefied ritual of the tea ceremony

In fact, a Kyoto artist holds tea ceremonies in a custom-built teahouse, complete with his naked body print embedded in the clay wall, exquisite tea accessories from Korea and China, Mariah Carey on the stereo and a fridge packed full of Yebisu beer for imbibing afterwards!

A traditional tea ceremony, however, must be infused with wakeiseijaku – harmony, respect, quiet and solitude. A full-on tea ceremony, or **chaji**, goes something like this: The guests, usually clad in kimono, assemble in a waiting room and select a member to act as the main guest. They then proceed to the garden and to the stone trough from which they ladle water to hand to mouth to purify themselves of worldly concerns. They enter the teahouse, admire the calligraphy work in the **tokonoma** (recess), and greet the host who presents the light **kaiseki** (Japanese formal cuisine), sake.

DRINKS

A bowl of koicha (thick green tea)

Whisking usucha (thin tea)

A **wagashi** (sweet) to offset the bitterness of the thick, green matcha that is to follow. Guests retire to the garden or the waiting room, and then re-enter the tearoom, stopping to admire the flower arrangement that has replaced the hanging scroll in the tokonoma. The thick **koicha** (first brew) is passed in a single bowl from the host to a guest, who savours the strong bitter taste that slowly overcomes the sweetness of the wagashi, before wiping the bowl and passing it on. Talk is purely of the tea – is it from Uji or Shizuoka or elsewhere? What is its poetic name?

Chasen (bamboo tea whisks)

The host then rebuilds the coals in the brazier, and prepares the thinner **usucha**, the second brew from the same tea leaves, which he whips to a delicately frothy consistency with the **chasen** (bamboo tea whisk), and passes to each person. There's more talk of the utensils, the lacquer of the container, perhaps ("It's a fine example, wajima-nuri, from Ishikawa Prefecture") and the fine-crafted curve of the tea scoop. Cultured conversation reigns. Then the guests depart, and the outside world seeps in. The chaji is over.

Yet, tea is certainly not for everyone, nor indeed for everyman. It could be argued that the tea ceremony has never shrugged off its 16th century role of, as Tsuji Shizuo plainly puts it, 'basic cultural training for the upper class'. There's a whiff of elitism about tea. It is also big business. The masters of the three tea ceremony schools, Urasenke, Omotesenke and Mushanokojisenke, are celebrities, forever seen dashing for their limos to avoid the snooping lenses of the Japanese tabloid press. There seems to be no shortage of alleged peccadilloes or scandals.

The tearooms are still full, though. One wonders just how many of the well-brought-up young ladies (**o-jōsan**) are adhering to Sen-no-Rikyū's dictum of simplicity, and how many are relishing the prospect of adding another skill to the CV one proffers to a potential marriage candidate – the **tsuri-sho**, the 'fishing list'.

Cha-kaiseki (Tea Ceremony Meal)

Kaiseki-ryōri, (or more specifically **cha-kaiseki**), usually shortened to kaiseki, is a quintessentially Japanese style of eating.

The tea ceremony meal begins with white rice, **misoshiru** (soup made from miso and fish stock) served in a lacquerware bowl, and plain or raw fish or **sunomono** (vinegared) vegetables placed on the far side of the tray.

Cedar chopsticks are used, and sake is served in an ironware pitcher. **Nimono** (simmered dishes) are served in lacquerware bowls, often so hot that it is difficult to remove the lid.

Yakimono (grilled dishes) are served on ceramic plates, with additional rice and soup.

During the following course of **yamanomono** (mountain dishes) and **uminomono** (saltwater fish), the host is served by the guests. Pickled vegetables, in this context called **kōnomono**, are served with browned rice in salted water.

Seasonal kaiseki, Hamasaku Restaurant, Kyoto

Interestingly, the word kaiseki can be written in two ways. In Tokyo, the Chinese characters, or kanji, for the words 'meeting' (kai) and 'seat' (seki) are often used, but essentially this is a modern coinage. In Kyoto, the kanji for 'inside sleeve' (futokoro), also pronounced kai, and 'stone' (seki) is used, alluding to the tea ceremony's origins as a Buddhist rite, when young, novice monks were given small, pebble-sized, heated stones to tuck into the inner sleeves of their kimono, to distract them from gnawing novitiate hunger.

Cha-kaiseki is seasonal to the nth degree, and its true practitioners are part-chef, part-visual artist, part-market gardener. Its greatest adepts are found, where else, but in Kyoto (see Kyoto in the Regional Variations chapter for more information on kyō-ryōri).

Kōcha & Kōhī (Black Tea & Coffee)

The Japanese do drink Indian- and Sri Lankan-style teas, and the big department stores are full of expensive delicatessens dispensing blends by Fauchon, Fortnum & Mason and Mariages Freres. But this tea drinking pales into comparison with the country's coffee intake, most of which is drunk in **kissaten** (coffee shops). Coffee is expensive, from ¥500 a cup, yet what you are really paying for is the location. In population-dense Japan, space is at a premium, and rather than rent a room for a business meeting, an English lesson, or a romantic tryst, the solution is to meet over a *cafe au lait* in your local kissaten.

Sofuto-dorinku (Soft Drinks)

The archipelago that long resisted western invasion has lost its battle with the forces of Coca-Cola, Pepsi and the like (helped not a little by its own conglomerates, Suntory and Kirin), and you can even find Dr Pepper, if needs be. Yet there are a few homespun drinks that catch the eye.

Cans of soft drink

First and foremost is Ramune, a sweet, lemonade concoction, that comes in a Victorian-style bottle, complete with marble in its crimped neck. It is sold at summer festivals, in shopping arcades, and on the approaches to major shrines and temples. For the Japanese it is the taste of nostalgia, of a time when things were scarcer, times harder, but pleasures simpler, when there was still fascination in lemonade.

Another throwback is Calpis, a lactobacillus, sweet concoction, sometimes mixed with the low-alcohol drink chūhai by adults, and forced on kids at breakfast – actually, most seem to lap it up. Another lactobacillus breakfast favourite is the equally sweet Yakult, which is delivered in mini glass bottles direct to your door by ladies in smart green uniforms driving refrigerated mopeds.

A popular sports drink is the bizarrely named Pocari-Sweat. Why sweat? What's a Pocari? No one seems to know or care, and it appears to outsell its nearest rival, the rather normal-sounding Aquarius.

Bottles of drink for sale at the Kōchi city asa-ichi (morning market)

DRINKS

Vending machines sell anything, from food to drinks to underwear

Jidōhanbaiki (Vending Machines)

Japan's legendary vending machines, which vend everything from fresh flowers to beer to individually-wrapped melons to schoolgirl underwear, are indeed everywhere. On Mt Fuji. In your local funeral home. On trains, boats and ... well, not planes. Not yet. Our definition of deep, rural countryside is 'the-place-without-vending-machines'.

Word has it they are environmental disasters (guzzling power 24 hours a day) and toxic nightmares. Yet they *are* irresistibly convenient. You can grab a can of hot or cold sustenance (with buttons marked red for the former, blue for the latter) for a handful of loose change. Here's a rundown on what's on offer at a typical machine. One may glimpse the deft hand of the Japanese copywriter: Fire (coffee – 'rest your mind', 'warm your soul & feel the fire'); Qoo (peach- and grape-flavoured juices); Boss and Emblem (coffee) and Gogo-no-Kōcha (black tea – 'tea can turn you into something new', 'tea – a natural gift of love'). Where else can you get a natural gift of love so cheap?

Alcoholic Drinks

The Japanese love to drink alcohol, and not simply for the pure, hedonistic fun of it (though they are no slouches at partying). Alcohol is the great social lubricant that sets the Japanese free from the intricate web of social and familial obligations that hounds them from cradle to grave. It gives them a socially valid excuse to boot society's rules into touch and have a good time. This 'let's party' determination gets intensified in the presence of guests,

Japanese Proverb

Sake wa hyaku yaku no chō

Alcohol's the best of a hundred medicines

not least foreign visitors. Don't be surprised if you're invited to join someone's party, end up drinking all night, then not pay a thing. As a general rule, the Japanese are inordinately generous to guests.

They might like to drink, but they are actually not too good at it. Japanese people tend to get drunk quickly. Japanese scientists attribute this to a deficiency in a component of the aldehyde dehydrogenation enzyme that aids the processing of alcohol. This is said to afflict 40% of the Japanese population. Thus, it is not unusual to see Japanese drinkers lit up like the red chōchin (lanterns) that adorn the **izakaya** (Japan's traditional restaurants-cum-bars), pubs and bars, however, it is very unusual to meet obnoxious drunks. Drinking in Japan is fun.

DRINKS

A trio of Sapporo wine

Sake/Nihonshu

From the first visit to a Shintō shrine at one month old, to the Buddhist funeral rites, the Japanese are accompanied by sake. Its place in religious life comes from its associations with rice – the food of the gods – and its symbolic purity. It is consumed at every major rite-of-passage in a Japanese person's life. In the Shintō wedding ritual, the bride and groom seal the marriage by exchanging sake cups and drinking sake. This invokes the gods to intervene to help the couple, and through the sharing of sake, to come closer together and create a bond of friendship. Sake is offered to the family butsudan, the altar that houses the spirits of departed ancestors, and at the feast of O-bon in mid-summer (when the spirits return to this world), at family graves (see the Celebrating with Food chapter). It is proffered to the roadside Buddha statues that dot the countryside, and is a feature both symbolic and practical, at every matsuri (festival).

> **Precepts for Drinkers**
>
> Sake by daylight is cruel
> Sake by twilight is mellow
> Sake at midnight intoxicates
> Sake at dawn entrances
>
> *Fujimoto Giichi*

The five prefectures from Akita to Ishikawa and Shimane on the coastal line of the Japan Sea have the serious sake drinkers, to the annual tune of more than 20L per person.

Precisely when the art of brewing reached Japanese shores is lost in the mists of time. Tradition ascribes its introduction to immigrants from Korea, at about the end of the 3rd century. They, no doubt, learned the technique from their omniscient neighbour China, where they had been knocking back a fermented rice drink since time immemorial. The *Kojiki* (Record of Ancient Things), however, adds 200 years to that estimate. The general populace started brewing sake in the 12th century, and by the end of the 15th, the districts of Itami in Osaka and Ikeda in Hyōgo had established their superiority, a position which, together with the city of Nishinomiya and Kyoto's Fushimi district, they hold to this day.

Often termed rice wine in the west, sake or nihonshu is actually made through a fermenting process using grain, somewhat akin to beer making.

Sake with gold flakes

Key to the sake-making process are good rice, good water and the absolutely magical **kōji**, a dark greenish-yellow, fine powder fermentation agent (converting sugar to alcohol) that is added to steamed white rice. From start to finish, the fermentation and refining process takes between one and two months, and the sake is ready to drink as soon as it drips from the barrel. It has an alcohol content of between 15% and 17%. Sake, unlike wine, does not have vintage years – its quality depends upon the conditions under which it is made, and foremost, the skill of the **tōji** (sake maker).

All sake is graded by the government into one of four categories: **chō-tokkyū**, a kind of 'especially special' class that is rarely available; **tokkyū**, special class; **ikkyū**, first class; and **nikyū**, second class. However, these classifications are based in part on volume produced, not quality, so prove of little value for the consumer.

Far more important for the layperson are the type of sake, and its classification of sweetness or dryness, based on a numerical scale (+20 indicating an extremely dry sake, -15 an ultra sweet one). The four main sake types are:

Dai-ginjōshu
Top of the heap, always a brewer's flagship sake. Made with rice milled so that 50% or less of the original size of the grains remain, it is always an intensely crafted, complex sake, and very expensive.

Ginjōshu
A complex sake made with rice milled so that 60% of the original grain remains. Ginjōshu is fermented at lower-than-average temperatures with special yeast.

Junmaishu
Pure sake, made simply of rice, water, and kōji without the addition of sugar, starch or additional alcohol. No more than 70% of the rice grain remains after milling.

Honjōzōshu
Similar to junmaishu, but with a small amount of alcohol purposefully added to enhance its fragrance.

The first two are generally reserved for special occasions, while the latter pair are for regular drinking. **Nama-zake** refers to sake that has not been pasteurised, and can fall into any of the classifications mentioned above. It needs to be drunk quickly once the bottle has been opened. **Nigori-zake** is a cloudy, whitish sake in which some of the lees have been allowed to remain. It is not a particularly delicate brew, as the sweetness of the lees swamps out any delicacy in the sake, yet it is a popular late-winter/early-spring bodywarmer. Its alcohol content is generally lower than other sakes.

DRINKS

Sake is generally drunk cold, when it is called **reishu**; hot, called **atsukan**; or warm, called **nurukan**.

Connoisseurs offer even finer classifications, including **hitohada** (luke-warm), **hanabie** ('flower-chilled' at 10 degrees), or **yukibie** (snow-chilled at 5 degrees). The finest sake is always drunk cold, the hot options reserved for cold winter evenings. Either way, it will be served in a ceramic sake pot, with a small **o-choko** cup for drinking (reportedly derived from the Korean word 'chonku', meaning 'a small, shallow cup or dish').

An older-style sake warmer

It is polite to fill your drinking partner's glass first (usually the younger person fills the older's glass), and then your partner in turn fills yours (a custom known as **hen-pai** – see Etiquette in the Culture chapter). However, by the end of a night's drinking, everyone usually ditches convention in favour of **tejaku**, pouring your own.

Cold sake is sometimes served in a wooden, square, open-topped box, or **masu**. Thus, it's known as **masu-zake**. The gentle pine aroma of the container mingles with the sake. Often, a small amount of salt is piled up on a corner of the masu, and the sake dissolves the salt as you take a sip.

At rural inns, sake may be served hot in freshly cut hollow cylinders of green bamboo, which are placed in the ash of a hearth to heat. This gives the sake a pleasant bamboo aroma, and is known as **take-zake**.

A professional sake expert, or **kikizakeshi**, will judge a sake using a **kiki-jogo** (a small white o-choko), which has an appraisal mark (two concentric circles) imprinted in the bottom, for judging colour and clarity. The best colour for sake is aozae, a slight yellow with a tinge of blue. If sake has a brown shading it most likely has too many subflavorings. A completely colourless sake will have a flat, two-dimensional flavor. Bouquet depends on a number of factors, and will indicate whether a sake is to be served by itself or with food. As with a wine sommelier, a kikizakeshi comes with an impressive arsenal of specialist phrases with which to praise or damn. Some of the simpler sake judging terms include amakuchi (sweet), karakuchi (dry), koku ga aru (a phrase implying an earthy depth), kuchi-atari (a sake's initial impression or impact), and its opposite, kire (the tail), and oku-bukai (which suggests deep complexity).

DRINKS

SAKE DRINKING TOUR

CHINA

NORTH
KOREA

Sea of Japan
(East Sea)

SOUTH
KOREA

Yellow Sea
(West Sea)

Prefecture Divisions

1 Hokkaidō
2 Aomori
3 Akita
4 Iwate
5 Yamagata
6 Miyagi
7 Fukushima
8 Niigata
9 Toyama
10 Ishikawa
11 Fukui
12 Gifu
13 Nagano
14 Yamanashi
15 Aichi
16 Shizuoka
17 Gunma
18 Tochigi
19 Ibaraki
20 Saitama
21 Tokyo
22 Kanagawa
23 Chiba
24 Shiga
25 Kyoto
26 Hyōgo
27 Osaka
28 Nara
29 Mie
30 Wakayama
31 Tottori
32 Okayama
33 Shimane
34 Hiroshima
35 Yamaguchi
36 Kagawa
37 Tokushima
38 Ehime
39 Kōchi
40 Fukuoka
41 Saga
42 Nagasaki
43 Ōita
44 Kumamoto
45 Miyazaki
46 Kagoshima
47 Okinawa

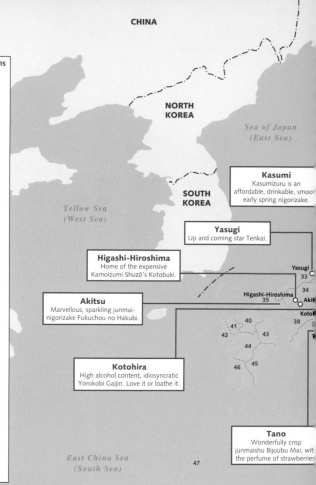

Kasumi
Kasumizuru is an affordable, drinkable, smoo
early spring nigorizake.

Yasugi
Up and coming star Tenkai.

Yasugi
33

Higashi-Hiroshima
Home of the expensive Kamoizumi Shuzō's Kotobuki.

Higashi-Hiroshima
35   34   Aki

Akitsu
Marvellous, sparkling junmai-nigorizake Fukuchou no Hakubi.

Koto

41 40
42   43
44
46 45

38

Kotohira
High alcohol content, idiosyncratic Yorokobi Gaijin. Love it or loathe it.

Tano
Wonderfully crisp junmaishu Bijoubu Mai, wit
the perfume of strawberries

East China Sea
(South Sea)

47

TAIWAN

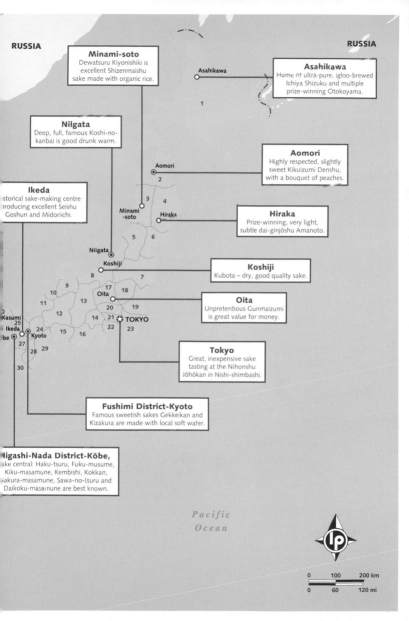

RUSSIA

RUSSIA

Minami-soto
Dewatsuru Kiyonishiki is excellent Shizenmaishu sake made with organic rice.

Asahikawa

Asahikawa
Home of ultra-pure, igloo-brewed Ichiya Shizuku and multiple prize-winning Otokoyama.

1

Nilgata
Deep, full, famous Koshi-no-kanbai is good drunk warm.

Aomori

2

Aomori
Highly respected, slightly sweet Kikuizumi Denshu, with a bouquet of peaches.

Ikeda
Historical sake-making centre producing excellent Seishu Goshun and Midoriichi.

3   4

Minami -soto

Hiraka

Hiraka
Prize-winning, very light, subtle dai-ginjōshu Amanoto.

5   6

Nilgata

Koshiji

8   7

Koshiji
Kubota – dry, good quality sake.

9
10   17   18
11   13   Oita   20   19
Kasumi   12   14   21 ✪ TOKYO
25   16   22   23
Ikeda   24   15
27   Kyoto
28   29
30

Oita
Unpretentious Gunmaizumi is great value for money.

Tokyo
Great, inexpensive sake tasting at the Nihonshu Jōhōkan in Nishi-shimbashi.

Fushimi District-Kyoto
Famous sweetish sakes Gekkeikan and Kizakura are made with local soft water.

Higashi-Nada District-Kōbe,
sake central: Haku-tsuru, Fuku-musume, Kiku-masamune, Kembishi, Kokkan, Sakura-masamune, Sawa-no-tsuru and Daikoku-masamune are best known.

Pacific
Ocean

0   100   200 km
0   60   120 mi

Home-Made Variations

Seriously rural communities produce their own home-made sakes, mostly drunk for their supposedly invigorating (read 'aphrodisiac') propensities. We have sampled **mamushi-zake**, sake containing a coiled poisonous pit-viper, in Gunma Prefecture, and, at a fire festival in Ishikawa Prefecture, **mukade-zake** – sake containing a poisonous biting centipede related to the scorpion. However, in neither case did we notice any major improvement in our mojo.

JI-ZAKE – Take the Taste Test

Here is a collection of ji-zake (local sakes) that you may wish to try. These are recommended by Narita-san, owner of the brilliant restaurant Sasagin, in Yoyogi-Uehara, Tokyo, and added to by recently departed film producer Tsuda Masanosuke. May he enjoy the good stuff upstairs. Almost all these ji-zake are junmaishu, unless otherwise indicated.

Kasumizuru *Hyōgo Prefecture*	Affordable, drinkable, smooth nigorizake for the early spring
Tenkai *Shimane Prefecture*	Hot tip for future stardom, from a small maker in backwoods Yasugi
Kubota *Niigata Prefecture*	Dry, good quality sake, popular in posher izakaya
Yorokobi Gaijin *Kagawa Prefecture*	Slightly dry, slightly acidic junmaishu with above-average alcohol content of 17% to 18%. Has many fans and just as many detractors.
Fukuchō no Hakubi *Hiroshima Prefecture*	Unusual, sparkling junmai-nigori-zake made in rural inland Hiroshima
Bijōbu *Kōchi Prefecture*	Junmaishu 'Mai', very crisp, semi-dry, fragrant, with the perfume of strawberries
Kikuizumi Denshu *Aomori Prefecture*	Classy sake by Nishida Shuzō, a company dating back to 1878, from Aomori at the tip of the Tōhoku region, Northern Honshū
Gunmaizumi *Gunma Prefecture*	Characteristic, unpretentious sake, great value for money – can be drunk warm
Higan *Niigata Prefecture*	Rare, expensive, ultra-smooth sake, available by order only or in good restaurants
Koshi-no-kanbai *Niigata Prefecture*	Highly respected, one of Japan's best-known sakes

Bīru (Beer)

The Japanese love beer **bīru** (rhymes with ear), and although their brews cannot compete with the variety and quality of, say, their European counterparts, beer drinking is an essential part of the culture. It's also the perfect antidote to those sweltering humid summer evenings, when most of the population seems to retreat to a hotel-rooftop beergarden, to sink icy steins of lager beneath tacky lanterns emblazoned with Sapporo or Kirin.

Beer is served either in bottles, or as draft, which comes in frosted, handled glasses in large, medium or small – **dai-jokki**, **chū-jokki** and **shō-jokki**. Often these are abbreviated to dai, chū and shō, and its quite acceptable for a parched customer to yell "nama dai chōdai!" (something like "gizza big draft!"). Beer gardens and izakaya are not places to stand on ceremony. Party groups often get a **pitchā** – a pitcher of beer to share. Kirin Lager and Ichiban-shibori, Sapporo Kuro-label and the all-malt Yebisu (pronounced Ebisu) and still topping the sales league Asahi Super Dry are some of the favourite brands.

Though few beergarden habituees know it, the Japanese have a Norwegian to thank for their suds. William Copeland – OK, he was Norwegian by way of the USA – opened the country's first brewery in Yokohama in 1868, having studied brewing in Germany and the US.

There's no record of why Copeland felt the urge to up sticks and traverse the globe to set up a beer-making concern, but it was an astute move. The Japanese had already tasted beer that had been imported from Britain and Holland to the treaty ports of Yokohama, Nagasaki and Hakodate, and the upper classes in particular took to the stuff. Copeland quickly picked up on a new invention, pasteurisation, and thus began selling gallon upon gallon of beer. Since then, Japanese consumers have continued to lap it up, to the tune of around 5,750,000kL per year, roughly 50L per person.

It was not until 1994 that the odd Japanese law demanding brewers have a yearly capacity of 2000kL was amended, so the Japanese microbrew industry is still in its infancy. However, the production of **ji-bīru**, literally, 'local beer' is on the rise. Here are a few you might try:

Hokkaidō

Japan's northernmost island is something of a ji-bīru leader. Sapporo's Kaitakushi-bīru and Muroran's dark pilsener Providence are two favourites.

Tokyo

Ryōgoku ji-bīru produced at the Ryōgoku Beer Station, is favoured by the local sumō wrestlers. The company does a German 'white beer', a pilsener and a 'Prague dark ale'. The suburb of Tachikawa offers the impressively titled Kami-kaze.

Nagano

In Karuizawa, Yona-Yona ale is produced using clear Nagano mountain water and the best-quality hops. Near the city of Matsumoto, Ji-bīru Azumino makes a tasty 'dunkelweisen Pilsener', again using Nagano's pure mountain water.

Kyoto

Liquor Mountain produces a good 'English-style' Shirakawa Baku-shu at its small brewery on Shirakawa-dōri.

Osaka

Right in the heart of Osaka foodie heaven, Dōtombori, Dōtombori-bīru produces a crisp Kolsh, a red Alt bitter, and wheaty, aromatic Special.

Kōchi

Yosakoi produces sharp, smooth 100% malt and barley Pilsener, and an aromatic, fruity, summer beer (Weissen), which still contains an active yeast because it is unfiltered. The deep, dark coloured alt is made with malt brought in specially from Munich.

Giant Kirin beer ice sculpture, Sapporo

Fukuoka

Hakata ji-bīru, right in the heart of Fukuoka, makes good amber and pale ales. Nagasaki's Unzen Yu-agari-bīru – 'Beer for getting out of the bath' – is a speciality of the dramatically volcanic hot-spring resort, the only place it is available. The light, golden Kolsch is slightly sweet but very smooth. The sweet, coppery-red alt is strong. Their special 'cloudy' lager is also excellent. Sasebo's Gamadas (the word is a local dialect equivalent of 'gambaru' – to do one's best, often heard in the aftermath of the Fugen-dake volcanic explosion here) is made on the north-west coast of Kyūshū. Its dark draft, yeasty alt beer and 'smoky beer' are especially good.

Yet it's the big makers that still have the beer market sewn up. For true beer lovers, the generic Kirins, Asahis and Sapporos are disappointingly similar. Nearly all are bottom-fermented brews using light malts and moderate hops content. Indeed when brewers *have* unveiled markedly different beers – for example, Sapporo's hoppy, very tasty lager Edel Pils – sales have been disappointing. The visiting connoisseur will simply have to make do, swallow a few dai-jokkis, and pick up a karaoke mike. Or else there's always that wonderful universe of **ji-zake** (local sakes) to explore ...

Friends enjoy a meal and a drink at an izakaya (a traditional restaurant-cum-bar) in Kyoto

DRINKS

Budō-shu or Wain (Wine)

At first glance, Japanese wine might appear to fall into the same category as Chilean sake, or Icelandic green tea. Yet while the country's vineyards are not yet threatening those of Bordeaux, Burgundy or the Barossa Valley, there's still some reasonable Japanese budō-shu out there. Suntory, Mercian and Manns have sown up the country's wine scene, usually offering 'Japanese wine' that is actually a mix of home-produced wine (nearly all of it from Yamanashi Prefecture), blended with foreign imports. Suntory's bordeaux and semillon are reasonable, but the star in Japan's wine firmament is Mercian's cabernet sauvignon (especially the 96 vintage) which is an exquisite, dense cab, and the first Japanese wine to be awarded a gold medal in France.

Shōchū (Grain Liquor)

Although it probably originated in Okinawa, shōchū is famously the drink of the southern island Kyūshū. It also has the reputation as the heavy drinker's tipple of choice. This may be because until the end of the Edo period it was in general use as a medical disinfectant. Yet not all of it is rough, cheap firewater. The better versions are actually rather pleasant.

Shōchū is usually drunk cold, on the rocks, or diluted with hot water. Ōita Prefecture produces **mugi-jōchū**, distilled from wheat, while Kagoshima Prefecture prides itself on shōchū made from potatoes, **imo-jōchū**. The Kōchi Mutemuka sake brewery uses the pure waters of the Shimanto-gawa river to produce the unusual **kuri-jōchū**, which is shōchū made from chestnuts. Unlike sake, this improves with ageing and is impressively smooth. However, few shōchū drinkers seem to have the patience to keep a bottle for more than a few days.

The southern tropical island of Okinawa produces its own version of shōchū called **awamori**, a powerful brew that the locals knock back, most often accompanied by Okinawa folk singing and dance. It is thought to have probably originated in Thailand (then Siam) and was brought to Okinawa during the Ryūkyū Kingdom's 'Golden Age', in the 15th and 16th centuries. Even the origin of its name is a little mysterious, and no one is sure whether the 'awa' refers to the foam that is created during distillation, the foam generated during measuring for alcohol content, or the foxtail-millet that it once contained. Serious awamori connoisseurs search out **kūsū**, awamori that has been aged for up to 20 years, a luxury that they are keen to shell out for.

home cooking
& traditions

A sharp knife and a chopping board are all you need to produce some startling Japanese food. Best of all, try to locate an obā-san (grandmother) to initiate you into the secrets of home cooking.

Illuminated by a shaft of light from the room's single, high skylight, the **daidokoro** (kitchen), the birthplace of so much marvellous Japanese cuisine, was a place of almost Mephistophelian darkness. Yet the gloom was dispelled by the flurry of activity that revealed the kitchen as the central focus in the daily life of a rural farmhouse. In the country they would be large spaces, with packed earth floors. In the cities, kitchens were much smaller, a situation that remains today. In Kyoto, the merchants' townhouses were built long and thin to avoid taxation, which was calculated by the size of a property's frontage. This earned them the nickname unagi no nedoko, the 'places of the sleeping eels'. Many Kyoto kitchens are, even today, impractical long thin slivers, with cupboards set so high that long-suffering housewives (yes, inevitably female) have to access them by way of short, portable stepladders.

A private house in the Tokushima countryside

Traditional & Modern-Day Kitchens

Traditional kitchens had a simple domestic setup. There would always be a **kamado**, the wood- or charcoal-burning stove that was used to heat the rice, and boil water, with a small separate fire (the precursor to today's heat-control switch) that allowed different parts of the stove to be heated to different temperatures.

Above the stove would be the kitchen's most important element, a protective amulet to ward off fires, in the form of a strip of calligraphy obtained from the local Shintō shrine. Even today these are very much in evidence, although the times of every house being made of wood are long gone. There would be no table, as the kitchens were designed solely for preparation, and eating would be in a neighbouring tatami mat room. There would be the basic utensils – the mortar and pestle for grinding sesame, ladles, sieves of either wood or metal, some simple knives, and metal **nabe** pans, either the single-handed **katate-nabe**, or the twin-handled **ryōte-nabe**, some the size of enormous soup tureens, used when the extended family were in town. Often the pans bore a hand-beaten, armadillo-scale pattern, which is known as yukihira-nabe, literally the 'flat snow pot'. Its name seems inappropriate, until you lift one up to see the snowflake design of the pan's bottom. There would also possibly be a mizuya-dansu, the glass-fronted chest of drawers used for storing the multitude of specially shaped dishes that Japanese cooking demands, and also a rectangular, wooden, ash-filled **hibachi** (hearth). The latter was used for heating, as an ever-ready source of fire, and as a secondary cooking area for preparing **yakimono** (grilled dishes). Suspended above the hibachi you would often find a fish-shaped rig-and-pulley contraption called a **jizai-kagi**, which was used for holding the cast iron nabe used in the preparation of **nabemono** (hotpot dishes).

Food preparation is usually labour intensive

Naturally, one would find chopsticks – such an indelicate phrase for such elegant utensils – the long variety, used for stirring, and for transferring food from pan to plate (much as tongs are used in western cooking), and shorter versions used for eating. Traditionally, men's chopsticks were longer than women's (to fit their larger hands) and as a result, the low tables on which food was served were slightly higher for women. This was so that the appropriate decorum could be maintained, and the unfortunate kimono-clad ladies didn't have to eat Quasimodo-fashion. Even today, a his-and-hers lacquerware chopstick set is a traditional wedding gift.

Finally, the traditional kitchen would posses its symbolic utensil, the **shamoji**, the flat, oval-ended wooden spoon used for serving rice. It had tremendous importance: as new brides entering a household were often regarded as little more than indentured servants to the omniscient, omnipresent mother-in-law. It was only after years of nagging and bullying that the new arrival was deemed to have earned her culinary spurs, which was signified by ma-in-law passing on the treasure – the family rice spatula! All that remained was for her to wait for her own children to grow up, marry, and ... payback time!

In the 1960s, when Japan discovered such modern artefacts as single-tub washing machines, hairdryers and the electric guitar (yes, it was for a short while dubbed the denki-shamoji – the 'electric rice spatula'), one might have expected there to be an avalanche of technical developments in the kitchen. Yet even today, some half a century later, the modern Japanese kitchen looks like a rather under-equipped, old-fashioned affair. OK, a **sui-hanki** (electric rice cooker) has been installed, with a fridge, neon lighting bright enough to melt one's eyeballs, and perhaps a microwave. Yet there's probably no dishwasher, no electric hotplate, maybe even no electric mixer. And cooking is done on a two-ring gas stove that in the west was long ago consigned to holiday caravans.

STOP THE CHOP

Waribashi, the 'chopsticks that split', are ubiquitous in modern Japanese life. Enough are used, and discarded, each year to build 30,000 homes. Most of the raw materials come from Japan's South-East Asian neighbours. If you don't wish to add to the environmental plunder, carry your own re-usable chopsticks, and simply refuse the disposable variety with a polite, "waribashi wa kekkō desu" – "thanks, but no thanks". If it causes a wee hiatus, worry not. You haven't mortally offended anyone, you've just done what 24,500,000,000 Japanese don't do, every year.

Cooking Methods

If Japanese kitchens haven't changed radically across the centuries, it comes as no surprise that the way in which food is prepared and served hasn't changed much either. Many families eat in the **osōzai** style (**obanzai** in Kansai), where the meal consists of several dishes, served centre table, from which the diners pick and choose. These will be accompanied by **gohan-mono** (rice dishes) and **shirumono** (soups) or **suimono** (clear soup). Really traditional households will still lay on a full restaurant-style spread, but for a family of eight (not uncommon with both sets of grandparents in residence) this necessitates preparing, then washing up, around 42 dishes, so it is fast losing favour. This labour-intensive (for mother and daughter – dad and the sons sit around watching TV) system stems from the way in which each meal is required to contain most, if not all, the different forms of cooking: **nimono** (stewed, simmered dishes), shirumono or **suimono** (soups), **yakimono** (broiled, grilled or pan-fried dishes), **agemono** (deep-fried foods), **mushimono** (steamed dishes), **sunomono** (vinegared foods), **aemono** (cooked leafy vegetables, poultry or fish blended with a dressing), and of course, gohanmono. No wonder then that the one exception to this style of eating, the nabemono, is so popular.

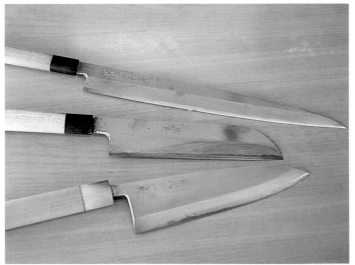

From top to bottom: yanagiba bōchō (a Kensai-style knife used for preparing sashimi), usuba bōchō (used for vegetables) and deba bōchō (used country-wide in the preparation of fish and fowl)

HOME COOKING

TREADING ON EGGSHELLS

Sawai Tomoko winced at the prospect. A British person coming for dinner. She knew, as do all Japanese, that the Brits drink warm beer and eat greasy fish out of old newspapers. Their cuisine is famously and unrelentingly, 'mazui' ('disgusting'). What could she possibly serve him?

Steve Jenkins was equally anxious. It was to be his first meal in a Japanese person's home. How would he negotiate the etiquette minefield that was surely awaiting him? He was sure to drop his chopsticks in his soup. And maybe worse. He nervously repeated his mantra … "Don't walk in the room wearing the toilet slippers".

Tomoko found her inspiration in an unlikely spot – history books. When the hairy western 'barbarians' first arrived in Japan they brought – besides gunboats, galoshes and golf courses – beef. Japan's favourite dish in the Victorian era (and Tomoko's choice for Steve) was a mix of Japanese one-pot, communal cooking (**nabe-ryōri**) and Meiji-period western trendiness, the once-so-daringly-fashionable **sukiyaki**.

Tomoko was proud of her selection. It is perfect winter food, fun to eat, requires little preparation, and even better, little washing up. And what's more it has that hint of an international heritage. Even the British might like it …

Using saibashi, the long chopsticks used for cooking

Steve was ushered to sit down at the **hori-gotatsu** (low, heated table), and Tomoko's husband, Yutaka, poured him a glass of hot, dry Niigata sake, which the guest sipped politely. The gentleness of its delicate rice aroma surprised him, but he welcomed the fiery warmth it spread through his chest. Tomoko, much to Steve's surprise, hauled out a circular cast-iron pan the size of a small gong, and a quaint single-ring gas stove.

Laid out on the table were the main ingredients. First and foremost, the sirloin beef, thinly-sliced and delicately arranged on a **zaru**, a flat, circular bamboo plate. The vivid red of the raw meat contrasted startlingly with the black lacquerware table. Beside this, on a larger flat lacquerware tray, were fresh green spring onions, mushrooms (both the brown **shiitake** and the white, thread-like, **enoki-dake**), a block of **yakidōfu** (grilled tōfu), green chrysanthemum leaves, and **ito-konnyaku**, a gelatinous, transparent, string-like entity. However, before he could enquire further, Tomoko had fired up the gas ring, and thrown a large lump of beef suet on to the hot skillet, which hissed and spat like an angry feline. The meal had begun.

Tomoko was cooking her native Osaka version of the dish. Similar to the Tokyo method she'd simply washed the vegetables, but rather than previously preparing a **warishita** sauce comprising a cup of shōyu, a cup of mirin and a little sugar, she put these directly onto the skillet with the suet, and two minutes later added the rest of the ingredients. She'd also chosen the rougher ito-konnyaku (she'd boiled it for two minutes, before slicing it into 10cm lengths) over its close relative, the smooth white **shirataki**. "Like life. Osaka rough, Tokyo smooth," she explained with a grin, as she stirred the mix with long cooking chopsticks in one hand, a beer in the other …

Tomoko passed him a cold Yebisu beer and Steve's worries about etiquette melted away like the suet. Yutaka showed him how to scoop whatever ingredients he wished from the skillet, and to dip them into the small bowl that Tomoko had placed in front of him, which contained a familiar yellow ingredient.

"Nama-tamago," she explained. Raw egg.

Steve looked nervously at the yellow mixture. Yet it was too late to back out now. He dipped the meat in the egg, raised it to his mouth, and … was gratefully surprised. As he held it between his chopsticks, the beef's heat had slightly cooked the egg. The delicate, succulent, tender sirloin tasted sublime …

As they slowly stuffed themselves, Yutaka talked to Steve about sukiyaki – how no one really knows the origin of its meaning, how a suki is a plough blade but also a homonym for 'to like', and how yaku means 'to cook'. They laughed as Tomoko used a dictionary to explain konnyaku as 'devil's tongue', 'elephant's foot' and 'a kind of processed starch'. Finally, as Steve wobbled to the door to take his leave, no one even noticed the 'Hello Kitty' toilet slippers on his feet.

HOME COOKING

Renowned author Susumo Hirayanagi (aka Robert Harris) and family eat osōzai style

Entertaining at Home

To many Japanese, entertaining guests at home is anathema. If they do even discuss throwing a hōmu pātī ('dinner party'), it is often said in the tones of someone about to undergo a bout of highly embarrassing, potentially life-threatening surgery. The reason for this is a combination of the esoteric – the cultural imperative that requires the separation of daily life and the celebratory, and the practical – most Japanese people believe they live in usagi-goya ('rabbit huts') that are too small, cramped and full of family to show outsiders. This, combined with the endless opportunity for eating out, makes it about as easy to get into a domestic kitchen as it is to get into the inner sanctum of the Imperial palace. One tried and tested ruse is to play on the fierce pride with which Japanese, most justifiably, regard their cuisine. Casually announce, with a theatrically wistful sigh, "Nn ... chotto ichi-do Nihon no katei-ryōri no tsukurikata o mite-mitai, ne ..." ("Oh, if only I could just once see Japanese home cooking ..."). It might take several months, but this is a hard one for any Japanese cook to resist.

foreign
infusion

Japan's chefs, like its mechanical engineers, love to 'adopt and adapt'.
Whether they're tinkering with **tempura**, honing the hamburger, or
redesigning **rāmen**, the result is inevitably a cross-cultural culinary
treat. Or fusion confusion? Witness the fruit sandwich and the rice
burger. Enjoy the diversity!

In a sense, all Japanese cuisine is 'fusion cuisine'. Almost everything was imported at one time from neighbours China or Korea, or from South-East Asia, India, Europe or the USA. Yet most imported cuisines have changed so profoundly that they are barely recognisable. **Udon** (wheat noodles) are a case in point. Wheat was imported from China via Korea as long ago as 239 AD, as were noodle-making techniques, but the Chinese don't eat udon, and the Korean version, 'udong', tastes markedly different. **Rāmen** (yellow wheat noodles) came from China, but has been so thoroughly adopted by the Japanese that the word 'rāmen' is as often written in the hiragana script, used for native Japanese words, as it is in katakana, the script reserved for words of foreign origin.

Katsudon, deep-fried pork cutlets served on a bowl of rice, is Japan's most common day-to-day 'fusion' dish. The katsu part, the cutlet, was introduced from Europe in the 16th century, but it really became popular during the Meiji era when Japan reopened to the west. It was served atop a dish of boiled rice, accompanied with sliced spring (welsh) onion, a well-beaten egg and **dashi** (stock).

Pan (bread) is a borrowing from the Portuguese, and Japanese bakeries can be both the foreigner's delight and horror house. Most starch-seeking foreigners enjoy the occasional sandwich as an alternative to noodles and rice, but often the joy is short-lived when they unexpectedly bite into **an-pan** (bread stuffed with sweet red beans), **karē-pan** (bread containing curry), and the **ichigo-sando,** a sandwich of ... strawberries and cream.

A master with freshly cooked Kyūshū-style Hakata rāmen (yellow wheat noodles in broth)

China

Similar to everywhere else in the big wide world, even a one-horse Japanese town will have its **chūka-ryōri-ya** (Chinese restaurant), which vary from tiny **shokudō** (cheap eateries) to opulent, palatial banquet halls. The largest selection is found in Kōbe's Nankin-machi, and Yokohama and Nagasaki's Chūka-gai, all huge, restaurant-packed Chinatowns filled with immigrants from the mainland and Taiwan, as well as Japanese-born descendants of Chinese traders. Szechwan, Cantonese, Beijing and Taiwanese are all well represented. While many establishments may offer a softer 'Japan-ised' taste, some remain truly authentic – though finding a blindingly spicy Szechwan meal might take some doing.

All the common Chinese dishes are there, though all too have Japanese names. **Harumaki** (spring rolls), **fū-yō-hai** (egg foo yung), **yakimeshi** (mixed fried rice), and **niku-man** and **shūmai** (dim sum) are popular. The spicy minced-beef and bamboo-shoot **mābō-dōfu** (known as 'acne-ridden grandma' tōfu), reputedly named after its less than pulchritudinous, but culinarily gifted inventor, is also popular. Kyūshū's Nagasaki,

A kanji paper lantern outside a Kyoto restaurant

historically the main point of entry for much Chinese trade, specialises in **chanpon** (noodle soup), and the refined banquet cuisine **shippoku-ryōri**, an amalgam of Japanese and Chinese dishes.

THE SOCIAL HISTORY OF CURRY RICE

Curry rice is the cheap and cheery, can't-be-bothered-to-cook food, a staple of winter school refectories, cut-price truckstops and **shokudō** (small, cheap eateries). Known as **karē-raisu**, it is prepared in seconds by adding hot water to an instant, sweet, spicy roux, mixing with vegetables or beef then adding to rice, is ubiquitous. Admittedly, it is the choice of flu-ridden children, and anyone in need of homely, junk food sustenance and is barely recognisable to visiting Indians or Pakistanis as 'curry' at all.

The first time Japanese citizens encountered curry is carefully documented in the diaries of a late-19th century Japanese sailor. In 1863, British warships were pounding Kagoshima into submission in retaliation for the murder of British citizen Charles Richardson by the Satsuma-han clan. Thirty-four Satsuma military officials were dispatched to France to lobby Napoleon III for support. They left aboard the French warship *Monsieur*, and later changed to a postal vessel, where they witnessed Indian passengers cooking up what they described as 'aromatic mud'.

Not surprisingly, curry didn't catch on, until Japan opened to the west during the Meiji period. It was then added to the local staple, to form **rice curry**. The Fūgetsudō restaurant in Tokyo began serving it as a luxury item, along with other such fashionable foreign imports as steak, omelettes, and pork cutlets, at 8 sen, eight times the cost of the poshest Japanese dish, **mori-soba** (cold buckwheat noodles).

By 1906, it was being advertised as the perfect addition to miso soup, or as an accompaniment to 'westernise' seaweed.

A decade later, *Nyokan*, a popular women's magazine, called it **curry rice**, and the name has stuck ever since. A curry revolution took place in 1931 when Britain's prestigious Crosse & Blackwell began selling domestic curry rice mix, which despite the manufacturing process, still tasted authentic. And it was cheap. Thus the modern, domestic curry rice industry was founded, aided and abetted by a new source of demand – the troops being shipped to fight wars in China. Over the next decade and a half it became used exclusively for military rations.

After WWII, the instant curry rice made by Hausu ('House') Shokuhin became a nationwide success, and its popularity remains huge today. By the early 1980s each household was consuming almost 2kg of curry rice mix per year, and an average of three curry rice meals per person per month – something in the region of 200,000,000 dishes annually.

Korea

Japan–Korea relations have long been characterised by periods of violent bloody war interspersed with peace, mutual distrust, and economic and technical exchange/forced appropriation. Similarly, Korean residents and Japanese-born children of Koreans have long been discriminated against, and denied from holding government jobs or even getting the vote. It is a sad fact that the reason so many excellent Korean eateries abound is that their owners have, in the past, been forcibly prohibited from engaging in other lines of work.

Most Japanese will visit Korean restaurants when they are prepared to spend a little more than usual, and want a party atmosphere but nothing *too* refined. These are not places that stand on ceremony, and if you're needing a break from the reserve of the posher Japanese establishments, look no further than the Korean barbecue specialists, or **yaki-niku-ya**. Recognise them by their Korean script, the Korean flag, and the powerful smell of roast beef wafting onto the sidewalk.

Osaka's Tsuruhashi, the country's biggest 'Korea Town', and Kyoto's Kujō and Sai'in are especially famed for **kankoku-ryōri** (Korean cuisine). In the popular imagination this really means beef and spicy **kimchee** (pickles). However, recent years have seen something of a Korean boom and the introduction of restaurants specialising in **ishiyaki-bibinbap** (mixed rice served on heated stones) and even Korean fast food.

Short-ribs, beef, tongue, the enticing **harami** ('cow diaphragm'), and **senmai** ('third stomach') are among the most common yaki-niku-ya meals. All are marinated in the establishment's special 'secret' sauce, served on a hotplate, then eaten with a dipping sauce most probably made of sesame oil, **kochijan** (a sweet spicy, pepper-miso paste) and grated apple. Cold jugs of beer are oft in evidence, as is **soju** (Korean shōchū), and very occasionally, the characteristic **makoli** (rice beer). It's a beef overload, so you might want to order fried vegetables, or cabbage leaves in which to wrap the beef before you put it in the dip.

In Korean-run restaurants, expect fiery sauces and more garlic. In those run by Japanese or Japanese-born Koreans, you might get a less-powerful version. Useful phrases include "Karakunai hō" ("less spicy"), "futsū" ("the regular") and, should you be brave enough, or foolhardy enough, "geki-kara" ("insanely hot").

The Korean equivalent of **nabemono** (hotpot dishes) is the **chige-nabe**, made most often with a mix of Japanese miso, cod, beef, tōfu, **shiitake** mushrooms, **harusame** (glass noodles) and leek. With the addition of **kimchee** it is called **kimchee-nabe**. Again, expect copious quantities of beef. In Japan, Korean restaurants are simply a vegetarian wilderness.

THE GREAT TEMPURA MYSTERY

Japan's best-known foreign import is **tempura** (lightly battered, deep-fried food). Yet rarely has the origin of a Japanese word been so mired in controversy.

Tempura shiso (perilla) leaf from the Yamadaya udon shop in Shikoku

The 'standard' encyclopedic definition states that it entered the language from Portuguese, some time in the late 16th century. Even here, however, food historians can't agree on how the word came about. Some say it refers to the Catholic Holy days – in Latin the 'Quattuor Tempora' – when, four times a year, the Portuguese traders were forbidden to eat red meat. Thus, they ate battered shrimp.

Others say it referred to the 'tempora', the time each week that eating red meat was prohibited, ie, Friday. Such an august tome as the *Kodansha Encyclopaedia of Japan* argues it is simply a corruption of the Portuguese word 'tempero', meaning 'cooking'.

Several Japanese historians attest it has nothing to do with the Portuguese, but originated in China during the 8th to 9th century Tang dynasty. Its current name, they argue, comes from the signboards that adorned temples (temp … oh, never mind) specialising in **shōjin-ryōri**, the Buddhist vegetarian fare that used the deep-frying technique of **abura-age**. The kanji characters for abura-age can be read as 'tem-pu-ra'.

A third school suggests that tempura was actually first created in 9th century India, and was then called tenjiku in Japanese. They say that the Edo period satirical novelist, Santō Kyōden, on one of the rare occasions he wasn't locked up in chains for lampooning the shōgunate, gave the nickname tempura to tenjiku-rōnin (a hapless masterless samurai), and it somehow got transferred to the food.

The least-known theory comes also courtesy of Santō Kyōden. It is rumoured that, in a creative moment, he described the dish as 'tenjiku kara furatto kita', the thing that 'floated over and popped in from ancient India'. As this was a bit of a verbal mouthful, it got abbreviated to 'ten-fu-ra'. Thus tempura was born, from poetry.

celebrating
with food

When the Japanese celebrate, it must include food and drink, and *lots* of it, whether it is in a rural festival to appease the rice gods (themselves not averse to the odd glass of sake), or in the party-hard **izakaya** (traditional restaurants-cum-bars) of the big cities. And it's fun. Everyone seems to know about the famous Japanese reserve — everyone, that is, except the Japanese themselves.

A Culinary Tradition

Every Japanese person's introduction to shoku-bunka, the 'culture of food' comes with the kuizome, when a baby is given its first morsel of solid food by the eldest member of the family. This custom symbolically invokes the fates to grant the child longevity and a life free from starvation. The traditional fare at kuizome is the **tai** (sea bream), with its connotations of wealth and the play-on-words congratulatory nuance of 'o-medetai', 'I wish to congratulate you'.

A young couple in traditional attire, about to be married in Kyoto

Sea bream pops up at every celebratory event in **honzen-ryōri** (formal celebration cuisine) and all rites of passage, notably in the marriage ceremony, where sea bream – real or symbolic – are often presented as gifts of thanks to the wedding guests. Most contemporary Japanese weddings take place in huge wedding halls, with specially constructed sugar-candy Disneyesque 'chapels', western-style buffet meals, several changes of clothes by the bride (into wedding dress, kimono and evening gown), and a general lack of frivolity. To some degree weddings are symbolic unions of families, and are also a chance to cement business and social connections. Yet even within a pseudo-Christian 'chapel', surrounded by guests clad in Armani and Missoni, toting Hermes bags, the bride and groom will seal the marriage by exchanging sake cups and drinking sake, a Shintō ceremony dating back centuries before the birth of Christ.

A month after the arrival of the couple's first child, the child will be whisked off in swaddling clothes to a Shintō shrine for the first shrine visit, which, once again, will be marked by a sake toast. Thus, begins a life attached to food and drink. The Japanese are born and marry Shintō, yet they die Buddhist. On the night preceding the funeral, mourners and relatives are served **butsu-ji** (Buddhist funerary cuisine). **Konnyaku** (devil's tongue – see the dictionary), **yuba** (soy milk skin), tōfu and vegetables are the main ingredients, with meat and fish strictly forbidden. The last relatives ever see of a departed one is when they pass the cremated, calcified, still-smouldering bones from the crematorium trolley to the funeral director, who arranges them in the funerary urn for burial. This transferring of the bones is from chopstick-to-chopstick, hence the strict taboo against passing food this way at the table.

Eateries and businesses sponsor lanterns hung at the entrances to Shintō shrines. One of these lanterns reads 'Kentucky Fried Chicken'.

A Food Calendar

The celebratory year begins in homes and restaurants on 1 January, with the multicourse, lavish, colourful **osechi-ryōri**. Served in **jūbako** (stylish lacquerware boxes with several layers), osechi originated mostly as a means of giving overworked Japanese housewives three days' of much-needed rest – its ingredients last well. Not only is it practical, it also contains linguistically symbolic references. Many ingredients have play-on-word meanings that are derived from the homonym-rich Japanese language. **Konbu**, or **kobu** (kelp), is served as it reminds one to yorokobu – 'enjoy'. **Kazu-no-ko** (salted or dried herring roe), with its many eggs, implies great fertility (kazu means number, or numerous; ko means child, although kazu-no-ko is actually named after the ancient word for a herring, **kado**). **Tazukuri** is a dish of **gomame** (a kind of small sardine) sauteed in shōyu with sugar. Its name exhorts one to be 'mame', in this sense 'dili-

A blossoming cherry tree in Ueno-koen (Ueno Park), famous for its 1200 cherry blossom trees, Tokyo

gently hard working' or 'persistent'. Even humble, compressed fish paste is dressed up in party colours as **kōhaku kamaboko**, white and pink, the colours of celebration. **Ise-ebi**, the Japanese spiny lobster, is commonly eaten at New Year, as its long beard and curved back symbolise longevity. Other osechi dishes include **surume** (dried squid), **dashi-maki tamago** (omelette roll), and **nishime** (a dried **nimono**, or simmered dish, containing such things as shiitake mushrooms, bamboo shoots, small potatoes and black soy beans).

The other great New Year delicacy is **o-zōni**, which is **mochi** (rice cakes) served in soup. Its precise ingredients vary extensively from region to region. In Kansai it is called **enman**, literally 'oval-full', conveying 'peace and harmony', and oval-shaped **mochi-gome** (glutinous rice) is used. Inhabitants of western Japan often also include yellowtail. Usually, o-zōni is a clear soup, though in Kyoto they use **shiro-miso** (sweet, white miso). In Kantō, the 'lucky', promotion-inducing ingredient is mustard spinach.

Mochi, ever-present in religious observations, is symbolic of New Year as **kagami-mochi**, an offertory decoration composed of two flat-bottomed rounds of mochi, a smaller one set atop a larger version. It is displayed with dried konbu and a **mikan** (mandarin orange) in homes and temples.

Hanging traditional Japanese carp kites used to celebrate the Boy's Day festival (5 May)

If your first dream of the New Year happens to contain an eggplant, you're also in for an auspicious 12 months. A cow's pretty good too, though Mt Fuji and a hawk are preferred. But if you should happen to have a nocturnal encounter with a horse or a fish, you're in trouble.

February 3 sees beans employed not as a meal ingredient, but as weapons in the fight against evil, at the Setsubun Matsuri. At shrines throughout the country, worshippers and tourists gleefully pepper costumed demons with hard soy beans, to the cry of "oni wa soto, fuku wa uchi" – "out with the demons, in with good luck". The ceremony traditionally marks the end of winter, though this must have been calculated by an obscure ancient calendrical theorem, because it is always bloody freezing. Householders scatter soy beans through their homes for similar protection against evil, and then, for added good luck, consume the number of beans equivalent to their age. The citizens of Kyoto, a city historically beset by fires, plagues and invasions, have adopted their own unique talismanic ritual in addition to the above. They face this year's 'ehō' (lucky direction), and consume, without talking, a double-sized roll of **maki-zushi** (nori-rolled sushi). We've been unable to ascertain who decides the lucky annual direction, or when or where this unique custom originated. One suspects the hand of the Kyoto Association of Sushi Dealers, but remains silent for fear of getting, er, 'beaned'. Kyoto's Yoshida-jinja shrine and Rosanji-jinja temple are both excellent venues for a spot of demon-expelling.

Common at many celebrations, but especially so at the 3 March Hina Matsuri (Girls' Day celebration) is **seki-han**, red rice, made from a mixture of glutinous and non-glutinous rice mixed with either **azuki** (red beans) or black-eyed peas, which give its sweetness and characteristic pink colour. This colour is the reason it is given to pubescent girls, to commemorate their first menstruation. The Hina Matsuri sees gender-role enforcement meeting culinary custom as young girls are given Venus clams, their two identical halves representing faithfulness, their closed shell chastity. However, the good folks of Gifu prefecture's Oagata-jinja shrine choose a rather bawdier parallel at their Hina Matsuri, where a young, local beauty pops out of a giant *papier mâché* clam shell. In addition to seki-han, diamond-shaped **hishi-mochi** rice cakes, **hina-zushi** (pink, yellow and brown sushi) and **shiro-zake** (white, cloudy sake) are all commonly served.

A masked festival participant celebrating the last day of winter

Late March or early April sees the much-anticipated coming of the cherry blossoms. The entire nation is glued to the TV to follow sakura-zensen, 'the cherry-blossom front', as it works slowly northwards from mid-Kyūshū, through Shikoku and Honshū, until it finally hits Hokkaidō sometime in May. Accompanying the front are hanami – 'flower-viewing' parties that during the brief, glorious reign of the pink blossoms, transform every inch of open space into a riot of alcohol-drenched, raucous contemplation of the evanescence of life and beauty. Actually, many people are too intent on consuming great quantities of cold beer and chatting up their newly found college classmates or company colleagues (the academic and business year begins in April) to notice the flowers.

Hanami (cherry blossom viewing), Ueno Park

The hanami at Tokyo's Ueno-kōen park is a wonder to behold, with groups sprawled across acres of blue tarpaulin sheeting, singing karaoke, dancing, and being anything but contemplative. It's noisy, good-natured chaos. Crimson-faced college students cover each other in beer. Best behaved are the group of middle-aged transsexuals, quietly toasting each other, while being photographed by every third passerby. A bald, elderly man in a kimono pretends to stab a teenage girl with a sword in a stunt to sell bottles of the dubiously titled 'bear oil'. Occasionally you'll spot someone eating **sakura-mochi**, mochi wrapped in cherry leaves, but more often the bill of fare is **yakisoba** (fried noodles with vegetables and meat), takeaway sushi, and more alcohol. Hanami parties are fun if you're in the mood, and the casual visitor will inevitably be invited to join in the revelry, but don't make any plans for the next morning.

The Tango no Sekku (5 May) Boys' Festival is an altogether more muted family affair. Its culinary highlight is ise-ebi, though here it is cleverly carved into the shape of a samurai's traditional armour. It is then served on a bed of vinegared rice, which resembles a flowing river. At the base of the stream are small fried fish, symbolising carp valiantly swimming upstream. Around the plates are iris leaves, representing swords. The overall picture is meant to champion those good ole pre-feminist boyish virtues of 'courage' and 'struggle against adversity', with a passing nod to bloodletting and armed warfare. Mochi is again present, as **kashiwa-mochi**, pounded glutinous rice with a sweet filling, wrapped in an oak leaf.

The Japanese summer is long, hot and extremely humid. Its star festival is Kyoto's Gion Matsuri, held in July and most commonly referred to as the Hamo Matsuri, the Pike-conger Festival, for the large quantities of the beast consumed during that time. Pike-conger and eel are famed for their invigorating qualities, and for their ability to restore flagging appetites. Both are favourite summer foods, especially in Kansai. Anyone unlucky enough to be trapped in ultra-humid Kyoto over the summer heads either for the nearest rooftop beergarden, or Kibune village the small mountain settlement just north of Kyoto, for the curious practise of **nagashi-sōmen**. Customers sit on yuka, straw platforms set over the flowing, cool, clear

All the accessories a girl needs – yaki-soba, chopsticks and a well-balanced handbag, Ueno Park, Tokyo

mountain stream. A restaurant employee, perched handily upstream, drops thin, white sōmen noodles into the river, which the downstream guests deftly pluck from the cold waters with chopsticks, and dip into a chilled **tsuyu** (dipping sauce). Nagashi-sōmen is not for the terminally clumsy or sorely ravenous, but it is great fun. A posher version with **kaiseki** (Japanese formal cuisine) and geisha, but no noodles, takes place on a specially constructed yuka set beside the Kamo-gawa river in the centre of the city, but it's not as cool. In either sense of the word.

Summer sees the festival of O-bon, the Buddhist equivalent of All Souls' Day, celebrated in most areas from 13 to 15 July, but in some areas a month later, when the spirits of the dead return to this realm. Obviously they're a bit peckish after the trip from the other side, so families gather (as they do at New Year) to pay respects, commune with their deceased ancestors, dance outdoors beneath lanterns, and eat. There's no specific o-bon cuisine, but miniature versions of a deceased relative's favourite dishes may be placed before a family's butsudan (Buddhist shrine) and Shintō kamidanà 'god-shelf' or altar. All families have the former. Many have both.

The harvest moon on 15 September is the time for tsukimi ('moon-viewing' parties). This aristocratic practise is somewhat in decline, though visitors to Kyoto at this time can hop in a boat and row out to the middle of the lake within Daikaku-ji temple grounds to compose the odd haiku or waka or two. Whichever poetic form you choose, make sure to have a handy supply of **tsukimi-dango**, rice dumplings on skewers, to fend off hunger. It is customary to offer these, or the newly in-season sweet potatoes, to the lunar object of your poetic meanderings. In the language of noodles, 'viewing the moon' refers to having a raw egg cracked onto your udon, soba or rāmen. In a fast-food joint, you may encounter a **tsukimi burger**. The egg in this case will be fried, unless you are singularly unfortunate.

Viewing cherry blossoms from rowboats at the Imperial Palace, Tokyo

Good eyesight is beneficial in the autumnal sport of collecting **sansai** (mountain vegetables), **sansai-tori**. Repeated in the late spring, hiking the mountains for sansai is popular mostly with middle-aged women and perpetually suntanned outdoorsy types. One goes hunting for vegetables such as **warabi** (bracken) and **junsai** (water shield), or wild mushrooms such as **hon-shimeji** or the valuable **matsutake**. It is an excuse to get out into the open air and drink lots of beer with friends, and is a potential source of sudden, unexpected, limitless wealth. Finding an undiscovered matsutake motherlode is a guarantee of instant wealth of El Doradic proportions. Mushroom greed in particular knows no bounds. The most spectacular wild mushroom we've witnessed featured a near- handbrake turn on Gunma Prefecture's Mt Akagi toll road by a gent in a large white Toyota sedan, who successfully spotted a matsutake at 40mph. There's a professional.

In a celebratory sense, the latter part of the Japanese culinary year is relatively quiet. In the autumn, the maples turn golden red, which brings hundreds of thousands of tourists to the famous maple-viewing spots across the country, most notably Kyoto. The **iroha-kaede** variety of maple is especially beautiful. One of the lesser-known delicacies of this time of year is – the maple leaf. Edible leaves can be served as tempura (**momiji-tempura**). Minō, north of Osaka, is one spot that is renowned for this.

On 15 November, families with children aged seven, five or three take them to the local shrine for the Shichi-go-san matsuri. Boys of five are decked out in the male kimono, while girls of seven and three wear their best kimono. It is a major source of tantrum throwing, as most kids are more used to jeans and Converse All-Stars than rope-tight silk, and wooden clogs. But the usual way to appease children is with the in-season, freshly roasted chestnuts, either served hot, as-is, from miniature flat-bed trucks parked outside the shrine, or in **kuri-gohan** (chestnut rice) prepared at home.

The year nears a close with that traditional Japanese ceremony, Kurisumasu, which begins some time in the early autumn and culminates in a department store shopping frenzy around, but not necessarily on, 25 December. Turkeys fill the department store food floors, alongside other delicacies such as Christmas compressed fish paste, Mickey Mouse yuletide chocolate logs, and snowmen sculpted out of mochi.

Old Year's night finishes with the ringing of the joya-no-kane (gong), 108 times, to relegate the traditional 108 Buddhist sins into a past life. The population then heads, en masse, for the country's Shintō shrines to offer prayers and alms to guide them into the New Year. Inevitably, it's a freezing mid-winter night, and the warm **ama-zake** (sweet sake) served at the shrine helps keep out the winter chill. The first dish of the year will be **toshi-koshi soba**, long buckwheat noodles symbolising long life, and wealth, as soba dough was once used by gold traders to collect gold dust. To cries of "yoi o-toshi o" – "Have a Happy New Year" and, after midnight, "akemashite omedetō gozaimasu" – "Happy New Year", the cycle of eating and celebration continues anew ...

regional
variations

The Japanese archipelago is blessed with ice-capped mountains, wide-open arable land, areas of fertile rice fields, and sub-tropical islands set in crystal clear seas. The variety of its cuisine, therefore, comes as no surprise. What astounds is the degree of specialisation that has given every minute settlement, from Northern Hokkaidō to Okinawa, its regional dish or ingredient.

REGIONS

Hokkaidō	Honshū	Kyūshū
Tōhoku (Northern Honshū)	Shikoku	Okinawa

Even the tiniest Japanese village has a **meibutsu** – a product, or dish, for which it is renowned. With the notable exception of Okinawa (see later in this chapter), it is this specialisation that gives Japanese regional dishes their unique quality, rather than major stylistic variations such as you find in, say, Chinese or Vietnamese. The prefectural governments of Kyūshū have even made this the mainstay of their island's economic development with their 'one village, one product' program.

Whether these meibutsu are really worthy of adulation is very much open to unbiased, non-partisan scrutiny. One Japanese adage drily observes "meibutsu ni umai mono nashi" ("lots of famous products, none of 'em any good"). It may be quite true that rampant commercialisation in heavily touristed spots has led to some dilution of quality. But, for the most part, sampling local specialities, with local vegetables, local rice and local grog, is a fine way to travel the country. And it certainly will endear you to the locals, who are fervent supporters of interesting products such as shiitake wine (Kiryū, Gunma) and **UFO-senbei** (flying-saucer shaped rice crackers from Anamizu, Ishikawa).

Hokkaidō

Hokkaidō, Japan's northernmost and second-largest island, has always been a place apart. Prior to Tokyo's decision towards the end of the 19th century to fill up the island with mainlanders, it was still, in essence, a wild, untamed frontier. Its indigenous peoples were the Ainu, peaceful, hirsute, primitive, tattooed worshippers of the bear and the otter. Sadly, they were over-partial to the cheap sake brought by the mainland colonists.

To some degree a frontier spirit remains in Hokkaidō even today. Its temperate summers, sub-zero winters and wide-open landscapes are a far cry from the mainland norm. Its potatoes, maize and wheat are crops belonging to different climes. Its capital, Sapporo, sits on the same latitude as such exotic places as Marseilles and Milwaukee. In winter, temperatures drop off the bottom of the thermometer. Its great rivers, the Ishikari-gawa, the Teshio-gawa and Tokachi-gawa provide water alluvial plains and fertile basins for agriculture. Its cattle and dairy ranches are such novelties for holidaying Japanese that it's not uncommon to see tourists stop their cars and jump out to photograph that rarest form of Hokkaidō wildlife, the dairy cow. Yet much of the island remains uncultivated wilderness, home to bears, serow, otters and foxes, and to violent, unpredictable volcanoes and exquisite, remote hot springs. Its cuisine springs from the confluence of salmon-filled mountain streams and the rich, cold-water ocean that surrounds the island.

Sadly, little tangible evidence remains of the indigenous cuisine of the Ainu, so thorough was their colonisation, assimilation – and almost annihilation – by the mainlanders. British missionary-anthropologist, the Very Reverend Doctor John Batchelor, one of the first to really document Ainu lifestyle and traditions in the late 19th century, was less than impressed. He described some of their favourite dishes: sea slugs; the root of the dog-tooth violet boiled and pulped into cakes for the long winter; horse cooked in bear grease; and stringy, antiquated dried fish. "In no sense," he observed laconically, "are the Ainu epicures".

Batchelor was not the first western observer in Hokkaidō. In 1878, an indomitable Yorkshirewoman and explorer had slugged all the way up from Tokyo to the northern island. Her name was Isabella Bird and unlike many of the effete, whinging early western visitors to Japan, she sought out the local cuisine. Her first Ainu repast is described by historian Pat Barr, in her magnificent *The Deer Cry Pavilion*:

"Soon the evening meal was prepared by the chief's principal wife, who tipped into a sooty pot swinging over the flames a mixture of wild roots, beans, seaweed, shredded fish, dried venison, millet paste, water and fish oil and left the lot to stew for three hours."

DON'T MISS – Hokkaidō

- **Ruibe** (frozen salmon sashimi)
- **Kani-ryōri** (crab cuisine) island-wide but especially in Wakkanai and Kushiro
- Seafood as fresh as it gets at Sapporo's bustling Nijō-ichiba market
- The rich, calorie-crammed **ishikari-nabe** (Hokkaidō salmon and vegetables hot-pot), island-wide
- Grilled smelt and Sapporo beer at one of the island's many **izakaya** (traditional restaurants-cum-bars)

SAPPORO

West 7   West 6   West 5   West 4   West 3   West 2   Ōdōri
Ōdōri-kōen
Ōdōri

Nijō-ichiba Market
Cheapest, freshest seafood in town. Great restaurants too, open from 7am.

Tanuki-kōji Arcade
Izakaya-hop in the cheaper alternative to Susukino.

Nishi-yonchōme

Tanuki-kōji Arcade

South 2

South 3

Sosei
Shōgakkō-mae   Susukino

Robinson's Susukino

Susukino
Search out the tiny bars and restaurants in Sapporo's high-octane party district.

Hōsui
Susukino

South 4

South 5

South 6

Higashi
Hongan-ji-mae

South 7

Higashi
Hongan-ji

0   100   200 m
0   100   200 yd

Rāmen Yoko Chō
Scores of noodle shops crammed into a single street.

Hyōsetsu-no-mon
Hugely popular crab specialist on six floors.

Toyohira-gawa

Yamahana South 9
-kujō

Nakajima-kōen

REGIONAL VARIATIONS

Interestingly, this sounds very much like a prototypical version of Hokkaidō's best-loved **nabemono** (hotpot dish), and its best-known dish, ishikari-nabe. A wonderful winter hotpot, **ishikari-nabe** is named for the small settlement near Sapporo that was once so dependent on salmon that it had its own 'Department of Salmon' in the town hall. No one goes much to Ishikari, but the dish it gave birth to is found in just about every Hokkaidō restaurant. It is satisfyingly simple, and very rich. Salmon is chopped and put into a heavy iron or earthenware **nabe** (pot), and slowly cooked in Hokkaidō miso, with potatoes, Chinese cabbage, tōfu, leek, **daikon** (giant white radish), carrots, **konnyaku** (devil's tongue – see the dictionary), **konbu** (kelp), shiitake or maitake mushrooms, and mirin, seasoned with salt. That's the theory at least. In reality as long as there's salmon, miso and tōfu, chefs seem to put in whatever they fancy. We've even had it with Hokkaidō-made cheese, which turned the dish into a heart-attack-inducing fondue-nabemono. Great way to die.

Hokkaidō's fresh seafood is legendary, and topping its list is salmon. It is charcoal-grilled, steamed in sake, added to **zōsui** (rice soup), and is served in any one of 1000 styles in the restaurants of Sapporo's foodtown, Susukino, and in **hokkaidō-ryōri** specialist restaurants throughout the country. It also appears in one dish we *can* thank the Ainu for, the sublime, unmissable, **ruibe**.

Ruibe is even simpler than ishikari-nabe. Get a salmon, leave it out in the Hokkaidō midwinter, cut it up, then eat it.

Or, to put it another way, take prime Hokkaidō salmon, freeze it to a temperature of -20 degrees Celsius or less, for more than 12 hours, slice it very thinly and eat it dipped in the best shōyu with just a small garnish of **benitade** (water pepper). As the raw salmon melts in your mouth ('thaws' in your mouth?), the effect is magical. It may sound like a fish popsicle, but once you've experienced the sublime suffusion of salmon and shōyu, you're hooked. And it may be simple, but that doesn't mean it isn't taken *very* seriously. Top Hokkaidō chefs won't slice it with knives, for fear of contaminating the salmon with a metallic smell. Instead they use the sharp edge of an abalone shell.

Hot on the heels of salmon in Hokkaidō cuisine is crab, the great winter cold-water speciality. The long-legged crabs of Wakkanai in the far north and Kushiro in the east are especially renowned, and are in season from December to April. Kushiro is also the smelt capital of Hokkaidō. Its season begins with Japanese railway-timetable precision on 10 October, but for the best fish, arrive in Kushiro a month later, when the fish are heavy with roe. Eat them broiled as an appetizer with sake. Wakkanai, bounded by the Sea of Okhotsk to the east and the Sea of Japan to the west, specialises in **tako-shabu** (octopus shabu-shabu). The unfortunate creature is speed-frozen while still alive, then sliced into thin pieces that you rapidly dip into boiling water flavored with konbu, using chopsticks. You then dip those into a thick sauce made of either miso, ground sesame seeds, or **nihaizu** – shōyu with vinegar.

Hakodate is famed for its chemical-free butter made by nuns at the city's Trappist monastery, and for **ika-sōmen** – squid sliced so thinly that they resemble sōmen noodles, served with a raw quail's egg, **wakame** (a type of seaweed) and **tsuyu** (dipping sauce).

Asahikawa, whose Ainu name means 'river where the waves are raging' (the mainland colonisers swiftly got rid of that one, and used Japanese characters to indicate the emperor-friendly 'river of the rising sun'), is best known for crab, and for its original rāmen. **Asahikawa-rāmen** features a shōyu-based broth, thin noodles and seafood, and has earned a reputation nationwide. Once nicknamed 'the Nada of the north' (in reference to Hyōgo's sake capital) for its plethora of breweries, Asahikawa produces some magnificent **nihonshu** (sake). Each year as the temperature drops to -10 degrees, Takasago Shuzō produces its **dai-ginjōshu** (top-quality sake), Ichiya Shizuku, in a specially constructed ice-dome. Its main rival is the local Otokoyama sake, which has consecutively won prizes for the last 24 years.

Obihiro, located in the south-east of Hokkaidō, was created during the Meiji period by government-sponsored militia-farmers. It is considered the breadbasket of Hokkaidō, lying as it does where the fertile Tokachi Plain is watered by the Tokachi-gawa river. In addition to being a major agricultural centre, it is famed for its sausages made at the government-sponsored Yachiyo-bokujō farm.

Last but not least is the island's major city, the thriving, oft-freezing Sapporo, where much of Hokkaidō's speciality products end up, either in the colourful Sapporo Nijō-ichiba market (its dozens of restaurants are good value) or in the countless **izakaya** (a traditional restaurant-cum-bar) and bars of Tanuki-kōji 'badger alley' and the Susukino entertainment district. Sapporoites are deeply proud of their miso-based **sapporo-rāmen**, which is popular nationwide, and their Yebisu and Kuro-label ('black label') beer. Also check out the wonderful trout from nearby Shikotsu-ko lake.

No culinary account of Sapporo is complete without mention of the highly dubious **jinghis ghan** (cooked mutton). A late, great British writer, Alan Booth, summed it up when writing of his experience in a Sapporo beerhall: "I ordered the largest mug of draft beer on the menu and a dish of mutton and cabbage which the Japanese find so outlandish that they have dubbed it jingisu kan (Ghenghis Khan) after the grandfather of the greatest barbarian they ever jabbed at. The beer, as always, was about one-third froth, but a single portion of Ghengis was so huge that it took an hour to eat – compensation for the loss of fluid ounces" from *The Roads To Sata*.

REGIONAL VARIATIONS

Honshū
Tōhoku (Northern Honshū)

The six prefectures that make up the Tōhoku district – Aomori, Iwate, Akita, Yamagata, Miyagi and Fukushima – are very much the boondocks, and great hunting grounds for **inaka-ryōri** (rustic cuisine).

Aomori is famous for its **hotate-ryōri** (scallop cuisine), with the specimens from Mutsu Bay being especially prized, and eaten as **sashimi** (raw fish) or in nabemono. As a whole, Tōhoku is partial to soups, not surprising considering the long, dark winters, and abundance of seafish and fresh vegetables. The fishermen and farmers of Aomori thrive on **jappa-jiru**, cod soup with daikon seasoned with miso. In summer, **ichigoni** soup with abalone and sea urchin is served in the ryokan (traditional inns) and minshuku (Japanese 'B&Bs') in and around Hachinohe

Assorted sashimi

city. The small port settlement of Kaijō-chō Ōaza Michibotoke on the Kofunawatari-kaigan coast even has its own Ichigoni Matsuri (Ichigoni Festival), on the fourth Saturday and Sunday of July, which features communal shiohigari (hunting for clams).

Expect to be greeted at an Iwate restaurant with the salutation "Yogu oden shitana han," the totally impenetrable local dialect equivalent of "Yoku oide kudasaimashita," "Welcome to our store". It will most likely specialise in Iwate's meibutsu **wanko-soba** (cold buckwheat noodles, served in small bowls). The noodles are delivered at a fast and furious pace one after the other. You try to keep up, and finally signal your imminent explosion by covering up your dish. On 11 February every year, the All-Japan Wanko-Soba Eating Contest takes place at Hanamaki-shi. The current soba-scoffing record stands at 189 bowls within two hours for men, 165 for

DON'T MISS – Tōhoku

- Iwate's soba – eat-till-you-burst buckwheat noodles
- **Jappa-jiru** (cod soup with daikon and miso) in Aomori
- **Wappa-meshi** (white rice steamed with wild plants and river fish) in Fukushima
- The deep, sweetish sakes of Akita, most notably Amanoto, Tenju or Dewatsuru

women. In summer, Morioka city specialises in a different kind of noodle, called **morioka-reimen**, which are frequently served with Korean **kimchee** (pickles). **Nambu-hittsumi** is the local nabemono dish containing stewed vegetable dumplings. The central part of the prefecture is renowned for its **iwate-gyū** (black-haired beef), while Yuda-Onsen (hot spring) prides itself on **suppon-ryōri**, cuisine featuring the soft-shelled turtles that are raised in its thermal waters. Locals wash these down with Nanbu Tōji sake, which rose from humble origins in Ishidoriya town to become one of the nation's 'big three' sake makers. Check out Ishidoriya's Nanbu Tōji Denshō Hōru (Sake Historical Museum) and, more importantly, the tasting corner at the nearby Sakesho Kaikan hall.

Akita produces some of the country's top-quality rice, most notably akita-komachi, and its sake is equally good, renowned for its characteristic depth and sweetness. Try Amanoto, Tenju or Dewatsuru. **Shottsuru** (shōyu distilled from sandfish or sardines, thus somewhat akin to Thailand's **naam plaa** or Vietnam's **nuoc mam**, is considered Akita's unique meibutsu (though, in truth, it is actually made in one other Japanese location, on the Noto-Hantō peninsula of Ishikawa, where it is called **ishiru**). The prefectural dish is **kiritampo** – rice balls on skewers, cooked in a stew of vegetables, chicken and mushroom. Inaniwa town's flat **inaniwa-udon** are also popular.

The brave folk of Yamagata combine fermented beans, taro and tōfu to make the adventurous soup, **nattō-jiru**. A winter speciality soup of the Shōnai region is **dongara-jiru**, in which a whole cod is chopped into a stew of miso and salt. **Tama-konnyaku** is konnyaku stewed in a shōyu broth and served on skewers. Shōnai is also a major producer of persimmons and cherries.

Miyagi, on the east coast, is well known for its saltier-than-the-Dead-Sea **sendai-miso**, oysters, and Kesennuma city's **fuka-hire** (shark's fin soup).

Tōhoku's southernmost prefecture, Fukushima, has a long, distinguished culinary pedigree, most noticeably in the historic castle town of Aizu-Wakamatsu, with sake and soba makers, and producers of **tamari-jōyu** (wheat-free shōyu) producers. Today, however, it is probably best known for its **kitakata-rāmen** made with thick, wavy noodles that are made in Kitakata. Its broth is a mix of shōyu and chicken broth. **Wappa-meshi**, found across the prefecture is white rice cooked with wild plants and river fish, steamed and served in bentō (lunch boxes) which are locally called 'wappa'. **Sanjin-ryōri**, literally meaning 'mountain man food', originated in Hinoemata village, and includes noodles and **yaki-mochi** (toasted glutinous rice). Mochi lovers will also want to seek out **shingoro**, balls of glutinous rice mixed with sesame seeds and potatoes and roasted **sumibi-yaki** style, over a charcoal fire.

REGIONAL VARIATIONS

Tokyo

"Every day we have excellent very fresh oysters, geese, ducks – open your eyes, be all ears you celebrated gastronomes" – Henry Heuksen, translator to the first US ambassador to Japan, Townsend Harris.

Tokyo is a *Mad Max*-meets-*Blade Runner* megalopolis, a 24-hour neon cyclone that chases its own tail and spins ad infinitum with limitless human energy. All life is there from the earthy, proletarian shitamachi ('downtown') to the unchanged-since-wartime backstreets of Asakusa, Ueno, Nippori and Katsushika-Shibamata, to trendy Aoyama and Harajuku.

All food life is present too, from Laotian to Lebanese, from deep-fried scorpions to haute cuisine served in transplanted French chateaux, from Shibamata's **tsukudani** (fish and vegetable pickle) streetsellers to Aoyama's snooty-but-irresistible street cafes. The city is just one giant revolving restaurant with a ravenous lunatic at the controls. Yet amid all this culinary 'noise' stands the Edokko, the true Tokyoite, as down to earth as a market-trader's boot, and forthright, proud and hungry.

When the powers that be decided to move the capital, and its emperor, from ancient Kyoto in the late 19th century, where it had resided for centuries, the effect on the country was profound. The site chosen for the new city was low-lying swampland where the huge Kantō plain that swept down from the mountains of Tochigi and Gunma met a huge, fish-filled bay. The name of the new capital was Edo. Its construction was a gigantic task, and carpenters and labourers were shipped in by the thousands. It was these rough and tough workmen who were to build, and settle in, the city that was later to change its name to Tokyo.

The Edokko, literally, 'children of Edo', were not the aesthetes and artisans of Kyoto, and their tastes, both culinary and otherwise, ran to the plain and direct. The Edokko loved the strong, dark brown **katsuobushi** (dried bonito fish)-based **dashi** (stock) that still characterises Tokyo cuisine today. They embraced buckwheat noodles with a vengeance, opting for a strong, dark tsuyu, a style found throughout the country.

Today the three great noodle restaurant rivals; Kanda Yabu Soba, Matsuya and Muromachi Sunaba, fight it out for the soba laurels, yet in all the unmistakable taste of Edo remains. The no-nonsense, middle-aged, smiling woman who manages Sunaba tells us that she's been out of Tokyo once – a weekend trip, 14 years ago. A true Edokko.

If Tokyoites love one thing as much as soba, it's sushi. In Ginza, and the streets that surround the Tsukiji wholesale market – that great pumping heart at the centre of the city's culinary system – the country's finest sushi chefs prepare its finest sushi. These itamae, 'the men who stand before the board' are a tough crowd, dry as 20+ sake, and wary of strangers. They proudly describe the fruit of their labours (as do all Tokyo-style chefs) as **edomae-ryōri**, 'the cuisine from in front of Edo'.

Two individual Tokyoites changed the course of sushi history. Matsumoto Yoshiichi in the 17th century introduced using rice vinegar in sushi rice, to cut down on preparation time. The populace loved the new tart flavour. In the 1820s, sushi visionary Hanaya Yohei added raw fish to vinegared rice, which he served directly from his sushi yatai (outdoor food stall), and sushi as we know it today, from the Ginza to the west coast, was born. Hanaya not only invented this **edomae-zushi**, or **nigiri-zushi** (hand-pressed sushi), he also popularised the concept of fresh sushi served as quickly as possible. It was not until 1923, when the great Kantō earthquake levelled the city and rendered its surviving chefs unemployed, that nigiri-zushi spread throughout Japan, because the skilled itamae were forced to move in search of work. Sushi consumption was revolutionised in the 1950s, when Osaka-born Shiraishi Yoshiaki invented 'conveyor-belt' sushi, where plates of sushi pass before the customer.

DON'T MISS – Tokyo

- The foodie voyeur paradise of Tsukiji Shijō external market
- **Edomae-zushi** – the origin of sushi, and a quintessential Tokyo dining experience
- Traditional shitamachi ('down-town') fare in the traditional restaurants of Asakusa and Ueno
- Kanda's and Nihombashi's three great buckwheat noodle restaurants, Muromachi Sunaba, Matsuya, and Kanda Yabu Soba
- Partying in Roppongi, Shinjuku or Shibuya, as suits your whim, wallet and age group
- **Yakitori** (grilled, skewered meat) under the tracks at Yūrakuchō

REGIONAL VARIATIONS

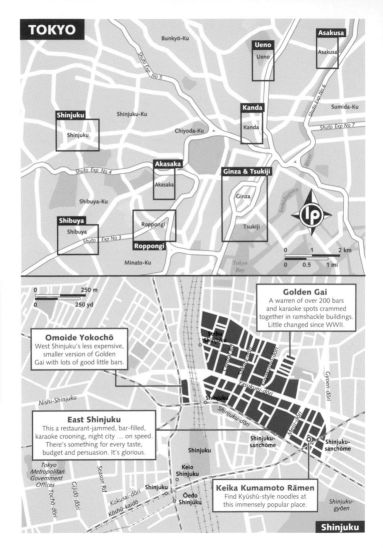

TOKYO

Bunkyō-Ku

Shuto Exp No 5

Ueno
Ueno

Asakusa
Asakusa

Sumida-Ku

Shuto Exp No 6

Shuto Exp No 7

Shinjuku
Shinjuku

Shinjuku-Ku

Chiyoda-Ku

Kanda
Kanda

Shuto Exp No 4

Akasaka
Akasaka

Ginza & Tsukiji
Ginza

Tsukiji

Shibuya-Ku

Sumidagawa River

Shibuya
Shibuya

Roppongi

Roppongi

Shuto Exp No 3

Minato-Ku

Tokyo Bay

| 0 | 1 | 2 km |
| 0 | 0.5 | 1 mi |

---

0 250 m
0 250 yd

Golden Gai
A warren of over 200 bars and karaoke spots crammed together in ramshackle buildings. Little changed since WWII.

Omoide Yokochō
West Shinjuku's less expensive, smaller version of Golden Gai with lots of good little bars.

Seibu Shinjuku

Yasukuni-dōri

Gyoen-dōri

Meiji-dōri

Shinjuku

Shinjuku-dōri

East Shinjuku
This a restaurant-jammed, bar-filled, karaoke crooning, night city ... on speed. There's something for every taste, budget and persuasion. It's glorious.

Nishi-Shinjuku

Shinjuku-sanchōme

Shinjuku-sanchōme

Shinjuku

Tokyo Metropolitan Government Offices

Keio Shinjuku

Shinjuku

Ōedo Shinjuku

Keika Kumamoto Rāmen
Find Kyūshū-style noodles at this immensely popular place.

Shinjuku-gyōen

Gijidō-dōri

Yotchō-dōri

Season Rd

Kokusai-dōri

Kōshū-kaidō

Shinjuku

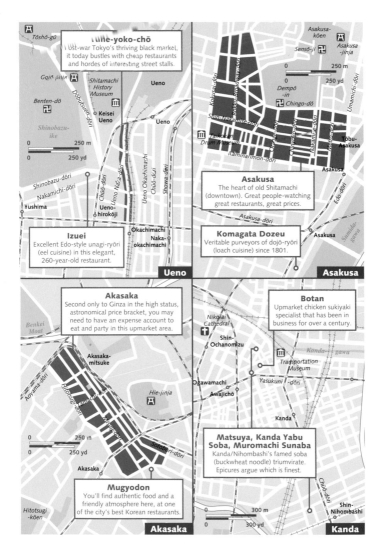

Amee-yoko-chō
Post-war Tokyo's thriving black market, it today bustles with cheap restaurants and hordes of interesting street stalls.

Tōshō-gū
Gojō jinja
Shitamachi History Museum
Benten-dō
Ueno
Shinobazu-ike
Keisei Ueno
Dōbutsuen-dōri
Shinobazu-dōri
Nakamichi-dōri
Yushima
Ueno Nizä-dōri
Chūō-dōri
Ueno Okachimachi
Showa-dōri
Ueno-hirokōji
Okachimachi
Naka-okachimachi
Okachimachi

Izuei
Excellent Edo-style unagi-ryōri (eel cuisine) in this elegant, 260-year-old restaurant.

Ueno

Asakusa-kōen
Sensō-ji
Asakusa-jinja
Umamichi-dōri
Dempō-in
Chingo-dō
Kokusai-dōri
Kaminarimon-dōri
Nakamise-dōri
Nakamise-dōri
Taikokan Drum Museum
Asakusa-dōri
Tōbu-Asakusa
Asakusa
Edo-dōri
Asakusa
Sumida-gawa

Asakusa
The heart of old Shitamachi (downtown). Great people-watching great restaurants, great prices.

Komagata Dozeu
Veritable purveyors of dojō-ryōri (loach cuisine) since 1801.

Asakusa

Akasaka
Second only to Ginza in the high status, astronomical price bracket, you may need to have an expense account to eat and party in this upmarket area.

Benkei Moat
Akasaka-mitsuke
Aoyama-dōri
Hitotsugi-dōri
Sotobori-dōri
Hie-jinja
Akasaka
Hitotsugi-kōen

Mugyodon
You'll find authentic food and a friendly atmosphere here, at one of the city's best Korean restaurants.

Akasaka

Botan
Upmarket chicken sukiyaki specialist that has been in business for over a century.

Nikolai Cathedral
Shin-Ochanomizu
Kanda-gawa
Transportation Museum
Ogawamachi
Yasukuni-dōri
Awajichō
Kanda
Chūō-dōri
Shin-Nihombashi

Matsuya, Kanda Yabu Soba, Muromachi Sunaba
Kanda/Nihombashi's famed soba (buckwheat noodle) triumvirate. Epicures argue which is finest.

Kanda

0 — 250 m
0 — 250 yd

0 — 250 m
0 — 250 yd

0 — 250 m
0 — 250 yd

0 — 300 m
0 — 300 yd

REGIONAL VARIATIONS

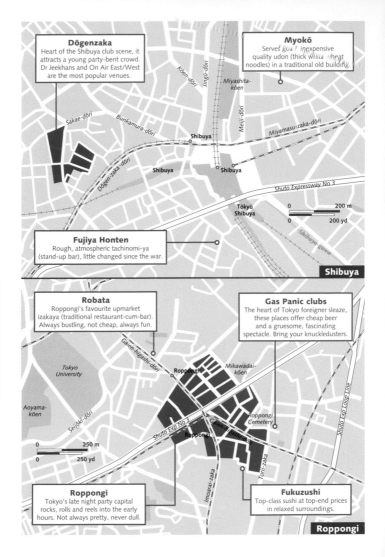

Dōgenzaka
Heart of the Shibuya club scene, it attracts a young party-bent crowd. Dr Jeekhans and On Air East/West are the most popular venues.

Myokō
Serves good inexpensive quality udon (thick white wheat noodles) in a traditional old building.

Kōen-dōri

Jingū-dōri

Miyashita-kōen

Sakae-dōri

Bunkamura-dōri

Meiji-dōri

Miyamasu-zaka-dōri

Shibuya

Shibuya

Dōgen-zaka dōri

Shibuya

Shibuya

Shuto Expressway No 3

Tōkyū Shibuya

0   200 m
0   200 yd

Shibuya-gawa

Fujiya Honten
Rough, atmospheric tachinomi-ya (stand-up bar), little changed since the war.

Shibuya

Robata
Roppongi's favourite upmarket izakaya (traditional restaurant-cum-bar). Always bustling, not cheap, always fun.

Gas Panic clubs
The heart of Tokyo foreigner sleaze, these places offer cheap beer and a gruesome, fascinating spectacle. Bring your knuckledusters.

Gaien-higashi-dōri

Tokyo University

Roppongi

Mikawadai-kōen

Aoyama-kōen

Seijoki-dōri

Shuto Exp No 3

Gaien-higashi-dōri

Roppongi Cemetery

Shuto Exp Loop Line

0   250 m
0   250 yd

Roppongi

Imoarai-zaka

Tori-zaka

Roppongi
Tokyo's late night party capital rocks, rolls and reels into the early hours. Not always pretty, never dull.

Fukuzushi
Top-class sushi at top-end prices in relaxed surroundings.

Roppongi

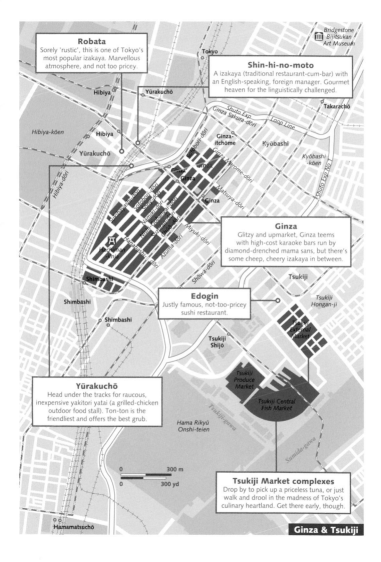

Robata
Sorely 'rustic', this is one of Tokyo's most popular izakaya. Marvellous atmosphere, and not too pricey.

Shin-hi-no-moto
A izakaya (traditional restaurant-cum-bar) with an English-speaking, foreign manager. Gourmet heaven for the linguistically challenged.

Ginza
Glitzy and upmarket, Ginza teems with high-cost karaoke bars run by diamond-drenched mama sans, but there's some cheap, cheery izakaya in between.

Edogin
Justly famous, not-too-pricey sushi restaurant.

Yūrakuchō
Head under the tracks for raucous, inexpensive yakitori yatai (a grilled-chicken outdoor food stall). Ton-ton is the friendliest and offers the best grub.

Tsukiji Market complexes
Drop by to pick up a priceless tuna, or just walk and drool in the madness of Tokyo's culinary heartland. Get there early, though.

Bridgestone Bijitsukan Art Museum

Tokyo

Hibiya · Yūrakuchō · Takarachō

Hibiya-kōen · Hibiya · Ginza-itchōme · Kyōbashi

Yūrakuchō · Kyōbashi-kōen

Ginza · Ginza

Tsukiji

Shimbashi · Shimbashi · Shimbashi

Tsukiji Hongan-ji

Tsukiji External Market

Tsukiji Shijō

Tsukiji Produce Market

Hama Rikyū Onshi-teien

Tsukiji Central Fish Market

Shuto Exp · Ginza Sakura-dōri · Loop Line · Shuto Exp No 1

Hibiya-dōri · Sotobori-dōri · Ginza Chūō-dōri · Ginza Nishi-dōri · Sukiyabashi-dōri · Ginza Suzuran-dōri · Ginza Yanagi-dōri · Ginza Corridor · Harumi-dōri · Hamaguchi-dōri · Ginza Chūōme-dōri · Matsuya-dōri · Miyuki-dōri · Azuma-dōri · Shōwa-dōri

Hachiman Jinja · Tsukiji-gawa · Sumida-gawa

| 0 | 300 m |
| 0 | 300 yd |

Hamamatsuchō

REGIONAL VARIATIONS

Ginza & Tsukiji

Today's cosmopolitan madhouse that is Tokyo features magnificent restaurants of every persuasion on every street corner. That's not hyperbole, just plain fact. But even within the metropolitan mayhem, some areas retain their old specialisations. The **ryōtei** (high-class restaurants) of Kagurazaka are still the venue for discreet, expensive rendezvous with geisha over **kaiseki** (Japanese formal cuisine). Kanda-Nihonbashi fairly teems with classy soba restaurants. Whereas Akasaka is all glitz and expense-account dining, Asakusa still has unpretentious loach, eel, **tempura soba** (soba noodles with tempura pieces on top) and rāmen restaurants that date back to a bygone age. Ginza is sushi mecca, from the posh refinement of restaurants such as Edogin to the impossibly fresh, inexpensive sushi of the restaurants surrounding Tsukiji's wholesale fish market. Across the Edo-gawa river in Katsushika-Shibamata, the streets approaching Taishakuten temple teem with **noshi-ika** (dried, hand-rolled squid), **senbei** (rice crackers) and tsukudani stores. The arches beneath the railway tracks at Yūrakuchō boast dozens of smoky, irreverent, convivial **yakitori** (grilled, skewered meat) shops.

If culinary freedom is the absence of choice, Tokyo's sheer size and mesmerising variety would drive a hungry soul to distraction. In the end there is but one option ... grab your wallet and follow your nose.

Grabbing a bite for lunch at the Imperial Palace, Tokyo

Kyoto

Moving the capital to Edo had devastatingly profound effects on Kyoto. In one fell swoop it lost its emperor (and the huge administrative and financial support system that came with the imperial household), its livelihood, its artisans, and a good percentage of its population. All that remained was its temples, its bruised pride, and its cuisine, **kyō-ryōri**. Even today, Kyoto retains its aristocratic, slightly haughty, slightly miffed demeanour, and this is reflected in its tastes. It eschews upstart Tokyo's blunt, no-nonsense directness, for an altogether more elegant, cultured grace. Kyō-ryōri is restrained, subtle and endlessly refined.

At the heart of all this cultured sophistication is the Gion district, with its geisha in all their powdered, deliberate beauty, its exclusive ryōtei, and its unforgiving mantra 'ichigen-san okotowari' – 'guests by introduction only'. Fortunately a combination of economic necessity and a grudging nod to the values of the 21st century means that many of the top Gion restaurants open their doors to those with the sole introductory power of a bulging wallet. Kinmata and Minoko, specialists in **cha-kaiseki** (tea ceremony cuisine) and **kaiseki** restaurants Hamasaku and Nakawa are some of the big names that open to the public. Ichi-riki still remains stubbornly closed to the mere passer-by.

If you do manage to get beyond the doors of a top Kyoto restaurant, you'll find either the Zen-inspired, frugal and unadorned cha-kaiseki, or full restaurant-style (read banquet) kaiseki. On the simplest level, a kaiseki meal is made up of one soup and three side dishes, served with rice and pickles, yet often the number of courses run into double figures, their content determined by season and the whim of the top chef. As many dishes originated in Kyoto's temples, expect Buddhist staples tōfu, fu (gluten), and **yuba** (soy milk skin) to be in evidence, along with bamboo shoots, and vegetables that originated in Kyoto: eggplant, daikon, and leek. Kyoto pickles include **takuan** (daikon), **senmai-zuke** and **suguki** (turnips), **mibuna-zuke** (greens), **nanohana-zuke** (rape shoots) and, most famously, **shiba-zuke** (cucumber, eggplant and Japanese ginger pickled with red beefsteak plant), adorn most menus.

Ironically, kyō-ryōri, famously so aristocratic and exclusive, evolved from a paucity of raw materials. Kyoto's distance from the sea, and the mountainous barrier that encloses its west, north and east sides, meant that Kyoto chefs had to devise new ways to eat the stuff no one else wanted. Thus, while the rest of the nation scoffed at herring and cod as 'cat stride' fish – even the cat would stride over them – Kyotoites actively embraced these 'inferior' species. They turned herring, by partly drying it, into its best-known dish, **nishin-soba**. Similarly, mackerel was widely discredited as a fish that soon rots, but in Kyoto it became a delicacy in **saba-zushi** (mackerel sushi).

DON'T MISS – Kyoto

- Posh **kaiseki** nosh at a Gion ryōtei
- **Yudōfu** (tōfu hotpot) in the temple-restaurants of Sagano or Nanzen-ji
- The Kyoto speciality **nishin-soba** – buckwheat noodles topped with a partially dried herring
- Nishiki-ichiba market, catering to emperors and restaurateurs since the 17th century
- Cheap dining and bar-hopping in downtown Kiyamachi
- Sake sampling at source in the sake warehouses and factories of Fushimi

The Kyoto chefs possessed such originality and innovative flair that they could even dish up less-than-pristine bone-filled pike-conger, which was long-considered the culinary lowest of the low (not least as it took half a day to get to Kyoto from Osaka, a full day from Wakasa Bay on the Japan sea coast) as haute cuisine. They patiently deboned it, boiled it, plunged it thereafter into ice-cold water, and served it with sour plum as **bainiku-ae**. It is still one of the city's greatest summer dishes.

In the nation's collective imagination, Kyoto is temple-town, and its **shōjin-ryōri** (Buddhist vegetarian cuisine) is unmissable. Try the **yudōfu** (tōfu boiled in a konbu broth) restaurants surrounding Nanzen-ji temple in the east, Sagano in the west, or Gion's Yasaka-jinja shrine. For shōjin-ryōri head to Arashiyama's Tenryū-ji, and for its Chinese-Zen equivalent, **fucha-ryōri**, go to Ōbaku south-east of the city.

Yet Kyoto today is equally secular. It is a thriving university town, which might account for its unusually large concentration of rāmen shops. There's no particular 'Kyoto style' of rāmen, although the dark, thick and peppery broth of Shinpuku-saikan is attracting much attention in rāmen connoisseur circles. Nationwide big names such as Dai-ichi-asahi and Tenkaipin originated here, while **Shinpuku-saikan**, Yonakiya, Kyōichi, Kin-chan and Chinyu all command many Kansai devotees. Yet the 'dark horse' vote must go to Teramachi-dōri's sublime, unpublicised Kyōhei.

Finally, make sure you don't leave Kyoto without sampling some of its famous sake, made in the Fushimi district several kilometres south of the main train station.

REGIONAL VARIATIONS

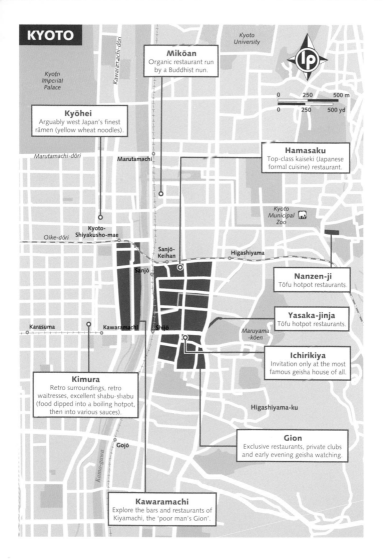

KYOTO

Kawaramachi-dōri

Kyoto University

Kyotn Imperial Palace

Mikōan
Organic restaurant run by a Buddhist nun.

0 250 500 m
0 250 500 yd

Kyōhei
Arguably west Japan's finest rāmen (yellow wheat noodles).

Marutamachi-dōri

Marutamachi

Hamasaku
Top-class kaiseki (Japanese formal cuisine) restaurant.

Kyoto Municipal Zoo

Kyoto-Shiyakusho-mae

Oike-dōri

Sanjō-Keihan

Higashiyama

Sanjō

Nanzen-ji
Tōfu hotpot restaurants.

Yasaka-jinja
Tōfu hotpot restaurants.

Karasuma

Kawaramachi

Shijō

Maruyama-kōen

Ichirikiya
Invitation only at the most famous geisha house of all.

Kimura
Retro surroundings, retro waitresses, excellent shabu-shabu (food dipped into a boiling hotpot, then into various sauces).

Higashiyama-ku

Gojō

Gion
Exclusive restaurants, private clubs and early evening geisha watching.

Kamo-gawa

Kawaramachi
Explore the bars and restaurants of Kiyamachi, the 'poor man's Gion'.

REGIONAL VARIATIONS

REGIONAL VARIATIONS

DON'T MISS – Osaka

- **Tako-yaki** (octopus balls) – streetside snacks, not social events (pictured)
- **Okonomi-yaki** (savoury pancake) on the restaurant-filled street of Dōtombori-suji
- **Izakaya**-hunting and karaoke in Namba or Shinsaibashi
- Shopping for that hard to find fish-deboner or wax sushi replica in Dōguya-suji, the kitchenware street in Sennichimae

Osaka

Japan's second-largest city is as food-crazed as they come. Osaka's mercantile and sea-going heritage has given it a rough-and-tough, no-nonsense image, and its industrious citizens have a reputation for partying as hard as they work. The saying goes that while Kyotoites will happily waste their fortunes on fine kimono, and Tokyoites on shoes, the Osakans have only one way to squander their riches – on food. There's even a word for it that has become Osaka's unofficial motto – kuidaore – the civilised practise of bankrupting oneself through sheer gluttony.

The city's love of good food is undeniable, from the entertainment districts of Umeda in the north to Shinsaibashi and Namba in the south. However, real foodie heaven is Namba's gourmet street, Dōtombori-suji, and the neighbouring area of Sennichimae. Dōtombori's fame and fortune began with the success of its kabuki theatres, but soon the area began to teem with restaurants to service the Osaka revellers' culinary needs. The entertainment connection remains strong even today, with the Yoshimoto manzai (stand-up comedy) television studios situated in the very heart of Sennichimae. Kuromon-ichiba market, nearby, still provides the raw materials for the countless restaurants that line the Dōtombori-gawa canal. Crab-cuisine specialists Kani-Dōraku and the rāmen shop Kinryū, with its fiery kimchee toppings and shōyu and pork-broth base, have become nationally famous, yet for most Japanese Osaka is synonymous with two dishes: **tako-yaki** and **okonomi-yaki**.

It says something about Osaka's lack of pretension, when one of its best-known epicurean delights is 'octopus balls'. Tako-yaki are tiny, spherical, wheat flour pancakes to which diced octopus, shredded cabbage and other vegetables are added. They are often grilled in front of the customer at yatai, and come topped with katsuobushi and a 'secret' sauce of the owner's invention. They are cheap, filling, fattening and seem to remain intact in one's stomach for several days following consumption. Needless to say this does nothing to lessen their popularity, not least for a midnight stop-off between izakaya and karaoke-den. Dōtombori's Ōtako store is nationally renowned.

Okonomi-yaki is perennially (and inaccurately) translated as 'a kind of Japanese pizza'. It is nothing of the sort. It's a discus-sized savoury pancake of wheat-flour, egg and water topped with your konomi – 'whatever takes your fancy'. Usually this means meat, squid, vegetables and finely chopped cabbage. Restaurant proprietors cook it in front of you on a flat hotplate and serve it with sweet brown sauce or mayonnaise, often garnished with dried and powdered **ao-nori** (laver seaweed,) or katsuobushi flakes that 'dance' as they heat up. Osakans can't get enough of the stuff, yet few know (or at least care to admit) that it was almost certainly invented in either Kyoto or Tokyo.

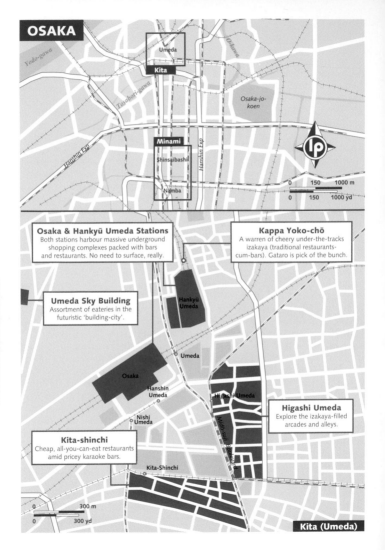

OSAKA

Osaka & Hankyū Umeda Stations
Both stations harbour massive underground shopping complexes packed with bars and restaurants. No need to surface, really.

Kappa Yoko-chō
A warren of cheery under-the-tracks izakaya (traditional restaurants-cum-bars). Gataro is pick of the bunch.

Umeda Sky Building
Assortment of eateries in the futuristic 'building-city'.

Higashi Umeda
Explore the izakaya-filled arcades and alleys.

Kita-shinchi
Cheap, all-you-can-eat restaurants amid pricey karaoke bars.

Kita (Umeda)

REGIONAL VARIATIONS

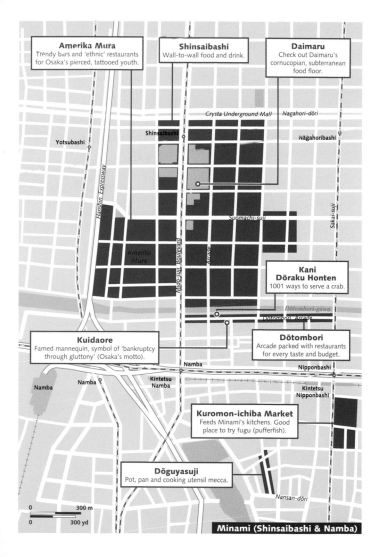

Amerika Mura
Trendy bars and 'ethnic' restaurants for Osaka's pierced, tattooed youth.

Shinsaibashi
Wall-to-wall food and drink.

Daimaru
Check out Daimaru's cornucopian, subterranean food floor.

Crysta Underground Mall

Nagahori-dōri

Shinsaibashi

Nagahoribashi

Yotsubashi

Hanshin Expressway

Suomachi-suji

Sakai-suji

Midōsuji Boulevard

Arcade

Amerika Mura

Kani Dōraku Honten
1001 ways to serve a crab.

Dōtombori-gawa

Dōtombori Arcade

Kuidaore
Famed mannequin, symbol of 'bankruptcy through gluttony' (Osaka's motto).

Dōtombori
Arcade packed with restaurants for every taste and budget.

Namba

Nipponbashi

Namba

Namba

Kintetsu Namba

Kintetsu Nipponbashi

Kuromon-ichiba Market
Feeds Minami's kitchens. Good place to try fugu (pufferfish).

Dōguyasuji
Pot, pan and cooking utensil mecca.

Nansan-dōri

0   300 m
0   300 yd

Minami (Shinsaibashi & Namba)

REGIONAL VARIATIONS

As far back as the Azuchi-Momoyama period, the masters of Kyoto's cha-kaiseki were rustling up a batter of flour and water mixed with wheat-gluten, which they grilled on a hotplate, brushed with miso, and the rolled up like a crepe. If this wasn't the proto-okonomi-yaki, then Tokyo's 18th-century **monji-yaki**, or the city's late 19th-century **dondon-yaki**, can almost certainly lay claim to the title.

It came to Osaka from Tokyo after WWII, and proved an immediate hit. The Osaka gourmands increased the variety of ingredients, added the sweet topping sauce and began serving it at a counter where the guest could sit and watch the okonomi-yaki being made. This cheery, informal style of serving an inexpensive, tasty meal suited the Osakans to a tee, and the rest is, as they say, octopus history.

Yet contrary to the commonly held belief, Osaka cuisine is not all balls and mistranslated pizza. An abundance of quality ingredients from Osaka Bay and the Seto-naikai Inland Sea, and the fertile plains surrounding the city, have meant that a sophisticated Osaka cuisine has evolved. At its heart is the light-coloured but salty **usukuchi-shōyu**, often combined with

GIFT-GIVING OBLIGATIONS

Gift-giving has had a long history in Japan as a means of cementing business deals or consolidating familial relationships. As the year grows to a close people give gifts such as canned beer, and gifts are also given during summer's O-bon festival. Sōmen noodles and again, beer, are popular choices.

Similarly, whenever a Japanese person travels domestically or abroad, they are duty-bound to bring back sackloads of 'souvenirs' for company colleagues, family members, neighbours, the neighbour's dog, etc. The shopping list is inevitably huge, and more often than not the chosen gifts will be **meibutsu** (local speciality products – see the beginning of this chapter).

Osaka station has an entire underground shopping complex devoted to meibutsu from the country's 47 prefectures. Primarily set up to relieve travelling salarymen from the irksome task of shopping between business meetings, or to allow last-minute purchases in case you forgot to get Auntie Sachiko's favourite smoked herrings, it is also witness to a roaring trade among the illicit lovers of Osaka. They use its products as irrefutable evidence of fictitious trips to furthest Hokkaidō or Okinawa, while in fact the unfaithful partner has all along been shacked up in a love hotel in Sakura-no-miya.

Osaka's entrepreneurial brilliance strikes again.

Street signs galore in Shinsaibashi, Osaka

konbu-dashi (kelp stock), a mix which so characterises the Osaka taste. **Semba-jiru** (mackerel soup); **udon-suki** (seafood and vegetables served with udon white noodles in a delicate light broth); pike-conger either served as teriyaki, or with sour plum as the exquisite **hamo no bainiku-ae; odamaki-mushi** (the savoury custard **chawan-mushi**, but containing boiled udon); **hansuke-nabe** (eel-head soup); and **tai no hako-zushi** (pressed sea bream sushi) are all bona-fide Osaka delicacies.

The city has also long been a sake-making centre, most notably Ikeda, which today still produces the excellent Seishu Goshun and Midoriichi varieties. The Yao suburb's Chōryū is also well received.

Osaka boasts one more culinary claim to fame, thanks to its favorite son Shiraishi Yoshiaki, who opened the nation's first conveyor-belt restaurant, Genroku-zushi, in Higashi-Osaka in the 1950s.

REGIONAL VARIATIONS

Hiroshima

Friendly and cosmopolitan, Hiroshima isn't exactly a major centre for regional cuisine, but it deserves mention for its oysters, **hiroshima-yaki** (okonomi-yaki with noodles), a few prefecture-wide specialities, and some fine sake.

From November to early spring, the folk of Hiroshima go oyster crazy, serving them as sashimi, dressed with vinegar, grilled, fried or as nabemono. **Kaki no dote-nabe** features oysters with **ito-konnyaku** (thinly sliced konnyaku) jelly 'noodles', burdock, shiitake mushrooms, bamboo shoots and tōfu in a soup of red and white miso mixed with egg yolk, mirin and white ginger. They also often appear in **kaki-meshi** (oyster rice).

There are around 2000 okonomi-yaki restaurants in Hiroshima, specialising in hiroshima-yaki. Typical varieties are **nikutama-soba** with pork, eggs and rāmen noodles, or **nikutama-udon** with udon noodles, although other types include squid and even oysters. The best place to explore is the Okonomimura, or 'Okonomi village' complex in central Hiroshima, which has 25 restaurants under one roof.

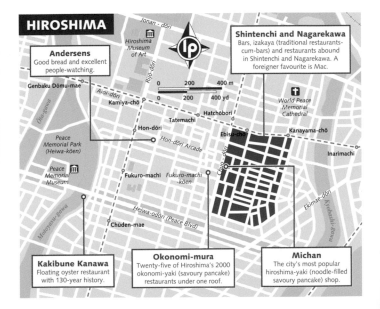

HIROSHIMA

Jonan - dōri

Hiroshima Museum of Art

Andersens
Good bread and excellent people-watching.

Genbaku Dōmu-mae

Ōtagawa

Aioi-dōri

Rijō-dōri

Kamiya-chō

0   200   400 m
0   200   400 yd

Tatemachi   Hatchōbori

Hon-dōri   Ebisu-chō

Peace Memorial Park (Heiwa-kōen)

Hon-dōri Arcade

Chūō-dōri

Peace Memorial Museum

Fukuro-machi   Fukuro-machi -kōen

Motoyasu-gawa

Heiwa-odōri (Peace Blvd)

Chūden-mae

Shintenchi and Nagarekawa
Bars, izakaya (traditional restaurants-cum-bars) and restaurants abound in Shintenchi and Nagarekawa. A foreigner favourite is Mac.

World Peace Memorial Cathedral

Kanayama-chō

Inarimachi

Ekimae-dōri

Kyōbashi-gawa

Kakibune Kanawa
Floating oyster restaurant with 130-year history.

Okonomi-mura
Twenty-five of Hiroshima's 2000 okonomi-yaki (savoury pancake) restaurants under one roof.

Michan
The city's most popular hiroshima-yaki (noodle-filled savoury pancake) shop.

REGIONAL VARIATIONS

DON'T MISS – Hiroshima

- Saijō's annual Sake Tasting Festival on 7 and 8 October
- **Hiroshima-yaki**, the city's noodle-filled take on **okonomi-yaki**
- **Kaki-ryōri** (oyster cuisine), especially in the early winter
- The bars, clubs and **izakaya** (traditional restaurants-cum-bars) of Shintenchi and Nagarekawa

REGIONAL VARIATIONS

The towns of Miyajima and Ōno specialise in conger-eel caught along the Miyajima shoreline, usually served as sashimi, tempura, or with rice as **anago-meshi**. Fukuyama city, and the nearby port of Tomonoura, have been renowned for their **tai-ryōri** (sea bream cuisine) for nearly four centuries, and throughout May the Tai-ami Matsuri festival, involving fishing for sea bream with nets, takes place. **Suigun-nabe** ('navy hotpot'), a speciality of Innoshima city, features fish, shellfish and seaweed. It was eaten in the 15th century by members of the Murakami fleet, who protected the transport of goods in the area. Hiroshima prefecture, too, boasts its own regional rāmen speciality, **onomichi-rāmen**, a beef- or pork-broth-based rāmen from the town of the same name. And finally, there's sake. The best place to sample the prefectures sake is at Saijō's annual Sake Tasting Festival on 7 and 8 October. Look out for the sparkling junmai-nigori-zake Fukuchō no Hakubi from Aki, or if the fates are smiling, Kamoizumi Shuzō's top offering Kotobuki. This deep, medium-dry sake from Higashi-Hiroshima usually retails at tens of thousands of yen a bottle.

Shikoku

Tokushima prefecture's Naruto is famous for its whirlpools and its wakame. The former bash the latter around, adding thickness and texture until the seaweed is perfect for making dashi. This features prominently in the local **kaizoku-ryōri** ('pirate food') consisting mainly of whelk, abalone, shrimp and other fresh seafood. Prefecture-wide **zomeki-ryōri** is a cuisine featuring local vegetables and seafood. Its odd name is a reference to Tokushima's raucous, ebullient, dance-crazed summer festival, the Awa-odori. Zomeki is a dialect word explaining the sound of the shamisen, zo meaning 'noise', and meki 'frolic'. Seafood and **sansai** (mountain vegetables) are presented as though they were 'dancing on the plate' and usually include the 'seven specialities of Tokushima' although no one, including Tokushima city hall, could conclusively identify for us precisely what these are. The inland Iya region, famed for its scarily wobbly straw bridge crossing the sweetfish-filled Iya-gawa river, specialises in **iya-soba**, plain, handmade, buckwheat noodles that border on the rough-hewn. Donari town offers **tarai-udon** (thick noodles served in a large bowl and eaten with fish broth), while Handa is known for the excellent, thin summer noodles, **handa-sōmen**. Since the Edo period Tokushima has been a producer of **wasanbon-tō** sugar. Refined, in both the literal and social sense, it is extracted from sugar cane and used in high-class confectionery. Tokushima city, Sanagōchi village and Kamiyama town all produce the wonderful citrus fruit **sudachi**.

Kagawa prefecture, once known as Sanuki, doesn't get enough rainfall for full-scale rice production, so it relies heavily on wheat. Thus, its meibutsu is **sanuki-udon**. Reputedly brought from Xian in China by Buddhist saint Kūkai in the 9th century, this tasty udon is most popular in Takamatsu city, although the most famous producer is Mure-chō's Yamadaya. **Kake-udon** is hot udon in hot soup, **zaru-udon** is cold udon eaten with dipping sauce and **kama-age** is hot udon eaten dipped in sauce. **Shōyu-mame**, eaten throughout the prefecture except on Shōdoshima island, are parched broad beans soaked in locally made shōyu containing sugar and red pepper. Other popular dishes include **manba no kenchan** (leaf mustard fried with tōfu and seasoned with shōyu), and **oshinuki-zushi**, prepared with small Inland Sea fish, served with locally grown rice. On Shōdoshima, **tenobe-sōmen**, made with finest quality wheat flour competes with Nara's **miwa-sōmen** for summer noodle laurels.

Famed for its **mikan** (mandarin oranges), Ehime also produces some great soups. **Imo-taki**, a speciality of Hōjō, Matsuyama and Ōzu cities, is a potato stew with chicken, burdock, fried tōfu and konnyaku. **Satsuma-jiru**, an Uwajima favourite, features a miso stock ground in an earthenware mortar and pestle. The stock is then ladled over a mix of rice and barley.

Imabari city serves the unusual **hōraku-yaki**, in which sea bream are grilled with shrimp, clams and other fresh fish arranged on small pebbles in a stoneware pan. Matsubara, Hōjō and Uwajima are well known for **tai-meshi** (sea bream rice). In east and central Ehime, whole sea bream are used, while in the southern area slices of the raw fish are dipped into a sashimi sauce and eaten with warm rice. Both styles are excellent.

Kōchi, was once the fiefdom of the fractious Tosa clan. Its inhabitants, most notably Meiji-era hero Sakamoto Ryōma, are renowned for being a rebellious lot. It's no surprise that these fishermen and farmers love to talk, drink and eat. And they're in the right place for it. Blessed by fertile soils, the pure fish-filled waters of the Shimanto-gawa river, and the warm current bringing fish from abundant southern waters, Kōchi is a gourmet's delight. The prefecture is also dotted with outdoor produce markets. Those in Kōchi city date back to 1690. Its Sunday asa-ichi (morning market) is teeming with locals and tourists and is unmissable. Where else can you find fresh fish, **yuzu** (citron) juice and the mysterious tanuki-abura (raccoon-dog oil)? Kōchi is synonymous with exquisite **katsuo no tataki**, where bonito fish is lightly braised over a charcoal grill (you can see this at the asa-ichi), left raw in the centre, and served sliced as sashimi in a light vinegar and shōyu sauce. Its salted offal is especially prized, and is nicknamed shutō ('sake theft') because it accompanies the drink so perfectly that sake-less gastronomes are forced to turn to crime. **Dorome**, found in Kōchi city and

DON'T MISS – Shikoku

- **Sansai-ryōri** (mountain vegetable cuisine), sweetfish and **ji-zake** (local sake) along the Shimanto-gawa river
- The Sunday asa-ichi (morning market) in Kōchi city
- Kagawa's **sanuki-udon** (wheat noodles)
- Kōchi's exquisite **katsuo no tataki** (bonito fish lightly braised over a charcoal grill)

dotted through the prefecture, are the best sardines. During early summer these are served with sake as **su-miso-ae**. The rest of Japan knows Kōchi for its celebratory cuisine **sawachi-ryōri**, in which local vegetables and seafood, **nimono** (simmered dishes), **agemono** (deep-fried food), and fruits are piled extravagantly on one large platter – the sawachi. However, it is so prohibitively expensive that it is rarely eaten outside the big tourist hotels. Much more common are the sweetfish from the Shimanto-gawa river, a region which also specialises in remarkable sansai-ryōri. In these stakes the Ichinomata Keikoku Onsen Hotel deserves special mention. Its chefs produce incredibly sophisticated dishes using sansai and fish and even algae from the upper reaches of the Shimanto-gawa. Local dishes include the splendid **tennen-ayu-no-shio-yaki** (salted and grilled wild sweetfish), the exotic-looking boiled **magani** (river crab), and the succulent crossover **masu** no *carpaccio* (trout carpaccio with capers and red peppers). Back down on the coastline look for Asian pears, each individually wrapped while still on the tree! Last but not least Monobe, Kitagawa, and Umaji-mura produce the marvellous yuzu. Stock up with yuzu juice for making your own **ponzu** dipping sauce (a mixture of dashi, shōyu, vinegar and citrus juice).

TON-CHAN'S LEGENDARY IZAKAYA

It perches on a non-descript corner in downtown Kōchi, but Ton-chan is one of Japan's finest, and truly original, **izakaya** (traditional restaurants-cum-bars). It was founded by the current owner's father – Ton-chan, on his return half a century ago from being a POW in Manchuria. It began life as a streetside **yatai** (outdoor food stall) selling **nikomi jingisu kan** (stewed mutton), as beef was too expensive. Ton-chan also set up shop in the roughest end of town, opposite the patch of green known as Kenka-kōen (the Punch-up Park), or Shonben-kōen (the Piss Park). Everyone marvelled at what they described as its hiden-no-aji, the 'secret taste', and it became a roaring success. Ton-chan designed and built his own izakaya, complete with retractable skylight for impromptu moon-viewing sessions, and a dumb-waiter to transport hot sake and beer up to the second-floor dining area. Now a spritely 90-something, Ton-chan pops in from time to time to meet old friends. Many are artists who devised and published the izakaya's own newspaper. The street fighting has long gone from Kōchi – this is a friendly, welcoming place. The taste remains unique. Try the mysterious **na-nashi**, the 'no-name dish'. And Ton-chan's inspiration for the secret cuisine? He was simply trying to ape the Manchurian prison-camp food – but, his son grins, 'hopefully a little bit better'.

Kyūshū

While there's no single 'Kyūshū cuisine' or 'Kyūshū style', the residents of the southern island might be characterised as hard-drinking sweet tooths. They love **shōchū** (grain liquor) and all things sugary. You'll find that the further you move south, the sweeter the food becomes, as even sushi is served without vinegar.

Most visitors enter Kyūshū through the northern-most prefecture, and international hub, of Fukuoka. It's a gregarious, thriving city, not least in the bar and restaurant enclave of Nakasu, where some of Fukuoka's best **karashi-mentaiko** (spicy cod roe) is to be found. Fukuokaites love **fugu-ryōri** (blowfish served as **tessa** – finely sliced sashimi – or in zōsui), and a dish called **gameni** or **chikuzen'ni** (vegetables stewed with chicken meat). They also occasionally consume live **shirouo** (see the Are You a Culinary Daredevil? boxed text in the Staples chapter). Yet for the rest of the country, Fukuoka means but one thing, **hakata-rāmen**. Originally Hakata and Fukuoka were separate cities, but today they make one huge, if slightly schizophrenic, metropolis – the airport is Fukuoka, the bullet-train station Hakata. It is Hakata that lends its name to the strong, white **tonkotsu-rāmen** (pork-broth rāmen) that is found on every street in the city, and nowhere is it more popular than at Fukuoka's famed yatai. Most are found in the central district of Tenjin, or west of the Canal City entertainment district on the banks of the Naka-gawa river. Eating at the noisy, people-filled yatai is a wonderful experience. Every local has their favourite, and comparing spots and trading secrets is half the fun.

Saga, Japan's smallest prefecture boasts excellent crab cuisine using the gazami or takesaki-kani crab from the Ariake-kai sea served as sashimi, fried or in zōsui. The Ariake-kai is the location of Japan's largest tidal flats, and the huge expanses of mud teem with bizarre looking, odd-tasting marine life. Try the prehistoric **mekaja** (a rare type of clam), or the **bizen-kurage** (jellyfish) finely sliced and served as **sunomono** (vinegared), the **warasubo** (the ray-finned goby), or most famous of all, the bog-eyed, multi-finned **mutsugorō** (mudskipper). It can be added to miso soup, or skewered from head to tail while still alive, and grilled over charcoal with a sauce of shōyu, sugar and water. That said, no one in Saga eats much mutsugorō anymore, not least as it has become the Ariake-kai's logo in fighting the developments and pollution that threaten the sea. It still crops up in **eki-ben** (station lunch boxes), though. Rather more-conventional fare is **yobuko-ika**, squid from the north-coast fishing village of Yobuko, eaten as sashimi or tempura, or Kanzaki town's **kanzaki-sōmen** noodles. A visit to Ureshino onsen hot spring is incomplete without trying yudōfu made using the alkaline thermal water that especially tenderises the ingredients.

REGIONAL VARIATIONS

FUKUOKA/HAKATA

Nakasu Entertainment District
Packed with karaoke bars and restaurants specialising in spicy cod roe dishes.

Ichiran
This 24-hour place has 'design-your-own' rāmen (yellow wheat noodles).

Fukuoka Asian Art Museum

Hakata Machiya Furusato-kan

Nakasu-Kawabata

Kawabata Shōtengai / Hakata-gawa

Kushida-jinja

Oyafukō-dōri
Fukuoka's youth party all night along here.

Former Historical Hotel

Naka-gawa

Nakasu

Tenjin   Tenjin

Shōwa-dōri

Tenjin

Haruyoshi-bashi

Meiji-dōri

Canal City

Fukuoka

0   150   300 m
0   150   300 yd

Naka-gawa
Fun al fresco dining at the riverside food stalls.

Kego-kōen
Kego-jinja

Watanabe-dōri

Sumiyoshi

Kokutai-dōri

Watanabe-dōri

Tenjin-nishi
The bars here attract an older crowd.

Canal City
Huge entertainment and restaurant complex, complete with artificial river and neon flamingos.

Nagasaki's best-known dish owes its existence to a homesick Chinese merchant who created **nagasaki-chanpon**, a stew of seafood, vegetables and pork in a thick rāmen broth, most famously served in Nagasaki's Chinatown. **Sara-udon**, also called **kata-yakisoba**, uses the same ingredients as chanpon without the broth, and is served on crunchy, hard noodles. **Shippoku-ryōri**, a mix of southern Chinese and Japanese cuisine, is Nagasaki's celebratory feast dish, which takes its name from the red laquerware table on which it is served. **Kaku-ni** (sweet stewed pork), often on the bone, is a typical ingredient. Coastal Shimabara boasts **guzōni** a colourful, rich soup combining seafood and sansai, while the typhoon-prone Gotō Rettō islands are renowned for **hako-fugu**, grilled blowfish stuffed with miso. Serious gourmands, however, will head to Iki-jima off the coast near Fukuoka for the exquisite **uni-meshi**, plain white rice cooked with sea urchin and shōyu. If that's a bit too exotic, return to Nagasaki for a spot of yellow sponge cake – the **kasutera** (from 'Castile'), a legacy of the Portuguese. Nagasaki is also famous for its delicate early-summer loquats, and **kara-sumi**, the dreadfully expensive dried mullet roe, a favourite accompaniment to sake.

The volcano-rich Aso-kōgen plain provides Kumamoto with **takana-zuke** (mustard-leaf pickles), and **basashi** (raw horse meat, thinly sliced 'sashimi' style, dipped in shōyu), which is the prefecture's culinary trademark. **Hitomoji no guru-guru** are small green onions rolled, wrapped, boiled and eaten with **su-miso** (vinegared miso). Another common dish is **karashi-renkon**, lotus root sliced and stuffed with Japanese mustard, dipped in soy powder, wheat flour, eggs and water and then deep-fried. It is a speciality of Uki town. In the Kikuchi district, **yubeshi** are yuzu rice cakes, with soy-bean paste, sugar and yuzu juice mixed with rice, then wrapped in bamboo wrappers and boiled. **Kumamoto keika-rāmen** is a local tonkotsu-rāmen that has found considerable popularity up in Tokyo.

Kyūshū's southernmost prefecture, the idiosyncratic Kagoshima, was once the fiefdom of the Satsuma clan, and that name often occurs in its regional speciality foods. Best known is **satsuma-age**, where fresh fish are ground into a paste, flavoured with local sake, and deep-fried. **Satsuma-jiru** is a miso soup with chicken, daikon, carrots and burdock. Legend has it that this originated during the Satsuma reign, as a way to dispose of unfortunate

---

DON'T MISS – Kyūshū

- **Tonkotsu-rāmen** (pork-broth rāmen), ingesting live fish and **karashi-mentaiko** (spicy cod roe) in Fukuoka/Hakata
- **Basashi** (raw horsemeat) in Kumamoto
- Fukuoka's myriad outdoor foodstalls, the **yatai**
- **Mugi-jōchū** and **imo-jōchū**, potato- or wheat-based firewater

losers in the fiefdom's then most popular sport, cock-fighting. Prefecture-wide, look for **karukan**, a sweet, dough-like confection made from yam, rice powder, and sugar, and **sake-zushi** (sushi made with sweet sake instead of vinegar), topped with seasonal fish and vegetables. The Ōshima district serves **keihan**, a dish of chicken, chopped vegetables, egg and wakame served on rice with a chicken broth, while Akune specialises in **kibinago**, a small blue sprat served as sashimi. Brown sugar as a raw, unrefined syrup is made in the Ōshima and Kumage districts. And everyone drinks shōchū, in this case mostly **imo-jōchū** made from sweet potatoes.

Head to the east coast of Miyazaki prefecture to Nobeoka city and Aya town to try their unique brand of **ayu-ryōri** (sweetfish cuisine). The fish are caught in man-made waterfalls and are eaten immediately beside the river as **shio-yaki** (roasted with salt). Miyazaki city's speciality is **hiya-jiru**, a cold summer soup made from sliced fish and sesame seasoned with miso, and poured over rice. Wash it down with **kappo-zake**, a Takachiho speciality, where sake is served in heated green bamboo cylinders, and takes on the bamboo aroma (this is the local name for **take-zake** – see Sake in the Drinks chapter). **Obi-ten** from Nichinan is a tempura made from ground-sardine paste, tōfu, miso and brown sugar, and right across the prefecture is the top-grade **miyazaki-gyū** beef.

Hot-spring festooned Ōita Prefecture uses its thermal waters to make **onsen-tamago**, spa-boiled eggs (perfect topped with ao-nori and a little dashi-ponzu), most notably in the port of Beppu. Also on the coast, Usuki and Saiki cities specialise in tora-fugu (raised in the narrow, fast-flowing Bungo Suido channel) deep-fried or eaten as tessa sashimi. The inland Taketa city is famous for **atama-ryōri**, literally 'head cuisine', which uses the parts of seafish that would normally be discarded. Its entrails are salted and boiled, and eaten with a mix of grated daikon, chopped spring onion and shōyu, vinegar and sugar. Even more exotic is Usuki's **ōhan**, rice that is boiled in water infused with the juice of gardenias, turning it bright orange! The practise arose in the late Edo-period when cash-strapped Usukiites could not afford adzuki beans. The resulting colour appealed as it resembled the latest in Spanish gastronomic fashion, paella. Further seafish specialities are seki-saba and seki-aji mackerel raised off the coast of Saganoseki in the Bungo Suidō channel, and shiroshita-garei flounder caught in the freshwater off Hiji-jō castle (see Saltwater Fish in the Staples & Specialities chapter), eaten as sashimi. Prefecture-wide, **dango-jiru** is a miso soup containing dumplings made of yams, daikon and burdock. It is often accompanied by the renowned **bungo-gyū** (marbled beef). Inland Yufuin and Ajimu both specialise in **suppon-ryōri** (snapping turtle served as nabemono, sashimi or deep-fried). The turtle blood mixed with alcohol is considered a 'tonic', ie, an aphrodisiac.

Okinawa

In the culinary lexicon of Japanese food, if **kyūshū-ryōri** is a different dialect, then Okinawan cuisine is a language unto itself. Reflecting its geographic and historical remove – Naha is actually nearer, both physically and culturally, to Taipei than Tokyo – the food of Okinawa shares little in common with that of mainland Japan. It was only a century ago that the Ryūkyū kingdom was incorporated into the country, and the southern islands still have a strong sense of being caught between the two behemoth cultures of China and Japan.

The island's cuisine either originated from the splendour of the Ryūkyū court, or from the humble lives of the impoverished islanders, and healthy eating has always been considered paramount. Indeed, it has long been held in island thought that medicine and food are essentially the same thing. The Okinawan language actually splits foodstuffs into kusui-mun, 'medicinal foods', and ujinīmun, 'body nutrition foods'. The island's most important staples are pork, which is acidic and rich in protein, and konbu, which is alkaline and calorie-free.

Okinawa is the nation's largest consumer of konbu (by far), but interestingly, it doesn't grow there. It is all imported from Hokkaidō. This seeming anomaly can be explained by looking at the political ambitions of the power-hungry Satsuma-clan that dominated Kyūshū and Okinawa during the Edo period. The Tokyo-based Tokugawa shōgunate had placed an embargo on marine product exports, allowing only Nagasaki to ship them overseas, of course under fierce taxation. China, however, had a huge demand for the iodine-rich konbu, which was recognised as a cure for goitre and an aid to longevity. The Satsuma clan soon struck up an illicit agreement with the medicine merchants shipping the seaweed gold through the Inland Sea to transport it a wee bit further, to Okinawa, whereupon it was passed on to the Chinese. The Satsuma clan made millions, and, inevitably, the Okinawans began to use kelp themselves in their own cuisine. It made a perfect match with pork and tōfu.

Not surprisingly, the names of Okinawa's principal ingredients don't sound even remotely Japanese. Okinawans also adopt a typically south Asian casual approach about how their dishes and ingredients are written, so expect to find menus with wildly different spellings.

The 'umble pig is very much in evidence. Every part of the animal is used, from top to bottom. **Mimigā** (pigs' ears) might not be at the top of every gourmand's must-try list, but on a sweltering hot summer night in Naha, these, washed down with cold Orion beer, are irresistible. **Rafutē**, very similar to the mainland buta no kakuni, is pork stewed with ginger, **kurozatō** brown sugar, shōyu and awamori until it almost falls apart. It is the most noticable remnant of the **kyūtei-ryōri** (palace cuisine) from the era of the

REGIONAL VARIATIONS

DON'T MISS – Okinawa

- Tōfu, one of Okinawa's staples – try **tōfuyō**, which is fiery, fermented, and bright pink
- **Gōya-champurū** (stir-fried bitter melon) in the rambunctious downtown **izakaya** (traditional restaurants-cum-bars) of Naha
- **Awamori**, the Okinawan **shōchū** (grain liquor) – finest as **kūsū**, awamori that has been aged for up to 20 years
- Cold Orion beer and **mimigā** – pigs' ears in vinegar. A match made in heaven
- **Sōki-soba**, udon with pork spare ribs and **kamaboko** topped with red peppers soaked in awamori

Ryūkyū kingdom. Okinawa's dish , **inamudotchi**, is also known as 'fake wild-boar soup' (**inoshishi-modoki**), and consists of pork, **kamaboko** (minced and steamed white-fish meat), shiitake mushrooms and konnyaku in a **katsuodashi** or **tonkotsu** (bonito- or pork-broth) mixed with **shiromiso** (white miso). **Ikasumi-jiru** is a stamina-inducing soup of pork stewed in squid ink. Another dish designed to pick you up in the enervating heat of an Okinawa summer is the enticing **irabu-jiru** (sea-snake soup). Dried sea snake is stewed for several hours with, you guessed it, konbu and pork.

While stewing is common, stirfrying, much like in Chinese chop suey, is even more common. The technique is called **champurū**, and follows the name of whatever ingredient is used. Best known is **Gōya-champurū**, which is stir-fried melon with the island's unique tōfu, **shima-dōfu**.

The hallmark of a great chef – sheer concentration

Shima-dōfu is distinguished from the mainland variety by being hard, and especially suited to frying, though there is a soft variety called **yushi-dōfu**. Shima-dōfu crops up as **tōfuyō**, the sorely fermented, violently spicy, bright pink tōfu. Fermented tōfu originated in China, some time before the beginning of the 17th century, and this is its Okinawan version. You eat small amounts from the end of a toothpick, a kind of culinary smelling-salts experience that jolts you from heat-induced slumber. Its colour comes from **beni-kōji** (a red fermenting agent) and it is as near as you can get to Okinawan camembert. As it was traditionally almost impossible to make, tōfuyō was once the sole domain of Ryūkyū kingdom aristocrats. *Don't* eat the whole block.

The Okinawa working folks' food is **okinawa-soba**. Don't let the name fool you, it isn't buckwheat noodles, but rather udon, served in a pork broth. The most common varieties are **sōki-soba**, with pork spare ribs and kamaboko topped with **kōregūsu** (pickled **tōgarashi** peppers soaked in **awamori** liquor) and **yaeyama-soba**, thin white noodles akin to sōmen. Okinawa does make buckwheat noodles, which are called **udunyama-soba**.

Other popular dishes are **hirayachī**, an Okinawan 'crepe' containing Chinese chives (this was once the staple dish when people were trapped in their house during typhoons); **hījā-jiru** or **yagi-jiru** (goat soup, a stamina-inducing, stinky reminder of when goats were traditionally slaughtered to celebrate the building of a new house); **fūchibā-jūshī** – rice gruel with mugwort that comes in two varieties, **kufa** with hard fried rice and **yafara** with soft zōsui; and **umi-budō**, literally, 'sea grapes'. Often termed 'green caviar' umi-budō is an oddly textured seaweed from Miyako-jima island.

The Okinawans are a gregarious, cheerful bunch, who love to eat, drink and party, yet, alas, the huge (and hugely unpopular) US military presence on the tiny island means that men will often be asked to show ID before being allowed to enter bars or restaurants. There's no malicious intent here, just pragmatics. The GIs do go nuts from time to time. Appearances may not matter – you could be asked to show your passport even if you are sporting shoulder-length dreadlocks.

shopping
& markets

Wandering through a Japanese market, supermarket or specialist shop is a fascinating gastronomic adventure in its own right. The variety is staggering, and you'll be guaranteed to find something you've never set eyes on before in your life.

Specialty Shops

Traditionally, Japan's stores were all family-owned specialists, and were gathered together in the typical Asian model. Today, remnants of this can be found in Kyoto, where streets are named for the specialist shops that once stood there. Abura-no-kōji is 'oil street', Shio-no-kōji 'salt street', Chaya-machi the 'tea town', and so on. Nowadays, across the country, independent stores are succumbing to the giant supermarket chains, and the ever-encroaching franchised convenience stores, yet if you take a walk down any of the remaining shopping arcades (most cities have them, built as all-weather, inexpensive retail and living space), you'll see that many of the small businesses remain.

While the generic word for a shop is mise, or more respectfully, o-mise, often a shop is denoted by placing the suffix -ya after the product the shop sells. Thus, an ice cream shop is an **aisu-kurīmu-ya**, a **pan** (bread) shop, is a **pan-ya**, etc, and the name comes to mean both the store and its owner. Another suffix indicating just the business is -ten. Finally, if one wishes to suggest a certain affection for the business and its owner, one can add -ya and -san.

Bentō-ya (Bentō Shops)

Japan's own answer to 'fast-food', the **bentō-ya**, or **o-bentō-ya**, serves cheap and filling takeaway rice lunches and dinners. The favourite of taxi drivers, students, salarymen posted to work away from home, and anyone who can't be bothered cooking. Some bentō-ya have become nationwide chains though the best are the family-run concerns.

Dagashi-ya ('Junk Sweet' Shops)

Every Japanese child below junior high-school age has at one time or another tried to sneak a sweet snack or two into their pockets from these irresistible treasure-troves of cheap and cheery junk food. Many of the five-for-100-yen **dagashi**, 'no good sweets', are no longer available anywhere except in these sweet shops, which seem to have changed little since the war. Alas, they are rapidly disappearing.

Old-fashioned sweets

Kanbutsu-ya (Dried-Food Shops)

Literally, the 'dried things' shop, these stores specialising in dried fish and vegetables for use in **dashi** (broth)-making and soups date back to the pre-refrigeration age, when drying (along with salting and pickling) was the only way to preserve foodstuffs over the humid summer months.

Konbini (Convenience Stores)

The ubiquitous Lawsons, Family Mart and 7-Eleven convenience stores swept through Japan in the last decade of the 20th century, killing off **yorozu-ya** (general stores), and preaching the commercial doctrine of the lowest common denominator. And convenient they damn well are. Open 24 hours a day, seven days a week, they sell every foodstuff from packaged Hiyayakko tofu to cup noodles to strawberry sandwiches (yes, strawberries between two slices of anaemic cardboard masquerading as bread). Budget travellers can live out of these places, if 'live' is the right word.

Korokke-ya (Croquette Shops)

Croquettes came with the Portuguese, and are now most often sold in butchers shops and supermarkets. They became hugely popular during the post-war years as a small luxury. Tiny croquette shops can still be found, usually run as a side business out of the front of a family home. The korokke, inevitably **niku-korokke** (meat), **yasai-korokke** (vegetable), or **kani kurīmu-korokke** ('crab-cream') are deep-fried to order.

Kudamono-ya (Fruit Shops)

Fruit is often the traditional summer and winter gifts that businesses give to their most valued customers, or that landlords give to tenants, and it is also considered an appropriate gift when visiting the sick. Thus, many kudamono-ya sell as much gift-wrapped expensive fruit as they do humble apples and bananas. Some even feature refrigerated fruit vending machines for 24-hour emergency gift buying.

Niku-ya (Butchers)

The skill, specialist knowledge and extra care taken by the niku-ya means that their products are always superior to the supermarket equivalent, and as prices are usually competitive, the niku-ya are amongst the most commonly seen independent shops.

The best butchers prepare their own smoked ham, and also meats ready for use in **shabu-shabu** (where thinly sliced meat is dipped into a boiling hotpot, then into various sauces), **sukiyaki** (beef, vegetables and tōfu cooked in an iron pan, then dipped in raw egg), as steak, or seasoned in the spicy Korean style.

SHOPPING & MARKETS

Pan-ya (Bakeries)

Japanese bakeries may outwardly resemble their western counterparts, but be ready for some surprises if you don't read Japanese. What looks like a doughnut might contain **an** (sweet-bean paste), **mochi-gome** (glutinous rice), or, in that bakery favourite **karē-pan**, curry! Many Japanese loaves are thickly sliced blocks of bleached white, tasteless sponge. A master breadmaker argues that this is a result of customers' wishes for a bread that mimics the soft consistency of plain, white rice.

Bread & pastries

Sakana-ya (Fishmongers)

With encroaching supermarkets and falling catches, fishmongers are slowly disappearing. However, the importance of fish in the average person's diet means that the sakana-ya will be around for a while yet. Also, few people possess the skill to fillet, for example, a pike-conger for sashimi, which the sakana-ya will do free of charge. They'll probably ask if you want to have the bones and head to use in **suimono** (clear soup).

Sōzai-ya (Delicatessens)

The Japanese equivalent of a delicatessen, the sōzai-ya sells foods such as salads, **nimono** (simmered dishes), and **yaki-zakana** (grilled fish), which are pre-prepared for consumption at home. The quality is often excellent.

Saka-ya (Sake Shops)

The traditional sake dealer also sells shōyu, mirin, salt and miso in addition to different varieties of alcohol. Look for the sugidama or sakebayashi, a large spiky ball displayed outside traditional sake stores. Some saka-ya will have their own warehouse where sake is made or stored, and the best will have samples to try.

Sushi-ya (Sushi Shops)

The best sushi is found in restaurants, also called sushi-ya, but the high street sushi shops selling take-out sushi are still a good stop for a cheap, tasty lunch.

Tōfu-ya (Tōfu Shops)

Every neighbourhood still has its own tōfu shop, dispensing freshly made tōfu from the early hours of the morning until late afternoon or early evening. Some shop owners still take to the streets pushing a handcart to sell the day's bean curd. Listen for their bicycle horn.

Tsukemono-ya (Pickle Shops)

Pickles, like fruit, are often sent as gifts, so expect to find elaborately packaged gift sets on the shelves alongside the stuff for household consumption. Kyoto's famed tsukemono-ya will even post tsukemono (within Japan only). Expect tasting samples for each type of pickle.

Tsukudani-ya (Tsukudani Shops)

Everything from shiitake mushrooms to **sansai** (mountain vegetables) is simmered in shōyu and mirin, to make **tsukudani**. These shops are also good hunting grounds for samples.

Yao ya (Greengrocers)

The greengrocery store will often, in practise, sell other foodstuffs such as canned foods, meat and fresh fish.

A local grocer in Kōchi

Yorozu-ya (General Stores)

Nowadays more commonly known as zakka-ya, yorozu-ya offer a charming, old-fashioned shopping experience. Yet, sadly, these 'something of everything' shops are fast being ousted by convenience stores.

In the Supermarket

The first thing you notice as you enter the Japanese **sūpā** (supermarket), is the light – bright neon, almost surgical, illuminating every furthest corner. Then of course the cleanliness. Followed by the wall-to-wall noise. From the "Irasshaimase!" ("Welcome!") to the mindlessly chattering recorded music, or taped invocations to buy! buy! buy!, Japanese supermarkets are incredibly loud affairs. The noise pollution as you shop goes unheard by regular customers, who instinctively block it out. The reason for it, one suspects, is that silence would imply neglect of the customer on the part of the store owner. Japanese shoppers themselves cannot give a clear account of why their **daikon** (giant white radish) buying should be accompanied by loud, up-tempo, pop muzak.

The supermarket shelves and refrigerators are jammed with goods. A time-honoured Japanese saying asserts 'okyaku-sama wa Kami-sama' ('the customer is God'), and the service is invariably precise, impeccable and formal to the nth degree. This is even from the dyed-blonde teenage part-time workers who are getting a pitiful hourly rate.

Generally, the greengrocery section is first. Many vegetables are individually packaged, usually wrapped in plastic on a white polystyrene dish, and are perfect. We don't mean in good shape. We mean Aldous Huxley *Brave New World* unnaturally pristine. Genetically modified foods are sold in Japanese supermarkets, driven by the cultural norm that requires products to look perfect. But you can always find the bargain bins if you don't mind putting up with a gently scuffed peach, or with a vaguely dog-eared cauliflower, when it comes at a quarter of the regular price.

The fruit and veg sections will have Philippine mangos, Chinese ginger and shiitake, and Taiwanese sansai. Even during the late spring, during the sansai and bamboo shoot season, Kyoto's supermarkets are full of those vegetables imported from China and Taiwan. There are also vegetables grown in Japan, with broccoli from Fukuoka, cauliflower from Tokushima and parsley from Shizuoka. The variety of in-season vegetables is considerable – some supermarkets offer eight varieties of tomato, from healthy **midi** to the intriguingly titled **natsukashii** ('nostalgic' tomatoes).

The **tsukemono** (pickle) section follows with unpretentiously packaged daikon in every shape, size and colour imaginable, **umeboshi** (pickled sour plums) and Korean spicy **kimchee** (pickles) in various guises.

The **tōfu** section not only has fresh bean curd, but mixes for the Chinese spicy **mābō-dōfu**, and packaged **konnyaku** (devil's tongue – see dictionary). There are no less than 16 varieties of konnyaku, from the thread-like **ito-konnyaku** to the bright red 'Kyoto-grown' **kyō-sodachi kado-konnyaku**, containing **tōgarashi** (hot red pepper).

Next comes a refrigerator packed with fresh noodles, with considerable regional variation. There's Nagano's **shinshū-soba** (buckwheat noodles); **kishimen** (flat **udon** – thick, white-wheat noodles) from Nagoya; **cha-soba** (green tea soba) from Uji, near Kyoto; Kyūshū's **hakata rāmen**; and Wakayama **shōyu-tonkotsu-rāmen**. Most come with pre-prepared dips and flavourings so you can instantly recreate the noodle restaurant in your own home.

In the fish section everything is shrink-wrapped on white plastic plates, even a large, whole squid from Shimane, which sits next to a refrigerator full of shrimp imported from India. Opposite that, another cold shelf heaves with **nattō** (fermented soy beans).

Finally comes the meat section. The beef is almost all from the USA or Australia, yet it is prepared in Korean 'Calbi' style (short-ribs), or sliced for shabu-shabu and stews. The small selection of home-produced beef is at least one-third more expensive.

There are no special rules for shopping in Japanese supermarkets, just bring ear-plugs, and be prepared to get bashed into by middle-aged women. The famous Japanese formality seems to disappear when bargain hunting is involved. Notice also, the near-complete absence of men.

Daikon (giant white radish) at Nishiki-kōji market, Kyoto

Local Kyoto yam (ebi imo) at Nishiki-kōji market, Kyoto

SHOPPING & MARKETS

At the Market

Japanese markets, or **ichiba**, fall into two categories – the covered or arcade variety, and the less organised, usually rural, **aozora ichiba**, literally 'blue sky' markets, set in the open air. At the latter, some farmers wheel the day's fresh produce into town by cart. Both types of market allow great people-watching opportunities, and are decidedly 'interactive'. Stallholders bellow "rashai!", the rough-and-tough version of "welcome!", and though touching the produce is frowned upon, you're very likely to be given a freebie with the invitation "tabete-mite kudasai" ("try a taste"). As at any market, caveat emptor is the order of the day, but it is very unlikely that Japanese stall-holders will brazenly try to rip you off. Bargaining at markets is quite acceptable, as long as you don't appear to be embarrassing the stall holder with a disrespectfully low offer. The safe bet is to try a combination of the regrettably pensive "nnn ... dhotto takai desu ne" ("mmm ... it's a bit pricey"); the wavering "dō shimashō ka?" ("what shall I do?") and the delicate but direct "chotto waribiite kudasai" ("please discount a little"). In Kansai, "chotto makete kurehen ka?" ("can't you lose a little?") will get at least a smile if not a discount – it is thick Osaka dialect.

Early morning at the Tsukiji fish market, Tokyo

Two of the country's best-known open-air **asa-ichi** (morning markets) are held in Kōchi city in Kōchi Prefecture, and Hida-Takayama in Gifu Prefecture. Yet the most famous markets of all are Kyoto's Nishiki Ichiba and Tokyo's Tsukiji.

Nishiki Ichiba (Nishiki Market), Kyoto

Nationwide it is known as Kyō no daidokoro (Kyoto's kitchen), and a market has existed on the site of the city's Nishiki Ichiba since the 17th century. Today around 130 stalls ply their wares in the covered arcade that stretches between Takakura-dōri in the west, and Gokōmachi-dōri in the east of downtown Kyoto. It is as much of a tourist attraction as the city's famed temples. In its heyday it had stretched a further kilometre westwards to Ōmiya-dōri. Nishiki (as it is often called) was founded on this site above an abundant natural spring, which provided the perfect water for rinsing and cooling fresh fish. The street was once called Kuso-no-kōji, a name that arouses much hilarity, as it is a homonym for 'shit alley', but it actually came about as an abbreviation for Gusoku-no-kōji 'warrior boot alley', as it was where the samurai footwear was crafted. The unflattering associations were disposed of in 1054 by renaming it Nishiki-dōri, 'the silk brocade' street – a good PR move, not least as silk brocade is strongly associated with luxury, and the imperial seal of approval.

Japan's imperial family was long Nishiki's most prestigious and wealthy customer. Even today, the imperial household, ensconced in the new upstart capital 500km east (Tokyo), orders its speciality foodstuffs from the market.

Since the Meiji era, the shops have maintained mutually agreed prices – ie, keeping them universally high – but recent years have seen even the Nishiki traditionalists bowing to the odiously vulgar 21st century concept of free competition. Nishiki is no longer as pricey as it once was, yet its reputation for excellence remains.

A stroll along Nishiki is a must for all Kyoto-bound food lovers. It is easy to spend several hours pottering, trying to fathom how to use many of the exotic wares on display. If you stop in at Aritsugu, knifemakers to the imperial family for four centuries, it is also easy to spend your entire vacation budget. Thankfully, just gawking is totally acceptable. Most Nishiki stalls open around 9am and close between 6pm and 7pm. Most are closed on Sunday.

A vendor proudly displays an octopus at the Nijō-ichiba market

TSUKIJI WHOLESALE MARKET

- **5pm** The market begins to receive goods from all corners of the globe, by plane, ship, and domestic trucks. Continues until the early hours.

- **3am** Wholesalers lay out the goods in preparation for the auction. Stallholders carefully examine quality and estimate a price.

- **5.30am** The tuna auction starts, with vigorous bargaining. It continues till 9am. The goods received on the day inevitably sell out.

- **7am** Stallholders carry the goods they have bought to their own shops and lay them out for sale to restaurateurs and retailers.

- **8am to 10am** Retailers load the goods that they have bought at auction or from stallholders into trucks and ferry them to their own shops in town.

- **11am** Stallholders begin to shut up shop.

- **1pm** The market is cleaned out. Heaps of polystyrene packages are heat-treated and recycled. A central sprinkler hoses the whole market down, and the working day is over.

Octopus on ice, Tsukiji fish market, Tokyo

Tsukiji Oroshi Uri Ichiba (Tsukiji Wholesale Market), Tokyo

Tokyo's monolithic Tsukiji Wholesale Market is justifiably famous for its sheer scale. Alas, its size (it serves around 12 million customers daily), and its location perched between Ginza and the waterfront, makes it less accessible than Nishiki. It also keeps a real market's insomniac hours (see the boxed text).

Eel for sale at the Tsukiji fish market, Tokyo

At the heart of the Tsukiji complex is the fish market. This market began around the same time that Nishiki started to flourish, in the 16th century, when He Who Must Be Obeyed, the mighty shōgun Tokugawa Ieyasu, decreed that what the new capital really needed was fish. As most of its new occupants were carpenters who didn't know a herring from a handsaw, he turned naturally to those inveterate gourmands, the good citizens of Osaka. Tokugawa invited the fishermen of Tsukuda-mura village up to Edo with the promise of lucrative fishing monopolies if they would provide seafood for himself and the residents of Edo-jō castle. Soon, the neighbouring Nihonbashi Uogashi fish market was formed to pass the surplus on to the rapidly expanding population. The fish market boomed as wholesalers favoured by the Shōgunate grew stinky and rich by bringing in fish from local ports, and selling it to market traders. Vegetable markets sprang up in the suburbs of Kanda, Komagome and Senju, modelled on the wholesaler-trader model of the fish markets, except that they also auctioned vegetables directly to the public.

In the Meiji restoration, the wholesalers were stripped of their privileges, and the public auction system that applies today was instituted. When the city, and most of its markets, was levelled in the Great Kantō Earthquake of 1923, Tsukiji became fish-and-veg central. Despite the fact that many of its post-war buildings are falling to bits, it still retains its dominance over Tokyo's food supply industry. The fish market alone sells an astonishing four thousand tons of seafood daily, worth millions of yen. Its most notable sale item to date is a single 202kg bluefin tuna, caught in the Strait of Tsugaru off Aomori Prefecture, which that went for a record 20.2 million yen in January 2001.

SHOPPING & MARKETS

Things to Take Home

Let's assume cost is no limitation, so we'll start with a table, basically a slice of tree, hand carved by Kyoto craftsman Tadaomi Inoue; a large, ceramic square bowl from Kyoto's 'ethnic Japan' ceramic collective Onokurimono-chōshinjo for main dishes, with five **kozara** (smaller serving bowls). Next we'll take Bizen-ware tōban from the Sanroku-gama kiln, each uniquely marked by a piece of straw pressed into the clay prior to firing. A tōfu heater and an **udon nabe** (udon hotpot) from Aritsugu in Kyoto's Nishiki Ichiba market are musts. If you're feeling extravagant, add in a hand-woven metal tōfu scoop. You'll also need a laquerware **katakuchi** (spouted bowl), and two 'Global' knives from Yoshikin Knife company, a **gyūtō** ('beef blade') and a petty knife, and an antique **tokkuri** (sake bottle) and five cups.

A rare bottle of sake to go with that is a must. We'd suggest an 1800ml bottle of Niigata's dry Higan. Oh, and small bottle of sparkling Hakubi too, from Hiroshima. Similarly good miso, perhaps a tub of three-year-old aged sweet miso from Hida-Takayama in Gifu, or some Akadashi Hatchō (red miso) from Aichi. Pick up packs of dried **wakame** (a type of seaweed), spring onion and shiitake to add. A block of dried **katsuoboshi** (dried bonito flakes) will let you create your own **dashi** (stock), so you should really have several bottles of good shōyu and mirin to make it authentic. We recommend Wakayama's Mukashi-zukuri and Aichi's Mukashi-jikomi respectively. Dried **soba** (buckwheat noodles) and udon are a must, with canned or vacuum-packed **tsuyu** (dipping sauce). Serious connoisseurs will want to smuggle home several pieces of fresh wasabi wrapped in wet news-paper. They'll keep refrigerated this way for up to two weeks.

An array of pottery, ceramics and jars for sale at the Nogi-jinja shrine flea market, in the Nogisaka district of Tokyo

SHOPPING & MARKETS

Japanese ceramics and handicrafts at a shop outside Yasaka-jinji shrine in the Gion district, Kyoto

The list is endless, from scissors designed to slice boiled quail eggs to beautifully packaged cans of dried **ocha** (green tea). So much of Japan's best food is rarely found outside Japan itself. One great, and cheap, souvenir is a packet of **ao-jiso-tane** (perilla seeds). Sow in late spring and they'll spring up like wildfire, providing you with an endless supply of the aromatic, basil-like seasoning (make sure to check your country's customs regulations before you purchase!).

where to
eat & drink

More than any nationality in the world, the Japanese love to eat out, and the cornucopia of culinary options, even in the smallest towns, is dizzying. There's something for every taste and budget, from the oft-excellent, humble workmen's canteens, to famous specialist restaurants that will satisfy even the most particular gourmets.

For the Japanese, eating out is one of the joys of life. Whether it is a company or school party, a date, a family treat or a get-together with friends, there is always an excuse to "Tabe ni ikō!" ("Let's go eat!").

There are strong cultural influences to explain the plethora of eating options that line the average Japanese high street. Eating out is an essential component in the cementing of relationships, paying back favours, and the general doing of business that is at the heart of Japanese social intercourse. Where else would one entertain, flirt, spouse-hunt, thank, celebrate, and, er, bribe, but in a restaurant?

Similarly, there's no tradition of bringing friends or colleagues back home to eat or to party – home life and business life are often lived quite separately. Indeed, a stereotypical Japanese male will work, eat and play separately from his wife and family, returning home to sleep, not eat. This may be changing, as lifetime employment, with its attendant joys of extended office hours, daily karaoke sessions and limitless expense accounts, is on its way out.

A group of salarymen eat and drink in a traditional osōzai (home-style cooking) restaurant

Where to Eat

If those salarymen husbands who still have their jobs are wont to eat out, their homemaker spouses most certainly want to do the same. Most Japanese food requires not only a great deal of preparation, and skill in execution, but to add insult to domestic injury, it also necessitates an equal amount of post-repast washing up. Long live the **nabe** (hotpot dish).

Fortunately, there are scores of different styles of cooking, and there are specialist restaurants to match. Here are some of the most common.

A group of young Japanese women enjoying their lunch at the Imperial Palace, Tokyo

Aka-chōchin

Literally, the 'red lanterns', aka-chōchin are downmarket, inexpensive bars-cum-eateries, serving regular izakaya fare in unpretentious surroundings. Find them by the red lanterns that give them their name in any neighbourhood, but especially in the backstreets near major transit terminals. Quality does vary massively, as does service, but a friendly, good-quality aka-chōchin establishment is worth its weight in sea urchin.

Fast-food Shops

Japan's version of western multinational junkmeisters is the home-grown hamburger chain Mosburger, which, though it has spawned several imitators (including Dom-Dom and First Kitchen), still remains the pick of the pack. Actually, the food there is quite palatable, as these things go. Sample such delights as the Mos Rice-burger, where the bun is replaced by rice, and the hamburger by, er, **kinpira-gobō** (thinly sliced burdock root). We doubt it will catch on in Arkansas. Be warned that Japan's fast-food isn't especially fast. The culturally required attention to detail seems to demand each chip be individually fried. Yoshino-ya, a place specialising in **gyūdon** (beef on rice); Matsuya, a soba specialist; and Nakau, an **udon** (thick white wheat noodles) establishment, serve cheapo fast-food Japanese cuisine. Yoshino-ya is way the best of these three national chains.

Salarymen queuing for a lunchtime bite at Yoshino-ya, Tokyo

Getemono-ya

Whenever the craving for assorted gastropods, vague amphibians, unidentifiable molluscs or miscellaneous insects becomes overwhelming, head for these oases of the weird and wonderful. Getemono-ya are devoted to culinary ingredients, that no one would eat unless they were on the verge of starvation. Thanks to the proliferation of such exotic comestibles as beans, vegetables, cows and fish, these places are a dying breed. Spot them by a dilapidated exterior, and the locals' warnings not to set foot within a mile of the place.

Izakaya

This is unmissable Japanese informal drinking and dining. From the moment you slide back the entrance door and step up from the hallway, to be greeted with the bellowing cries of "irasshaimase!" ("welcome!"), it becomes apparent that izakaya are going to be fun. You'll be welcomed by an enthusiastic worker (always – izakaya are the antithesis of reserve) clad in traditional festival jackets, and headbands, who asks "nan-mei-sama deshō ka?" ("how many are in your group?"). Feel no compunction to answer in perfect Japanese. The appropriate number of raised digits, assuming you are a party of less than 10, is actually how most Japanese customers respond. You'll be either asked to wait – "shōshō o-machi kudasai" – or be shown directly to your table, or seat at the counter, and asked what you want to drink. Once the drinks arrive, you toast "kampai!" and the waiter takes the food order.

At this stage you might get a chance to look round the room. Slumped at one end of the counter will be a drooling salaryman who came in early, got drunk and is waiting for someone to throw him out. In the corner will be earnest students competing for the attention of their classmates. A couple of middle age will be scrutinising the menu with aficionado intensity, there'll be a group of partying foreigners in another corner, and at the heart of the maelstrom stands the 'master'. Impassive, calm, intense or plain tyrannical, he's in charge of the whole thing. The menu features a wide variety of fried goods, from **poteto furai** (chips) to **kara-age** (fried chicken) to **nabemono** (hotpot dishes), rice dishes, and a fair amount of pseudo-western fare. This is where you'll find **hamburg steak** (hamburger, but without the bun) and **nattō** (fermented soy-bean) pizza!

Welcome to the izakaya, part-restaurant, part-pub, part rural hideaway, part trendy city date spot. Visually, they are a mixed bag, from the cool-looking bars set in authentic wooden buildings, to cavernous German-type 'beer halls'. Most offer some rustic hints – a wheelbarrow here, a barrel there. They are never exorbitantly pricey, and are often good value. The name means 'the place where there is sake', and they are simply unmissable. Quality is not guaranteed, but then again, that may not really be the point. Celebration. Food. Drink. Communion. These qualities are what make izakaya irresistible. Kampai!

Kamameshi-ya

These are restaurants specialising in vegetables, meat and fish, cooked with dashi in white rice in small **kama** (literally, 'kilns'). The dish is a winter speciality, and as it's a little expensive, a trip to a kamameshi-ya is considered a small luxury.

Kappō Ryōri-ya

If you've the yen for good food, in both senses of that phrase, **kappō** restaurants are the place to go. They are usually small, and are run by self-confessed food lovers. Kappō ryōri-ya are upmarket equivalents of **izakaya** (a traditional restaurants-cum-bars – see izakaya earlier in this chapter), but with clearly more expensive tastes in decor and the

Sharing a meal, a beer, and a good laugh

food they offer. Often there will be seats at an expensive wooden counter – made, perhaps, from a single block of cedar – where the diner can chat with the 'master' as he offers up classic dishes and those of his own creation. Chances are the chef will have served an apprenticeship in the kitchen of a luxury hotel prior to branching out on his own. Expect the top-end hors d'oeuvres such as sea urchin and **kani-miso** (crab reproductive organs), as well as some creative main dishes. Fusion cuisine may well be on offer – this is poached egg and blowfish territory! Balancing out the new will be standards such as sashimi and **katsuo no tataki** (seared bonito with a dipping sauce), with emphasis on the freshest regional ingredients. Rounding it off will be a fine wine and sake selection. Make sure you scout out the prices first though, and reservations are recommended.

Kissaten

In space- and privacy-starved Japan, its **kissaten** (coffee shops) serve more as a cheap place to meet rather than as centres of culinary excellence. However, for the casual visitor, they serve the essential role of providing that early morning, low-cost godsend, the **mōningu-setto**. Served until around 11am, the 'morning set' is coffee with toast and jam (or marmalade), or in its slightly pricier version, with toast, ham and egg. They are the perfect antidote to too many breakfasts of raw egg on rice, and green tea.

Kushi-ya

Kushi-age (deep-fried, skewered food) restaurants fall into two distinct categories – the cheap and cheerful, and the posh and pricey. Both serve a variety of vegetables, meat and seafood ingredients grilled on skewers. With the former you order individual dishes, with the latter you select a price ceiling and the chef keeps flinging kushi at you until you're bursting. Both are likely to feature shrimp, scallops, crab claws, green peppers, shiitake mushrooms, and beef. Best of all is **guji-shiso** (tilefish wrapped in beefsteak plant leaf).

THE FINE ART OF NOODLE DIVINATION

Professor X, as he prefers to be called, teaches at a prominent Kyoto arts university. A certifiable noodle addict, here are his top ten rules for finding perfect soba-ya or udon-ya.

1. Avoid famous tourist spots and train stations. Restaurants that are busy and isolated are winners.

2. Handwritten menus are a good sign, as long as the script is flowing, precise and elegant. Distrust noodle shops with photo menus.

3. Ditto English menus.

4. Go at lunch or in the early evening. If the place isn't busy, there must be a better shop nearby. If you go too early, the broth won't have reached sufficient strength.

5. Look out for evidence that the proprietor makes his own noodles. A soba-giri-bōchō, the huge soba-slicing knife straight out of a low-budget horror film, is a dead giveaway. In the event that the shop is closed, root around near the garbage bins looking for empty flour sacks.

6. Noodle shops with plastic food replicas outside may be fine, but quality deteriorates according to how many millimetres of dust have accumulated upon them. Sun-bleached specimens are not at all a good omen.

7. Regard shops that advertise with roman letters, or emulate western-style architecture, as suspect. If their advertising boasts any French imagery, they are to be avoided at all costs.

Tokyo's Genkotsu-ya noodle shop

8. Station employees, barbers, and anyone sporting a beret or using a walking stick, can be relied upon as a good source of local noodle knowledge. For rāmen (yellow wheat noodles), however, truck drivers are the only people to ask.

9. Taxi drivers, dentists and policemen are known to provide the worst noodle information.

10. Every town has at least one good noodle shop, one awful one, and one that has yet to be discovered.

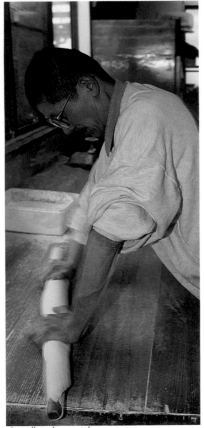

A noodle maker at work

Men-dokoro

These restaurants, specialising in noodles made from wheat and buckwheat, can be discovered on almost every Japanese street. Often run by families, with the best known dating back through several generations, their name simply means 'noodle place'.

The butterfly-inducing, palm sweating anticipation that approaching a hitherto untried noodle shop affords is the Japanese food-lover's greatest pleasure. As menus are quite similar at every restaurant, most **udon-ya** (wheat noodle shops) and **soba-ya** (buckwheat noodle shops) look more or less alike superficially, and there's no overt advertising (Japan's **menrui** chefs guard the secret of their dashi) so you never know what you're going to find. One surefire indication of quality is the appearance of the Japanese word 'honke' ('original house') indicating a shop's pedigree. The word **te-uchi** may indicate high quality, as it signifies 'hand-rolled' noodles, but, alas, the phrase has been much watered-down by overzealous use. Everyone claims to be 'hand-rolling'. Soba shops, especially the artfully decorated variety, can be a little pricey, or even a little snooty – some will refuse to admit children. Udon shops tend to be humbler, which may be a reflection of the comparatively high skill needed to make buckwheat noodles. This would also explain why soba shops often sell udon, but udon shops *never* make soba.

Nabemono-ryōri-ya

Whilst most **nabemono** (hotpots) are offered up in private homes, izakaya or as part of a ryōri-ryokan menu, some establishments specialise in one particular type. Best known are the **chanko-nabe** restaurants serving the high-calorie, multi-ingredient sumō wrestler favourite, and Kyoto's **yudōfu** (tōfu hotpot) specialists. While Kyoto's yudōfu spots are rather refined, nabemono restaurants often feature a deliberately rustic atmosphere, be this authentic or contrived. Given the cheery communal nature of this one-pot eating, few people bother whether the cast-iron pot suspended over the hearth is real or not. There's too much gossiping, partying, drinking and arguing going on to worry about the minutiae. Nabemono restaurants are designed to accommodate groups for communal drinking and eating parties and are therefore a favourite with students and businessmen, not least for the end-of-year and New Year shindigs. Other nabe specialisations include soft-shelled turtle, wild boar, and pheasant.

Tokyo's Isegen in Kanda Suda-chō is a venerable nabe specialist dating back to the Taishō period.

Osōzai

For great home cooking outside the home, osōzai can't be beaten. Small places, usually run by a 'mother', perhaps with help from another family member, they are little more than a line of chairs at a counter. However, atop the counter are a series of large bowls, perhaps a dozen, containing today's mama's specials. You pick and choose from such dishes as sardines marinated in vinegar, seaweed salad, mixed bean salad, or beef and potato stew. Rice, and miso soup, will be offered automatically. Osōzai restaurants are great places to sample good-quality food at budget prices. Kyoto, where the idea originated, is especially known for its osōzai havens.

Oden-ya

Cheery, working-class hostelries serving a hotpot of vegetables, meat and compressed fish paste, these down-to-earth establishments are, due to some unwritten law, always run by middle-aged women. The stock, in which the boiled eggs; potato; burdock (wrapped in fish paste and fried); and **gan-modoki** (tōfu dumplings containing beans and woody ear tree fungus) are simmered, is never allowed to fully evaporate. In western Japan, gan-modoki are marvellously called **hirōsu**, literally, the 'flying dragon head'. The previous oden day's stock forms the basis for today's, and some oden shops claim to have used the same base for decades. Tokyo's oden sauce is notably stronger than Kansai's. Countrywide, oden is perceived as winter fare, though the oden-ya are open year-round.

Okonomi-yaki-ya

These are cheery, noisy, no-frills establishments, where part of the fun lies in cooking up your own **okonomi-yaki** (savoury pancake) mix under the stern gaze of a demanding proprietress, or else enduring her torrent of advise/abuse while she does it for you. They are often pretty rough and ready places.

Whipping up a batch of okonomi-yaki

Rāmen-ya

Japan's love affair with **rāmen** (yellow wheat noodles) knows no bounds. Part of the attraction of this economical noodle dish is in each store's individuality. Almost anyone can set up a rāmen shop with relative ease, and its blue-collar roots lend it a certain macho mystique. It is only recently that young women have been venturing into the stores. Quality ranges from the sublime to the outstandingly awful, and even cleanliness can't be equated with culinary godliness.

WHERE TO EAT & DRINK

Robata-yaki

Originally, robata-yaki referred to izakaya in which the individual dishes were passed out to customers from the central kitchen on long wooden paddles. Of late, however, the word has come to mean any generic izakaya, especially those in which the customers eat around the central serving area. This arrangement is a true foodie's dream, as you can watch precisely what the chef does. They also like to talk with the customers, even more so if you buy them a beer.

A Kōchi restaurateur updates the chalkboard menu

Ryōri-ryokan

Whereas all **ryokan** (traditional Japanese inns) serve food, ryōri-ryokan in particular pride themselves on their food. Most likely this will feature regional and seasonal specialities, and those that boast their own onsen (hot-spring baths) are especially convivial. Quality does, however, vary considerably, and cost is not a guarantee of great food. Some travelling epicures prefer to stay at a more modest **minshuku** (family-run inns), and eat out at a regionally famed kappō restaurant or good-quality izakaya.

When you make a reservation at ryōri-ryokan, the 'mother' (the managers are inevitably older women) will automatically assume – unless you specify otherwise – that you want to eat a full meal on the evening of your arrival, with a full Japanese breakfast the following morning. This is ippaku-nishoku-tsuki (one night with two meals). If you decide to eat out – common in the larger resorts and big cities, but rare in rural districts – ask for chōshoku-tsuki ('with breakfast'). That will be a Japanese-style breakfast, complete with **yaki-zakana** (grilled fish), **misoshiru** (miso soup), **tsukemono** (pickles) and green tea, along with raw egg to crack on your rice, and dried **nori** (sea laver) in which to wrap the gloopy rice-egg mix.

If you're really on a budget, or you can't stomach the idea of a Japanese-style breakfast for the third consecutive day, ask for "Sudomari" ("Just staying"). However, ryōri-ryokan are unlikely to allow this except during the quietest periods. Not only are they proud of their cuisine, it also makes for a large part of their profits.

Ryōri-ryokan come in all shapes and sizes, from modern multiroom mega-complexes to old-style, rustic inns. Even today, some of these old-style places eschew ugly modern conveniences such as karaoke rooms, TVs and credit card facilities for a slower, simpler rural luxury. Try to find one that openly claims to be dentō-teki – traditional, or, even better, soboku na – stubbornly, primitively, unchangingly cool.

The family-owned Ton-chan izakaya in Kōchi city

Ryōtei

Japan's luxury restaurants are not for everyone. At least one visit is a must, for these traditional, top-notch establishments offer the full-on Japanese dining experience, whether they serve **kaiseki/cha-kaiseki** (tea ceremony cuisine) or **honzen-ryōri** (celebration cuisine). Pristine tatami rooms, hanging calligraphy scrolls, seasonal flower arrangements, and politely aloof kimono-clad waitresses are *de rigueur*, and even jaded gourmand-travellers will be impressed by the restrained elegance of it all. Yet, they will cost you an arm, a leg and perhaps several other appendages too. You are paying for the whole experience, the ambience, and the status inferred by being a patron of these famed eateries, but be warned that, in gastronomic terms, some ryōtei are something of a letdown. Whether it is because their fame allows them to become complacent, or because some deeper cultural over-emphasis on form-over-function is at work, is a moot point. The fact remains that a good kappō restaurant can often be better than a so-so ryōtei.

Shokudō

Often family run, these canteens, used by students and blue-collar workers, are quality-meets-value-for-money options. Their **higawari-teishoku** (lunch sets that change daily) are filling and inexpensive. Pick them in shopping arcades or near universities and stations, by their plastic displays that reveal a huge variety of dishes. Some have a large refrigerated display case, from which you lift several plates of your choice. You carry these to the register where you'll be offered mis-oshiru and white rice. Expect to discover **yaki-zakana** (grilled fish), tōfu, **nattō** (fermented soy beans), some noodle dishes and that bizarre Japanese novelty/anomaly **hanbāgu** (hamburgers without bread) – doused in ketchup, but tasty all the same.

A shokudō set-up in Kōchi. Shokudōs are general eating places, often with set meals.

Sukiyaki & Shabu-shabu

When Japanese go out to eat **sukiyaki** (beef, vegetables and tōfu cooked in an iron pan, then dipped in raw egg) or **shabu-shabu** (where thinly sliced meat is dipped into a boiling hotpot, then into various sauces), there is always the sense of it being a special occasion, even more so than a trip to the sushi-ya. Sukiyaki restaurants grill mainly beef, sometimes chicken, on a hot skillet with spring onions, shiitake and enoki-dake mushrooms, **yakidōfu** (grilled tōfu) and the thread-like **ito-konnyaku** (thinly sliced konnyaku), most often with beef suet (see the Treading on Eggshells boxed text in the Home Cooking chapter). Some add a last-minute raw egg. Tokyo's Botan is its best-known sukiyaki shop, specialising in chicken sukiyaki. In Kyoto the splendid downtown Kimura hasn't changed in decades.

Sushi-ya

Despite its fame in the west, eating out at a sushi-ya (sushi restaurant) is usually considered a special event for a Japanese family, a chichi date spot, or a celebratory post-work slap-up.

Unless, that is, you stop off at a **kaiten-zushi** (conveyor-belt sushi) spot for lunch or dinner, to snatch tasty vinegar-rice morsels from colour-coded plates as they frenetically whizz – is it always anticlockwise? – by. Your bill is totted up at the end, according to how many plates are at your side. Rumour has it that Osaka conveyor belts move 14% more quickly than their Tokyo counterparts, which, though as yet unconfirmed, would surprise no one. Quality ranges from adequate to dire, but nonetheless it's a hands-on, fun, inexpensive sushi experience. Expect to find, in equal amounts, **gaimai** (imported rice), monosodium glutamate, and lack of service.

Sublime sushi

Top-notch sushi-ya are characterised by their subdued but rather classy exteriors. Inside you'll find seats at a wooden counter, backed with the refrigerator containing today's offering of the freshest seafood. Behind that, there'll be a row of fierce-looking itamae (sushi chefs), all in pristine, white starched shirts, wielding knives of malevolent sharpness, to prepare delicacies such as **toro** (the finest, priciest tuna), **ika** (squid) and **anago** (the magnificent conger-eel) brushed with teriyaki sauce. It is correct form to announce your order in a confident subdued bark that suggests you know your ika from your elbow, and have chosen this restaurant out of a favour to the chef. You might like to practise at home first. Don't be surprised if the itamae plonks your order directly onto the marble ledge in front of the cold case. He's not upset, although he'll *look* upset. That's how its done. Keep barking until you're full.

Tempura

This well-known dish is often served as part of a course at a **ryōtei** (high-class Japanese restaurant), in cheap canteens, or in the stand-up noodle restaurants on the platforms of major railway stations. The latter are cheap, and immensely satisfying in that junk-food-fix fashion. The most common oil used for tempura is soy bean oil, followed by cottonseed, sesame and rapeseed oils. A full tempura course will feature seafood such as giant prawn, squid, octopus and sardines, with vegetables such as **renkon** (lotus root), shiitake mushrooms and onion. Dip them in a **tsuyu** (dipping sauce) of shōyu, mirin and **dashi** (stock), perhaps with grated daikon or grated ginger. Alternatively, dip them in **matcha-shio** (a mix of salt and powdered green tea). Eating good tempura doesn't come cheap, especially at nationally acclaimed tempura specialists such as Kyoto's Tenki.

Teppanyaki

Better known abroad than in-country, thanks to the major success of Japanese–American Rocky Aoki's chain of Benihana restaurants, it's relatively difficult to find a solely **teppan** (hotplate) restaurant outside the plush major hotels. The ingredient of choice is prime steak, grilled in front of you to your requirements. Side orders include assorted vegies, and shrimp. Teppanyaki isn't cheap.

Tonkatsu-ya/Katsudon-ya

These pork cutlet specialists are easy to locate. Almost all have some large, often hilarious, representation of the porcine form adorning the shopfront. At tonkatsu-ya, price does generally reflect quality, with the top of the heap being the succulent **hirekatsu** (fried pork fillet).

Katsudon, a dish of deep-fried pork cutlets served on a bowl of rice, is probably Japan's most widespread 'fusion' dish. The **katsu** part, the cutlet, was introduced from Europe in the 16th century, but it really became popular during the Meiji era when Japan reopened to the west, when it was served atop a dish of boiled rice, accompanied with sliced spring onion, a well-beaten egg and dashi. It is warming fare, and is also inexpensive.

Food being prepared at a Sapporo night stall

Unagi-ya

Eel specialists are more likely to be busy in the hot summer months, when eating the slippery morsel is said to defeat the enervating heat. It comes at its most delicious in **unagi no kabayaki**, charcoal-grilled eel, dusted with a sweet teriyaki sauce and topped with powdered **sanshō** (prickly ash pepper). Recognise unagi-ya by the sign featuring the hiragana character for 'U' shaped like an ascending eel, or the magnificent, irresistible aroma of the charcoal-grilled fish. It is one of the Japan's marvellous streetside smells that will stay permanently in your memory.

EEL MUSIC

I was once warned never to venture into the rooms behind the kitchen of a busy eel restaurant. Legend has it that if you do, you'll hear a mysterious rustling sound that appears to be coming out of thin air. Brave souls might venture into the Stygian gloom, where you'll find its source. Tucked away, out of sight, is a metal bucket. Peer inside at your peril, for it contains the still wriggling, whispering spinal chords of freshly filleted eel that the staff, in their haste, have been too busy to throw away. So they twist, rustle and hiss, headless, tail-less in the dark twilight between this life and the next. "Gasa goso, gasa goso," they cry. The Song of the Eels.

John Ashburne

The 103m-tall Tsūtenkaku Tower, an Osaka landmark

Yaki-shiitake (Grilled shiitake mushrooms)

Ingredients
16   shiitake mushrooms
2 Tbs   grated ginger

Sauce
20ml   shōyu
10ml   katsuo-dashi (bonito-fish stock)

Remove the mushroom stems and make a crisscross incision on the caps. Heat the mushrooms in a thick-bottomed pan over a medium to medium-low heat, until both sides of the mushroom become tender. Serve on small individual plates, topped with the grated ginger. Mix the sauce ingredients together, and pour them onto the mushrooms.
    Serves 4

Vegetarians

For a nation that embraced vegetarianism for centuries, Japan is a surprisingly carnivorous society, and vegetarians can have a hard time of it. Vegans even more so. First, the good news. The traditional staples of soy beans, tōfu and seaweed, along with a huge selection of fruit and vegetables, means that the vegetarian-friendly raw materials are very much in evidence. The problem actually comes when one walks into a restaurant. Nearly every dish contains dashi that is made using either meat products, or is derived from **kat-suobushi** (dried bonito fish flakes). You can't simply walk into a noodle shop and ask for "noodles without the meat".

A vegetarian meal and an ice-cold Kirin

Here lies the larger hurdle for vegetarians. Asking a chef, or by proxy the waiter, to remove any item from a dish on offer is simply anathema to the average Japanese diner. It's not that chefs will even take umbrage, though the prickly ones might. It's simply that it is far from the cultural norm. So when you say "I'll have the potato salad but without the egg topping please," it comes as something of a surprise. See the 'Eat Your Words' section at the back of this book for help with ordering vegetarian meals.

The good news lies in the accommodating nature of people working in the Japanese food industry. It is not unheard of for waiters to lead you out of the door and down the street to a place where non-meat dishes are available. However, be warned that the general awareness of what constitutes 'vegetarian' and 'vegan', even in the big cities, is suspect. So where to go? Best options are the few 'natural food' macrobiotic and health-oriented restaurants that pop up in most urban centres, but they are often hard to locate. Try asking for "ōganikku restoran" ("organic restaurants"). Many have particularly good-value lunch deals. Otherwise, a fantastic vegetarian option is **shōjin-ryōri** (Buddhist vegetarian cuisine). This really is sublime, delicate, creative fare, but the downside is the expense.

The most reasonable, tasty option may be to head for our old friend, the izakaya. Order fistfuls of **yaki-shiitake** (grilled shiitake mushrooms – see the recipe), **yaki-yasai** (grilled assorted vegetables), **hiya-yakko** (cold tōfu), fresh **yuba** (soy milk skin) with wasabi dipped in shōyu, **morokyū** (sliced cucumber with a miso dip), perhaps with some **ume-shiso-maki** (sour plum and beefsteak plant sushi rolls).

Yakitori-ya

Post-work refuge for frazzled salarymen; students' small luxury; and non-vegetarian foreigner favourite, yakitori-ya (grilled chicken restaurants) are inexpensive, informal, and usually very good indeed. They are often just small establishments with rows of stools at a counter, or are even **yatai** (outdoor food stalls), they serve bite-sized chicken pieces on skewers, either basted with **tare** (a sweet shōyu) or sprinkled with salt. In Tokyo, the 'master' will ask you which you want. In western Japan almost all yakitori is served as tare.

Most bits of the fowl are on offer. Expect to see skin, cartilage, liver, heart and head, in addition to the less exotic thigh, wings, and chicken breast. **Negi** or **negima** is chicken served with spring onion. **Tori-dango** are balls of chicken mince, served on skewers dipped in tare.

Traditionally, yakitori is washed down with cold beer, accompanied with beans, yaki-shiitake and other assorted vegetables. When you order, you'll need to use the Japanese grammatical counter for long cylindrical objects: ippon (one), nihon (two), sanbon (three) or yonhon (four), but raised fingers are quite acceptable. In fact, no one stands on ceremony at yakitori-ya, making them one of Japan's friendliest dining experiences. Their smoke-filled intimacy means it is almost impossible not to strike up a conversation with the locals, who will inevitably offer to buy you a beer.

Salarymen queue at a stand-up restaurant on the way home from work, Tokyo

Yatai

These 'portable kitchens' are found in the big cities, around railway stations (and everywhere in Fukuoka, Kyūshū), specialising in either rāmen, yakitori, yakisoba or udon. Most stallholders set up, or wheel in their stands, just before dusk to service the post-office salaryman crowd and the late night post-karaoke clientele.

The ritzy Ginza district is the yakitori capital of Tokyo. This restaurant can be found tucked away underneath the railway lines in Yūrakuchō Yakitori Alley

Where to Drink

It is rare for the Japanese to just go out for a drink. Eating and drinking are almost always done at the same time, whether it be in a robata-yaki, an izakaya or another type of restaurant. It is inevitably a communal event, the sole exception being the workers who stop off for a beer en route for home at the tachinomi-ya (see the tachinomi-ya entry later in this chapter). Alcohol is the glue that binds much of the Japanese social fabric together, and though you'll see plenty of drunks, they're rarely obnoxious. Watching the Japanese rid themselves of their binding social obligations is entertainment of the highest order (they'd be the first to agree). Here are some spots to join in the fun.

Karaoke pub

Karaoke pubs are certainly not pubs in the western sense, but are tiny clubs where you can make a total fool of yourself with your cacophonic rendition of such classics as *Tie A Yellow Ribbon 'Round the Ole Oak Tree*, and miraculously, no one will hold it against you. You may well come across a perfume-drenched hostess in four-inch-high Prada stilettos, who will ply you with the world's most expensive peanuts. The only escape is to jump back to the mike to strike into *I Left My Heart in San Francisco*, or an impossibly melodramatic enka melody about your impoverished childhood as the son of a tough but fair Hokkaidō fisherman. Clip joints abound, glacial toughies outnumber pleasant-fun hostesses by 10 to one, and the bill can reach Sotheby's proportions. Yet, if you go with friends to a recommended spot, and lubricate one's vocal chords with flagons of foamy ale, you'll have a great time. Best of all is when you discover your mousy librarian friend, (or even better, your spouse or sibling) does a hot version of Ozzy Osbourne.

Let me sing you a love song

Karaoke 'boxes' are just that. Often shipping containers decked out for the purpose, they offer the same acoustic debauchery without the hostesses at a fraction of the cost.

Okama Bar

These bars are a take on the classic karaoke pub, but they manage the impossible – to be noisier, trashier, and even more fun than their forebears. The 'ladies' hostessing are drag queens, and they inevitably fall into two categories, the lusciously authentic (often professionals visiting from Thailand or the Philippines) and the commendably absurd. The customers, incidentally, are mostly a straight crowd out for a good time, which they inevitably get.

Shot Bars

These places often follow a western theme – The Beatles, reggae, surfing, etc – and offer beers and cocktails at reasonable, fixed prices, along with snacks of dubious quality. There may be a cover charge, with beers at the same price, hard drinks a little more. They're a safe bet before you venture off into the pleasure districts of Tokyo's Shinjuku.

Partying hard at a Tokyo nightclub

Tachinomi-ya

There's a retro, spit-and-sawdust charm, and also a hint of Wild West saloon-meets-neighborhood sake dealer about Japan's tachinomi-ya, which literally means, 'The standing drinking shop'. Many of these leftovers from the Meiji, Taishō and early Shōwa periods are still sake shops, but they are also allowed to serve food and drink, as long as they observe two prohibitions: the food cannot be cooked, and the customers cannot sit down. Found mostly in working-class neighborhoods, they are almost solely the domain of men, mostly old-timers who've been regular customers since time immemorial, or labourers and salarymen stopping off for a cheap beer or sake on the way home. Prices are the same as in retail liquor stores, and the food, itself often the product of a bygone age, is unpretentious and cheap. Potato salad, boiled eggs, and processed cheese in triangular segments wrapped in tin foil are a reminder of times when western culinary chic didn't include foie gras or french fries. Recognise tachinomi-ya by the antique, Meiji-era style woodblock advertising signs, menus that are blackboards, and early-evening bursts of raucous laughter. Tachinomi-ya can become very ebullient.

understanding
the menu

A challenge indeed. But you should take comfort in the fact that many native Japanese speakers have to ask for explanations, and there is inevitably someone on hand willing to help you sort out your **ankō** (angler fish) from your **an** (sweet-bean paste), and your **nama-tamago** (raw egg) from your **nama-bīru** (draft beer).

Most ordinary restaurants in Japan have either menus on the wall (such as at aka-chōchin, shokudō, yakitori-ya or sushi-ya), usually written in Japanese only, or table menus, often written in both English and Japanese (perhaps with a picture). Foreign food restaurants usually have a mix of Japanese and English.

In exceptionally traditional Japanese restaurants, the menu may be a rather beautifully handwritten affair. However, in expensive establishments, there may not be a menu at all – the owner will most likely have built up a clientele of reg-

Menu from the Hamasaku Restaurant in Kyoto's Miyako Hotel

ular customers who are quite prepared to trust their favourite chef to serve up dishes to their taste. The customer allows the chef to exercise his or her creativity, and to use seasonal ingredients to create the best meal possible on the day. Come bill time, he can charge the fee he thinks is fair. Westerners may find this an odd concept, but relationships in Japan are built on trust, with obligation and counter-obligation ensuring you are rarely ripped off.

Should you need help deciphering a Japanese menu, your two greatest aids (in addition to the 'Eat Your Words' section of this very tome) are your own mastery of a single five-word sentence – "kore wa nan desu ka?" ("what's this?") – and the inordinate helpfulness of 99% of Japanese people. You really have to go out of your way to find surly Japanese restaurant workers, and inevitably someone will come forward to help translate. This may take time, as most Japanese are nervy about talking with foreigners in English. Yet in this highly literate society, nearly all have had around six years of English teaching in school, so someone can probably hazard a "Sorry, that's not available". It might be less easy to locate a "Well, madam, that's actually the reproductive organs of a sea creature that yet has to be discovered in the English-speaking world". Which is, of course, part of the fun.

If you do have to decipher a Japanese menu, all is not lost. The Japanese kanji script employs ideograms that occur again and again. For example, **niku** (meat), will pop up in **gyūniku** (beef), **niku-dango** (meat balls),

toriniku (chicken meat), and **yaki-niku** (grilled meat, Korean style). A swift rearrangement of the same characters gives you **tori-dango** (chicken balls) and **yakitori** (fried chicken). Minor additions will give you such staples as **butaniku** (pork) and **gyūnyū** (milk). If you can manage to memorise oft-recurring parts of the visual jigsaw puzzle, it makes life much easier – see the 'Eat Your Words' section at the end of this book for Japanese script.

Yet of course there's a catch. Japanese menus, as with everything else, are written in three ways, with kanji (Chinese characters), and in the two native scripts, the cursive, flowing hiragana and the angular katakana. While the kanji carry implicit meaning, and may be pronounced in a multitude of different ways, hiragana and katakana simply convey sound, as does the western alphabet. Actually, they can be learned without *too* much difficulty. Visitors planning a trip to Japan can crack them in several weeks. However, don't fall into the trap of learning only hiragana because it is used to convey Japanese words. And this is the good news. The Japanese language possesses a huge number of loan-words imported from other languages. All are written in katakana. Thus, such Japanese staples as **kōhī** (coffee), **pan** (bread), **sutēki** (steak), **aisu-kurīmu** (ice cream), **sarada** (salad) and **bīru** (beer) will all be rendered in the script. As will the word **menyū** – menu.

From the cheapest aka-chōchin to the poshest ryōtei, menus are constructed in the same basic manner. You will be encouraged either to order **tanpin** (a la carte) or a **setto** (set menu). Often the set menus at more exclusive establishments will be given names that rise in grandeur according to the lavishness of the ingredients: humble **ume** (plum), slightly posh **take** (bamboo) and top-of-the-range **matsu** (pine), is a common ranking.

For an a la carte dinner, the menu follows the logical order in which you eat. At the top of the menu will be the list of **o-tsumami** (small starter dishes), followed by the speciality of the restaurant in which you are dining. Next come assorted dishes, perhaps fried, grilled, steamed or raw, and finally, rice-based offerings, most likely **zōsui** (rice soup) or **ochazuke** (where green tea is poured onto white rice). When you order rice, it is a signal that you are about to finish eating. Right at the bottom of the menu will be the drinks list.

In restaurants that offer daily specials, and most do, it is likely that they'll be listed on a separate blackboard, as 'kyō no o-susume' ('today's specials') or perhaps 'kisetsu no ryōri' ('seasonal cuisine'). Be a little wary of the latter. They are no doubt excellent, but are also not cheap.

You don't have to order your entire meal at once, and it's probably best to do as the Japanese so often do, and select several items and then say "tori-aezu ii desu". It means "that's enough for now", with the implication that you'll be ordering more. In **izakaya** (traditional restaurants-cum-bars) this often gets shortened to the informal, but quite OK, "toriaezu".

MENU

I AM ENCHANTED TO COOKING, PROBABLY

Just because a menu is written in English doesn't mean that it is necessarily comprehensible. As far back as 1981, humorist and Japan scholar Basil Hall Chamberlain quoted the following advertisements, in his Things Japanese:

Fuji Beer
The efficacy of this beer is to give the health and especially the strength for Stomach. The flavour is so sweet and simple that not injure for much drink.

Japan Instead of Cofee
More men is not got dropsg of the legs who us this coffee, which is contain nourish.

More recently, the good people of the Sapporo Lincle Web site, who provide excellent help in understanding the vagaries of eating out and shopping in Hokkaidō, listed food and shop descriptions on their site. Their information is much appreciated, although one may wonder about the sobriety of their translation software.

On 'Alcohol carpenter' Kobayashi:
Real cheap spirits, additive-free wine and also bottle and cup etc. of we handle. The offer of the that abundant knowledge, information is the service of our shop regarding the local brew. 'It is more cheerfully. Deeper'.

On 'Cheese workshop Kakutani':
It is a Camembert cheese speciality. The Camembert cheese of the 1st ALL JAPAN natural cheese contest excellent prize winning a prize yes whether.

On 'Asoniel Kazaka french restaurant':
The store of the chef of KAZAMA where takes the trouble of granting the request of the customer quickly be the store which wants to go going up the dress a little bit. I used a fresh food material nice furthermore it is the intention that I am enchanted to cooking probably. It is possible even the takeout of dessert.

a japanese
banquet

You might have to hop on a plane to get the best ingredients, the right serving dishes, and that hard-to-find fresh Japanese mountain vegetable, but preparing your own authentic Japanese feast will delight both eyes and palate.

Japanese feasting isn't what it once was, it must be avowed. Back in 1866, when two British officers, R. Mountney Jephson and Edward P. Elmhirst, accompanied British diplomat Sir Harry Parkes to Kagoshima, they were greeted with a 40-course meal. Forty courses that is, until even the British army's stiff-upper-intestine gave in to the might of Japanese gastronomic hospitality, and the officers fled to watch troops marching, rather than risk a diplomatic incident of potentially explosive proportions. Their Japanese hosts steadfastly munched on. The menu included: "item #1 Bitter green tea (whipped); item #11 Fish,

Presentation is an important element of each meal

with salted Plums and Vegetables (NB plums not unlike tobacco); item #17 Small Fried Trout; item #34 Gelatine Sweetmeat (like stewed India-rubber), a Chestnut, and Pickled; item #35 Bitter Green Tea; item #37 Bitter Green tea again; and Item #39 Red Berry Syrup, Slices of Turnip, Salt etc".

If you are to lay on your own formal, Japanese-style restaurant banquet, some advance preparation needs to be done. A low table set with lacquerware **obon** trays is a handy thing to have around. If you can't rustle up the trays, place mats will do. Make sure that the **hashi** (chopsticks) and **hashi-oki** (chopstick holders) contrast nicely with the mats or trays – the classic style is red chopsticks on a black background, or vice versa. Selecting the right dishes and bowls is also extremely important. Miso should be served in a **shiruwan** (a lidded bowl of either wood or black lacquer); fried fish on a **kakuzara** (a flat square dish); sashimi needs its own plate and an **o-teshō** (small plate – also called a **kozara**) for the shōyu-based **tsuyu** (dipping sauce); and rice is served in a **meshijawan** (rice bowl). Each guest should have their own plate, onto which they transfer morsels from the other plates. Similarly, you'll need a **tokkuri** (sake bottle) and **o-choko** (sake cup) for serving sake. If you *really* want to do it right, you'll need to invest in a hanging scroll to decorate your walls, and to create a flower arrangement to suit the season. Again, seasonality is important in your choice of ingredients – serving spring bamboo with frozen saury, an autumn speciality, for example, would destroy the all-important thematic harmony.

Obviously, this degree of authenticity demands careful preparation, and some considerable expense. The good news is that if you visit Japan you can pick up beautiful but inexpensive tableware in all the big department stores, or at the flea markets that regularly take place in the big cities (Kyoto's monthly markets at Tōji temple on the 21st, and Kitano-Tenmangū on the 25th, are especially good hunting grounds). If you're unable, or simply can't be bothered, to go to this degree of preparation (or you don't have a specialist Japanese interiors store nearby), plain, white porcelain western-style dishes have that suitably Zen-minimalist effect. Another stylish way to avoid the need for an entire new culinary wardrobe is to do as the posh **ryōtei** (high class restaurants) do, and serve ingredients on a bed of crushed ice (a **kōri-zara**).

For a seriously formal meal, you don't need to go to the extent of Jephson and Elmhirst's Kagoshima hosts, but at least five separate dishes would be considered the norm. Welcome your guests with sake, and a "kanmpai!" ("cheers!"), or beer in chilled mugs, and then offer them an appetiser (salted beans are the classic offering) to nibble while you dive back into the kitchen and they engage in civilised conversation. Next, bring in the three 'main' dishes – a combination of cooking styles such as **aemono** (cooked leafy vegetables, poultry or fish blended with a dressing), **mushimono** (steamed dishes – see the Hamaguri no sakamushi recipe) and **yakimono** (grilled dishes – see the Tai no shio-yaki recipe) is appropriate, and everyone can begin eating. If it is a celebratory occasion, it is nice to include sea bream, the traditional dish for special occasions. Keep filling your guests' sake cups, and as they near the end of these three dishes, serve miso soup, and then a rice dish. Round everything off with fruit, and **hōjicha** (roasted tea) to cleanse the palate.

Many ingredients in the recipes throughout this book are available in western countries at Japanese, Chinese or Korean supermarkets. However, at a pinch, you can use the following substitutions: basil instead of **ao-jiso**; very thinly sliced western ginger instead of **myōga**; lemon instead of **yuzu**; and hen's egg (yolk only) instead of quail's egg.

Creating a Japanese banquet is labour intensive, in terms of preparation and cleaning up the aftermath. A fun way around it is to gather a group of friends, and, as the large ryōtei do, assign each person to create one or two dishes, either beforehand or there and then. You may need to reach agreement on a theme. If so, remember that 'shun' (seasonality) is paramount, or, if you are preparing a meal in Japan itself, take a leaf from **kyōdo-ryōri**, a regionalised speciality cuisine, where all the ingredients, even the sake, originate in the same locality, and you can't go far wrong. And don't forget the wonderfully convivial, preparation-nearly-zero hotpot cuisine known as **nabemono**.

JAPANESE BANQUET

Kinpira-gobō (Spicy sliced burdock root)

Ingredients

2	full roots **gobō** (burdock root)
¹/₂	carrot
2 Tbs	sesame oil
1	dried red pepper
1 Tbs	sugar
1 Tbs	shōyu
1 Tbs	mirin
1 Tbs	sake
	a sprinkle of roasted white sesame seeds

Peel the burdock and cut it lengthways into thin strips of 5cm in length. Soak the strips in water for at least 10 minutes. Peel the carrot and cut it into thin strips, again 5cm in length. Slice the red pepper and remove its seeds. Heat the oil in a frying pan, add the red pepper and burdock, and fry over a high heat for about 4 minutes. The burdock will not change colour. Add the carrot and fry for about 2 minutes. Add the sugar, shōyu, mirin and sake, and simmer over a low heat until the liquid has almost evaporated. Make sure it does not burn. Garnish with the sesame seeds.
    Serves 4

Yōfū-miso (Fusion miso)

Ingredients

2	medium potatoes
2	rashers bacon
2	medium spring (welsh) onions or leeks
3 Tbs	miso (any miso, but not excessively sweet)
1	beef, chicken or vegetable bouillon cube
5 cups	water

Garnish
sanshō (prickly ash pod), **tōgarashi** (red chilli pepper) or black pepper

Peel the potatoes and slice them as thinly as possible. Slice the bacon into 1cm-wide strips. Slice the spring onion or leek into 1cm-wide pieces. Put the bouillon cube, bacon and potato in a medium-sized pan with the water, and bring to the boil. As soon as it begins to boil, turn down the heat, and let it simmer for approximately 3 minutes. At this point add the miso and the spring onion, and gently simmer until the miso has dissolved. Serve into individual dishes, and garnish with sanshō, tōgarashi or black pepper.
    In this dish, the spring onion can be replaced with nearly any green vegetable. Trial and error is best.
    Serves 4

JAPANESE BANQUET

Kinpira-gobō (spicy sliced burdock root)

Kōmi-yasai no sengiri sarada
(Japanese aromatic vegetable salad)

Ingredients

10	**ao-jiso** (green beefsteak plant) leaves
4 or 5	**myōga** (Japanese gingers)
2	green peppers
½	onion
½	carrot
3	leaves cabbage
1	**gobō** (burdock root)
5 or 6	spring onions

Dressing

1 cup	**dashi** (stock)
3 Tbs	sesame oil
4 Tbs	**yuzu** (citron) or lemon juice
3 Tbs	shōyu
salt to taste	

Finely slice all the vegetables. Blanch the burdock and drain the water. Allow the burdock to cool. Soak the rest of the vegetables and ao-jiso in iced water for 10 to 15 minutes, to make them crispier. Finally, drain all the vegetables, serve in a bowl, and pour the dressing over the top.

Serves 4

Sake no teriyaki (Salmon saute Japanese style)

Ingredients

4	unsalted salmon fillets	1 Tbs	sake
1 or 2	white leeks	3 Tbs	shōyu
2 or 3	**tōgarashi** (red chilli peppers)	a little salad oil	

Sprinkle salt on to the salmon fillets and allow them to sit for 30 minutes. Cut the leek diagonally in 5cm- to 6cm-long pieces. Heat the salad oil in a frying pan, add the fillets and leek and fry gently until golden brown. Add the sake and shōyu, cover the frying pan and cook for a further 2 to 3 minutes. Serve immediately.

    Serves 4

Tai no shio-yaki (Grilled and salted sea bream)

Ingredients

1	large sea bream	**Garnish**	
3 Tbs	sake	2	**yuzu** (citrons)
		2 Tbs	sea salt

Clean the sea bream by wiping it down with a damp cloth. Cut a shallow cross-shape (no more than 1cm deep) into both sides of the fish's flesh. Sprinkle sake onto both sides of the fish, then rub the sea salt along both sides. Grill the sea bream over a medium heat (about 7 to 10 minutes each side). Serve garnished with the yuzu, halved. Squeeze the yuzu onto the fish if desired.

    If sea bream isn't available, you can substitute snapper, or any other similar white fish.

    Serves 4

Hamaguri no Sakamushi
(Venus clams steamed in sake)

Ingredients

12	Venus clams
²/₃ cup	sake
1 tsp	salt

Garnish
grated **yuzu** (citron), finely chopped spring onion, or chopped **mitsuba** (Japanese wild chervil)

Wash the clam shells thoroughly. Place a frying pan over a medium heat, and when it appears hot, add the clams, sake and salt, and cover the pan. Cook for about 5 minutes (or until the shells open). Serve in a large dish immediately, while still hot, and garnish.

If Venus clams aren't available, you can substitute clams, mussels or any similar shellfish. For a fusion take on this Japanese classic, add a little butter and a dash of shōyu when you add the clams, sake and salt to the pan. Serve this alternative version with warm, fresh country bread, or pancetta.

Serves 4

Yuzu no Shābetto (Yuzu citron sorbet)

Ingredients

1	large **yuzu** (citron)	2 cups	water
¹/₃ cup	sugar	2 Tbs	Cointreau

Wash the citron skin well, and grate the yellow (or green) zest finely, making sure not to include any of the white flesh of the fruit. Squeeze the citron and reserve the juice. Put the sugar, juice and water into a thin-bottomed pan and heat over a moderate heat until the sugar dissolves. Allow this mixture to cool. Add the grated yuzu zest, Cointreau, and freeze. Prior to serving, place the frozen block in a food processor and whisk it into a mouldable consistency. Serve in small ball shapes, garnished with fresh mint.

If yuzu is not available, this can be done with a mixture of lemon and orange zest. Similarly, very finely chopped **ao-jiso** (green beefsteak plant) leaf can be used, in which case substitute the Cointreau with white wine.

Serves 4

fit & healthy

Low fat, packed with minerals and vitamins, Japanese cuisine is one of the healthiest cuisines in the world, and it is considered a major factor in Japan's remarkable longevity rates. The Okinawans, with their diet heavily dependent on **konbu** (kelp) and **butaniku** (pork), live longest of all.

Don't plan on hitting the ground running. Allow yourself time to adjust physically and mentally to your new environment, especially if you plan visiting during the hot and humid summer months. Factor in some time to take a breather, recover from jet lag and catch up on sleep. Don't over-do the sake or the temple-hopping; work up to your usual party vigour slowly. For a comprehensive health guide, look no further than Lonely Planet's pocket-sized *Healthy Travel Asia & India*. If you need medication, pharmacies are everywhere and are easily recognisable. Most pharmacies in Japan can summon up an English speaker. However, as many drugs that are sold in the west as over-the-counter medications are actually prescription drugs in Japan, it is wise to bring a supply of your own medicines.

DRINK TO YOUR HEALTH

Ever since the monk Eisai brought **ocha** (green tea) from China to Japan, it has been recognised as a health drink. Its initial use was medicinal, as a blood-cleansing agent, and a perceived prolonger of life. Recent studies in both the west and Japan have confirmed that the 12th century scholars weren't wrong. Catechins, the powerful antioxidants in green tea, destroy free radicals that can damage the body at cellular level, leaving it susceptible to cancer, heart disease, and other degenerative diseases. There is also strong evidence to suggest that the chemical structure of ocha works in a sum-of-the-parts-greater-than-the-whole way to combat sickness and promote health. Epidemiological studies have shown that the group who drink large volumes of strong green tea, the female teachers of Japan's **sadō** (tea ceremony), have high rates of longevity, and are documented as almost never dying as a result of cancer.

Hygiene

Japan's cultural obsession with cleanliness means that hygiene is of an exceptionally high standard. Most visitors suffer no ill effect whatsoever from the food. One should be somewhat wary when consuming **sashimi** (raw fish), as the very cheapest fish have been known to harbour the anisakis parasites, roundworms that have a penchant for burrowing into the stomach wall to reproduce. Fortunately, instances of this are extremely rare. Common sense will tell you what's safe

Taking a break in rural Kōchi, Shikoku

and what isn't. If raw fish smells too 'fishy', and you're dining in a less than salubrious establishment, play it safe. The good news is that vinegar and wasabi are to fish parasites what kryptonite is to Superman.

Water

Japanese water is perfectly safe to drink in all areas of the country, though the stuff coming out of city taps tastes pretty grotty. Many Shintō shrines are constructed on sites with natural springs, and water there is free and uncontaminated. Nashi-no-ki jinja, in the heart of Kyoto, is one such place, its water long-used in the tea ceremony. The Muroto district of Kōchi prefecture is making big yen selling its desalinated 'deep-sea water', taken from 200m below the surface of the ocean. Rich in nitrogen and phosphorus it is said to be exceptionally pure.

Fluid Balance

You're unlikely to get dehydrated in Japan, unless you're lugging a backpack repeatedly across cities in the sweltering summer heat, or trekking long and hard in the high mountains. However, if you do become dehydrated, plain water is the best antidote. Always have a supply and remind yourself to sip from it regularly. Air-conditioned convenience stores are ubiquitous oases of cool in the summer months. Although you may find that stocking up on fluids gets expensive, and, in the case of 'sports drinks', calorific, the water at shrines is free.

Diarrhoea & Indigestion

The most serious threat to your digestive and corporeal wellbeing is likely to be the generosity of your Japanese hosts, who are given to plying guests with food and drink well beyond the realm of what is sane or sober. It is often very difficult to refuse this hospitality, but an oft-repeated "Mō onaka ga ippai desu" ("I'm full")', a "Tabe-sugimashita" ("I ate too much"), or a "Nomi-sugimashita" ("I drank too much") should at least stop the deluge. If

"Tabe-sugimashita" ("I ate too much")

all else fails, try a worried-sounding "Hakisō" ("I think I'm going to vomit").

Inveterate party animals for centuries, the Japanese have developed a veritable pharmacoepia of remedies for post-party dyspepsia and hangovers. Best known is Seirogan, the emperor's anti-diarrhoea pills of choice. This remedy is swiftly effective, but a close look at the bottle will reveal it contains mostly creosote, so one might simply prefer to squat and suffer. A popular cure for an upset stomach is the herbal mixture Solmac, sold over convenience store counters. The Japanese have been swift to appreciate the role of vitamin U, found in largest quantities in cabbage, for soothing stomach disorders, and Kyabejin pills, available at pharmacies, which soothes indigestion. As abstemiousness is frowned upon in social circles, the medicine companies have even adopted a 'prevention is the best cure' philosophy, producing pre-party, cabbage-based tonics that are said to protect the stomach wall. Kyabe2 is the best known.

The generic word for stomach medicine is 'ichō-yaku'. If you want the non-pharmaceutical Chinese herbal type, ask for 'kampō no ichō-yaku', otherwise you'll be given an Alka-Seltzer-style western cure.

Several ingredients commonly used in Japanese cuisine come with their own digestion-aiding propensities. Top of the list is grated yam. **Udon** (wheat noodles) and **sōmen** (thin white noodles) are also especially easy on an upset stomach.

Diabetics

If you are diabetic, bring plenty of supplies and everything you will need, then pack some more. If you're travelling with a companion it's a good idea to split your supplies between you in the event that your luggage is lost. Medicine for diabetes *is* available in Japan, but getting it will be time-consuming and expensive, so its best to come prepared. Venus clams help to rid salt from the body, so are naturally good for diabetes.

Heat & Cold

Japan's summers, especially from mid-July to late August, are hot and humid, so take it slow until you've acclimatised. Drink plenty of liquids to replace all the water lost via perspiration. Use sunscreen, even when overcast. If you are regularly using Japan's sentō (public baths), beware that they are a favourite haunt for athlete's foot, which can totally ruin your trip. Slip an anti-fungal foot powder in your bag for emergencies. Be aware that temperatures may fall below zero in winter, especially up in Hokkaidō. Pumpkin, spinach, **myōga** (Japanese ginger), spring onions and **shiso** (beefsteak plant) are all said to protect against and alleviate colds and flu.

Mid-winter in the Susukino entertainment quarter of Sapporo, Hokkaidō

Allergies

Anyone with an allergy to shellfish should be aware that Japanese dishes can contain shellfish in a dried and powdered form that is not easily detectable, though this is rare. If you are in doubt, ask "Kairui wa haitte-imasu ka?" ("Does it contain shellfish?"). If the answer is "hai" ("yes"), desist. A traditional remedy for seafood allergy is to take juice of shiso.

There are a few unfortunate individuals who are allergic to **soba** (buckwheat noodles). Clearly, these people have committed some drastic sin in a previous existence, though this punishment seems unduly harsh. If you haven't had buckwheat before, just wait a moment or two before you take a second mouthful. The symptoms of soba allergy are instant, the same as for a heavy asthma attack, and can be quite scary, but this type of allergy is mercifully rare.

Enjoying an ice cream

Children

Travelling with children in Japan is easy, as long as you come with the right attitudes, equipment and the usual parental patience. There's such a variety of food on offer that even the most particular eaters can find something to their liking, and if noodles and rice begins to pale there's always McDonald's and Japanese fast-food chains in almost every city. During the day at most budget restaurants, you can find 'okosama-ranchi' ('the children's special'), which is often western style, and actually rather good, although its mini-hamburgers and wiener sausages won't appeal to non-meat eaters.

In the event that you're seriously concerned about your child's health, take them immediately to a 'shōni-byōin' (paediatric specialist), or 'kyūkyū-byōin' (emergency hospital).

eat your words
language guide

Pronunciation

The Romanised transliteration of Japanese words in this book is based on the Hepburn system (**Hebon-shiki**), the most widely used system in Japan. Reading Japanese words is easy. Words are made up of syllables, which comprise either a single vowel or consonants plus vowel pattern (e.g. su-ki-ya-ki). The only exception to this is 'n' which is sometimes found on its own (e.g. o-ya-ko-do-n). Japanese has no tones, unlike other languages in the region, and many of its sounds are found in English. The few points to watch are explained below.

Vowels

a	as the 'a' in 'father'	**a**
e	as the 'e' in 'get'	**e**
i	as the 'i' in 'pin'	**i**
o	as the 'o' in 'lot'	**o**
u	as the 'u' in 'put', not the 'yu' sound as in 'use'	**u**

Long Vowels

Long vowels in this book are represented by double notations or a line written above the vowel (macrons). In both instances the vowel must be pronounced twice as long as a short vowel. This is important as vowel length can change the meaning of a word: **suki** means 'to like', while **sukī**, means 'ski'.

Consonants

Most consonant sounds are similar to English, with the following important exceptions;

f	before u – 'fu' is pronounced by releasing the vowel 'u' while the lips are held as if you were about to whistle. If you find this difficult you can also pronounce the 'f' like an English 'f'	**f**
g	always hard as in 'good', never soft as in 'general'	**g**
r	made with a single flap of the tip of the tongue against the ridge behind your front teeth. It's almost a cross between English 'r' and 'l'.	**r**
ts	as the 'ts' in 'cats', even at the start of a word	**ts**

Double Consonants

There is a slight pause between double consonants, as in the English word 'part-time': For example, **nettō**, 'boiling water', is pronounced **ne** (pause) **tō**.

Useful Phrases
Eating Out

restaurant	**resutoran**	レストラン
cheap restaurant	**yasui resutoran**	安いレストラン

Do you speak English?	**eigo ga dekimasu ka?**	英語ができますか？

Table for (one/two/three/...), please.
  (hirori/futari/san-nin/...-nin), (一人／二人／三人／...人)、
  onegai shimasu お願いします。
I'd like to reserve a table for
  eight o'clock (tonight/tomorrow night).
  (konban/ashita no ban) hachi-ji ni (今晩／明日の晩)
  yotaku shitai no desu ga 八時に予約したいのですが。
We have a reservation.
  yoyaku shimashita 予約しました。
We don't have a reservation.
  yoyaku shite imasen 予約していません。
Do you accept credit cards?
  kurejitto-kādo ga クレジットカードが使えますか？
  tsukaemasu ka?
Do you have a highchair for the baby?
  kodomo-yō no isu ga 子供用の椅子がありますか？
  arimasu ka?
Can I smoke here?
  koko de tabako o sutte mo ここで煙草を吸ってもいいですか？
  ii desu ka?
Can I pay by credit card?
  kurejitto-kādo de クレジットカードで支払えますか？
  shiharaemasu ka?
Waiter/Waitress!
  ueitā-san/ueitoresu-san! ウエイターさん／ウエイトレスさん！
No-smoking table, please.
  kin'en-seki o onegai shimasu 禁煙席をお願いします。
Tatami-room, please.
  o-zashiki o onegai shimasu お座敷をお願いします。

Just Try It!
What's that?
  are wa nan desu ka? あれは何ですか？
What's the speciality of this region?
  kono tochi no meisan wa この土地の名産は何ですか？
  nan desu ka?
What's the speciality here?
  koko no tokubetsu ryōri wa ここの特別料理は何ですか？
  nan desu ka?

What do you recommend?
  o-susume wa nan desu ka? おすすめは何ですか？

What are they eating?
  **ano hito-tachi wa nani o あの人たちは何を食べて
  tabete imasu ka?** いますか。

I'll try what she/he's having.
  **ano hito to onaji mono o あの人と同じものをお願い
  onegai shimasu** します。

At the Restaurant or Shop

Do you have ...?   **... ga arimasu ka?**   ... がありますか？
Great!   **subarashii!/sugoi!**   すばらしい！／すごい！

The Menu

Can I see the menu, please?
  menyū o misete kudasai メニューを見せてください。

Do you have a menu in English?
  eigo no menyū wa arimasu ka? 英語のメニューはありますか？

What are today's specials?
  **kyō no supesharu wa 今日のスペシャルは何ですか？
  nan desu ka?**

We haven't made a choice yet.
  mada kimete imasen まだ決めていません。

I'd like ...   **... o kudasai.**   ...をください。

I'd like the set lunch, please.
  ranchi-setto o kudasai ランチセットをください。

What does it include?
  **sore ni wa nani ga それには何が含まれていますか？
  fukumarete imasu ka?**

Is service included in the bill?
  **o-kanjō wa sābisu-ryō-komi お勘定はサービス料込みですか？
  desu ka?**

Does it come with salad?
  sarada-tsuki desu ka? サラダ付ですか？

What's the soup of the day?
  kyō no sūpu wa nan desu ka? 今日のスープは何ですか？

Throughout the Meal

What's in this dish?
  **kono ryōri ni wa nani ga この料理には何が入っていますか？
  haitte imasu ka?**

How do you eat this?
  kore wa dō yatte tabemasu ka? これはどうやって食べますか？

Do you have sauce?
  sōsu wa arimasu ka? ソースはありますか？

Not too spicy (hot) please.
   amari karaku nai yō ni　　　　あまり辛くないようにお願いします。
   onegai shimasu

Is that dish (spicy) hot?
   ano ryōri wa karai desu ka?　　あの料理は辛いですか？

I like it hot and spicy!
   karai no ga suki desu!　　　　辛いのが好きです！

It's not hot (spicy).
   karaku nai desu　　　　　　　辛くないです。

It's not hot (temperature).
   atsukunai desu　　　　　　　　熱くないです。

I didn't order this.
   kore wa chūmon shite imasen　これは注文していません。

I'd like something to drink.
   nomimono o kudasai　　　　　飲み物をください。

Can I have a (beer/water) please?
   (bīru/mizu) o onegai shimasu　（ビール／水）をお願いします。

This food is cold.
   kono ryōri wa tsumetai desu　この料理は冷たいです。

This room is cold.
   kono heya wa samui desu　　　この部屋は寒いです。

It's taking a long time,
please hurry up.
   osoi desu ne
   isoide moraemasu ka?　　　　　遅いですね。急いでもらえますか。

Please bring me ...	... o onegai shimasu	...をお願いします。
an ashtray	haizara	灰皿
some/more bread	pan	パン
chopsticks	hashi	箸
a cup	kappu	カップ
a fork	fōku	フォーク
a glass	koppu/gurasu	コップ／グラス
a knife	naifu	ナイフ
a napkin	napukin	ナプキン
some pepper	koshō	コショウ
a plate	sara	皿
a small plate	ko-zara	小皿
some salt	shio	塩
soy sauce	shōyu	醤油
a spoon	supūn	スプーン
a teaspoon	tī-supūn	ティースプーン
a toothpick	yōji	楊枝
some water	mizu	水
some wine	wain	ワイン

This food is ...	kono ryōri wa ...	この料理は ...
awful (very strong word)	mazui desu	まずいです。
bitter	nigai desu	苦いです。
bitter (like a young persimmon)	shibui desu	渋いです。
brilliant	subarashii desu	すばらしいです。
burnt	kogete imasu	こげています。
cold	tsumetai desu	冷たいです。
delicious	oishii desu	おいしいです。
not delicious	oishikunai desu	おいしくないです。
fresh	shinsen desu	新鮮です。
hard	katai desu	かたいです。
hot (spicy)	karai desu	辛いです。
very oily	aburakkoi desu	油っこいです。
old	furui desu	ふるいです。
salty	(shoppai/shio-karai) desu	（しょっぱい／塩辛い）です。
soft	yawarakai desu	柔らかいです。
sour	suppai desu	酸っぱいです。
spoiled	itande imasu	いたんでいます。
stale	shinsen dewa arimasen	新鮮ではありません。
sweet	amai desu	甘いです。
undercooked	hi ga tōtte imasen	火が通っていません。

Thank you, that was delicious.
gochisōsama deshita — ごちそうさまでした。

This isn't to my taste.
amari kuchi ni aimasen — あまり口に合いません。

Please pass on our compliments to the chef.
shefu ni oishikatta to tsutaete kudasai — シェフにおいしかったと伝えてください。

The bill/check, please.
(o-kanjō/o-aiso) o onegai shimasu — （お勘定／おあいそ）をお願いします。

Can I pay by credit card?
kurejitto-kādo de haraemasu ka? — クレジットカードで払えますか？

Can I have the receipt?
reshīto o itadakemasen ka? — レシートをいただけませんか？

This bill is wrong.
kono (o-kanjō/o-aiso) wa machigatte imasu — この（お勘定／おあいそ）は間違っています。

We wish to pay separately.
betsu-betsu ni onegai shimasu — 別々にお願いします。

How much all together?
zenbu de ikura desu ka? — 全部でいくらですか？

Can you please bring me more ... ?
... no okawari o onegai shimasu — ...のおかわりをお願いします。

| I'd like ... | ... o kudasai | ...をください。 |

I'd like something to drink.
nomimono o kudasai 　　　　飲み物をください。
Let's give her/him a tip.
chippu o watashimashō 　　　チップを渡しましょう。
Let's not give her/him a tip.
chippu o watasu no 　　　　チップを渡すのはやめましょう。
wa yamemashō
Can I drink this water?
kono mizu wa nomemasu ka? 　この水は飲めますか？

You May Hear
irasshaimase/irasshai!
　May I help you?/Welcome! 　いらっしゃいませ。／いらっしゃい！
o-hitori-sama desu ka?
　By yourself? 　　　　　　　お一人さまですか？
(ni/san/yon) -mei-sama desu ka?
　(Two/Three/Four) persons? 　（二名／三名／四名）さまですか？
kochira e dōzo
　This way, please. 　　　　　こちらへどうぞ。
(go-chūmon wa) o-kimari desu ka?
　May I take your order? 　　　（ご注文は）お決まりですか。
... wa ikaga desu ka?
　Would you like ...? 　　　　　...はいかがですか？
hoka ni nani ka?/ijō desu ka?
　Anything else?/Is that all? 　ほかに何か？／以上ですか？
kyō, ... wa (arimasen/gozaimasen)
　We have no ... today. 　　　　今日、...は（ありません／ございません）。
dōzo o-meshiagari kudasai!
　Enjoy your meal! 　　　　　　どうぞお召し上がりください！
o-matase shimashita
　Here you are. 　　　　　　　お待たせしました。
　(lit: Sorry to let you wait)
nani ka o-nomimono wa?
　Do you want anything to drink? 何かお飲み物は？

Family Meals
Can I bring anything?
nani ka motte ikimashō ka? 　何か持って行きましょうか？
You're a great cook!
ryōri ga jōzu desu ne! 　　　料理が上手ですね！
Can I watch you make this?
tsukuri-kata o mite mo ii desu ka? 作り方を見てもいいですか。

| Let me help you. | **tetsudaimasu** | 手伝います。 |
| This is brilliant! | **subarashii!** | すばらしい！ |

Do you have the recipe for this?
tsukurikata o shitte imasu ka?

作り方を知っていますか？

Is this a (family/local) recipe?
kore wa (katei/kyōdo) -ryōri desu ka?

これは（家庭／郷土）料理ですか？

Are the ingredients local?
zairyō wa kono tochi no mono desu ka?

材料はこの土地のものですか？

I've never had a meal like this before.
kono yō na ryōri wa hajimete desu

このような料理は初めてです。

I've never eaten food like this before.
**kono yō na ryōri wa tabeta
koto ga arimasen**

このような料理は食べたことが
ありません。

If you ever come to (Australia)
I'll cook you a local dish.
**(ōsutoraria) ni kuru koto ga attara
(ōsutoraria) no ryōri o tsukurimashō**

（オーストラリア）に来ることが
あったら（オーストラリア）の料
理を作りましょう。

Could you pass the (salt) please?
(shio) o totte kudasaimasen ka?

（塩）を取ってくださいませんか？

One is enough, thank you.
hitotsu de kekkō desu

ひとつで結構です。

Do you use ... in this?
kore ni ... o tsukaimasu ka?

これに ... を使いますか。

No thank you, I'm full.
mō kekkō desu
onaka ga ippai desu

もう結構です。
おなかがいっぱいです。

I've already eaten.
mō tabemashita

もう食べました。

Thanks very much for the meal.
gochisōsama deshita

ごちそうさまでした。

Vegetarian & Special Needs

I'm a vegetarian.
watashi wa bejitarian desu

私はベジタリアンです。

I'm a vegan, I don't eat meat
or dairy products.
**watashi wa saishoku-shugisha desu kara,
niku ya nyūseihin wa tabemasen**

私は菜食主義者ですから、
肉や乳製品は食べません。

Is it cooked with pork lard
or chicken stock?
**kore wa rādo ka tori no dashi o
tsukatte imasu ka?**

これはラードか鶏のだしを
使っていますか。

I only eat vegetables.
yasai shika tabemasen

野菜しか食べません。

I don't want any meat at all.
niku wa issai tabemasen

肉は一切食べません。

Don't add egg.
tamago wa irenaide kudasai

卵は入れないでください。

I don't eat ...	... wa tabemasen	... は食べません。
chicken	toriniku	鶏肉
fish	sakana	魚
meat	niku	肉
pork	butaniku	豚肉
poultry	tori no niku	鳥の肉
seafood	shīfūdo/kaisanbutsu	シーフード／海産物

Do you have any vegetarian dishes?
bejitarian-ryōri ga arimasu ka?　　ベジタリアン料理がありますか?
Can you recommend a vegetarian dish, please?
o-susume no bejitarian-ryōri wa　　おすすめのベジタリアン
arimasu ka?　　料理はありますか?
Does this dish have meat in it?
kono ryōri ni niku ga haitte imasu ka?　　この料理に肉が入っいますか?
Can I get this without the meat?
kore o niku nashi de dekimasu ka?　　これを肉なしでできますか?
Is the sauce meat-based?
kono sōsu no bēsu ni　　このソースのベースに
niku ga haitte imasu ka?　　肉が入っていますか?
Does it contain eggs/dairy products?
kore ni wa (tamago/nyūseihin) ga　　これには(卵／乳製品)が
haitte imasu ka?　　入っていますか?
Does this dish have gelatine?
kono ryōri ni wa zerachin ga　　この料理にはゼラチンが
haitte imasu ka?　　入っていますか?

carbohydrate	tansuikabutsu	炭水化物
fat	shibō-bun	脂肪分
high fibre	kō-sen'i	高繊維
low fat	tei-shibō	低脂肪
organically-grown produce	yūki-saibai no seihin	有機栽培の製品

Is it ...?	sore wa ... desu ka?	それは ...ですか?
gluten-free	guruten-nashi	グルテン無し
lactose-free	nyūtō-nashi	乳糖無し
salt-free	mu-en	無塩
sugar-free	mu-tō	無糖
wheat-free	komugi-nashi	小麦無し
yeast-free	īsuto-nashi	イースト無し

Is this organic?
kore wa yūki-saibai desu ka?　　これは有機栽培ですか?
I am a diabetic.
watashi wa tōnyō-byō desu　　私は糖尿病です。
I'm allergic to (peanuts)
watashi wa (pīnattsu)　　私は（ピーナッツ）アレル
arerugī desu　　ギーです。

I follow a particular diet.
  shokuji-seigen o shite imasu　　　　食餌制限をしています。
I follow a ... diet
  ... no daietto o shite imasu　　　　... のダイエットをしています。

Children
Are children allowed?
  kodomo-zure demo ii desu ka?　　　　子供連れでもいいですか？
Is there a children's menu?
  kodomo-yō no menyū wa arimasu ka?　　子供用のメニューは
　　　　　　　　　　　　　　　　　　　　ありますか？

Do you have a highchair for the baby?
  bebī-yōno isu wa arimasu ka?　　　　ベビー用の椅子は
　　　　　　　　　　　　　　　　　　　　ありますか？

At the Market/Self-Catering
Where's the nearest (market)?
  ichiban chikai (ichiba) wa doko desu ka?　一番近い（市場）はどこで
　　　　　　　　　　　　　　　　　　　　すか？

Where can I find the (sugar)?
  (satō) wa doko ni arimasu ka?　　　（砂糖）はどこにありますか？

Can I have a ...	... o kudasai	...をください。
bottle	bin/botoru	ビン／ボトル
box	hako	箱
can	kan	缶
packet	pakku	パック
tin of ...	... no kanzume	... の缶詰

How much is it?　　　**ikura desu ka?**　　いくらですか？

How much is (a kilo of cheese)?
  (chīzu ichi-kiro) ikura desu ka?　　（チーズ一キロ）いくらですか？
How much altogether?
  zenbu de ikura desu ka?　　　　　　全部でいくらですか？

How much (for) ...?	... ikura desu ka?	...いくらですか？
this	kore	これ
both	ryōhō de	両方で
per piece	hitotsu/ikko	一つ／一個

Do you have anything cheaper?
  motto yasui mono ga arimasu ka?　　もっと安いものがありますか？
Give me a kilo, please.
  ichi-kiro kudasai　　　　　　　　　一キロください。
I'd like (six slices) of ham.
  hamu (roku-mai) kudasai　　　　　　ハム（六枚）ください。
I don't want to buy anything.
  nani mo kaimasen　　　　　　　　　何も買いません。

I'm just looking.
  mite iru dake desu 見ているだけです。
No!
  irimasen! いりません！

I'd like to buy ... **... ga kaitai desu** ... が買いたいです。
Where can I buy ...? **... wa doko de** ... はどこで買えますか？
  kaemasu ka?

Who's next? **tsugi no kata?** 次のかた？
I'd like some ... **... ga hoshii desu** ... が欲しいです。
Best before ... **shōmi kigen ...** 賞味期限 ...

Can I taste it?
  ajimi o shite mo ii desu ka? 味見をしてもいいですか？
Will this keep in the fridge?
  reizōko de totte okemasu ka? 冷蔵庫でとって置けますか。
Is this the best you have?
  kore ga ichiban ii mono desu ka? これが一番いいものですか。
Do you have anything better?
  motto ii mono ga arimasu ka? もっといいものがありますか？

I'd like some ... **... o kudasai** ... をください。
  bread **pan** パン
  butter **batā** バター
  cheese **chīzu** チーズ
  chocolate **chokorēto** チョコレート
  eggs **tamago** 卵
  flour **komugiko** 小麦粉
  frozen foods **reitō-shokuhin** 冷凍食品
  fruit & vegetables **kudamono to yasai** 果物と野菜
  ham **hamu** ハム
  honey **hachimitsu** 蜂蜜
  jam **jamu** ジャム
  margarine **māgarin** マーガリン
  marmalade **māmarēdo** マーマレード
  milk **miruku/gyūnyū** ミルク／牛乳
  olives **orību** オリーブ
  pasta **pasuta** パスタ
  pepper **koshō** コショウ
  rice (uncooked) **kome** 米
  salt **shio** 塩
  sugar **satō** 砂糖
  vegetable oil **shokubutsuyu** 植物油
  yoghurt **yōguruto** ヨーグルト

What's the local speciality?
  kono tochi no tokusan wa nan desu ka? この土地の特産は何ですか？

Can you give me a discount?
waribiki shite kuremasen ka?

割引きしてくれませんか？

When does this shop open?
kono mise wa nan-ji ni akimasu ka?

この店は何時に開きますか？

I am looking for ...
... o sagashite imasu

...を探しています。

Where can I find ...?
... wa doko ni arimasu ka?

...はどこにありますか？

Where/what is the expiry date?
shōmi kigen wa (doko/itsu) desu ka?

賞味期限は（どこ／いつ）
ですか？

At the Bar

Shall we go for a drink?
nomi ni ikimashō ka?

飲みに行きましょうか？

I'll buy you a drink.
ippai ogorimasu

一杯おごります。

Thanks, but I don't feel like it.
arigatō. demo amari nomitaku nain desu

ありがとう。でもあまり
飲みたくないんです。

I don't drink (alcohol).
o-sake wa nomimasen

お酒は飲みません。

What would you like?
nani ni shimashō ka?

何にしましょうか？

You can get the next one.
tsugi wa onegai shimasu

次はお願いします。

It's on me.
kore wa watashi no ogori desu

これは私のおごりです。

It's my round.
tsugi wa watashi no ban desu

次は私の番です。

This is your shout, right?
kore wa anata no ogori desu ne?

これはあなたのおごりですね？

Okay.
ōkē

オーケー。

I think I've had a little too many.
sukoshi nomi-sugita yō desu

少しのみ過ぎたようです。

I can't drink any more.
mō nomemasen

もう飲めません。

One more and I'll be under the table.
ato ippai nondara taoremasu

あと一杯飲んだら倒れます。

I'm never, ever drinking again.
mō nido to nomimasen

もう二度と飲みません。

I'm next.
tsugi wa watashi desu

次は私です。

Excuse me.
sumimasen/suimasen

すみません／すいません。

I'll have ...	... o onegai shimasu.	... をお願いします。
I'll have (a) ...	... o (nomimasu/ onegai shimasu).	... を（飲みます／お願い します）。
beer	bīru	ビール
brandy	burandē	ブランデー
Champagne	shanpen	シャンペン
cider	saidā	サイダー
cocktail	kakuteru	カクテル
Japanese spirit	shōchū	焼酎
Japanese spirit with mixer	chūhai	チューハイ
liqueur	rikyūru	リキュール
rum	ramu	ラム
sake	o-sake	（お）酒
cold sake	reishu	冷酒
hot sake	o-kan	お燗
vodka and lemonade	uokka to remonēdo	ウォッカとレモネード
whisky	uisukī	ウイスキー
(red/white) wine	(aka/shiro) wain	（赤／白）ワイン
Cheers!	kampai!	乾杯！
No ice.	kōri-nashi.	氷無し。

Can I have ice, please?
kōri o onegai shimasu.　氷をお願いします。
Same again, please.
onaji no o onegai shimasu.　同じのをお願いします。
Is food available here?
taberumono wa arimasu ka?　食べるものはありますか？
Where's the toilet?
toire wa doko desu ka?　トイレはどこですか？
I'm a bit tired, I'd better get home.
chotto tsukaremashita.　ちょっと疲れました。
mō, kaetta hō ga ii desu.　もう、帰ったほうがいいです。

I'm feeling drunk.	yoimashita	酔いました。
I'm pissed!	yopparatta!	酔っ払った！
I feel ill.	kibun ga warui desu	気分が悪いです。
I want to throw up.	hakitai/ modoshitai desu	吐きたい／もどしたいです。
She/he's passed out.	(kanojo/kare) wa yoi-tsuburemashita	（彼女／彼）は酔い つぶれました。
I'm hung over.	futsuka-yoi desu	二日酔いです。

Do you come here often?
yoku koko ni kimasu ka?　よくここに来ますか？

I really, really love you.
  hontō ni anata ga suki desu

本当にあなたが好きです。

What did I do last night?
  watashi wa yūbe nani o shimashita ka?

私はゆうべ何をしましたか？

Good health!
  kenkō ni kampai!

健康に乾杯！

Wine

May I see the wine list, please?
  wain-risuto o onegai shimasu

ワインリストをお願いします。

I'd like a glass/bottle of ... wine
  ... wain o (ip-pai/
  ip-pon) kudasai

...ワインを（一杯／
一本）ください。

Champagne	**shampen**	シャンペン
red	**aka**	赤
rose	**roze**	ロゼ
sparkling	**supākuringu**	スパークリング
white	**shiro**	白

What is a good year?
  nannen ga ii toshi desu ka?

何年がいい年ですか？

Which wine would you recommend
with this dish?
  kono ryōri ni au wain wa
  nan desu ka?

この料理に合うワインは
何ですか？

Please bring me another bottle.
  mō ippon motte kite kudasai

もう一本持って来てください。

This wine has a nice/bad taste.
  kono wain wa (oishii/mazui) desu

このワインは（おいしい／
まずい）です。

Sake

What is a good local sake?
  kono tochi no ii ji-zake wa
  nan desu ka?

この土地のいい地酒は
何ですか？

Cold/warm sake please.
  (reishu/o-kan) onegai shimasu

（冷酒／お燗）お願いします。

Where is this sake made?
  kore wa doko no o-sake desu ka?

これはどこのお酒ですか？

I like sweet/dry sake.
  (ama-kuchi/kara-kuchi)
  no o-sake ga suki desu

（甘口／辛口）のお酒が好きです。

English–Japanese Glossary

All verbs listed in the following section are noted in the -masu form, as this form is most often used in everyday conversation. Please note that standard dictionaries do not list verbs in this way.

A

abalone	awabi	あわび
air-conditioned	eakon	エアコン
ale	ēru/bīru	エール／ビール
allergy	arerugī	アレルギー
allspice	ōrusupaisu	オールスパイス
almond	āmondo	アーモンド
anchovy	anchohi/katakuchiiwashi	アンチョビ／カタクチイワシ
anise	anisu	アニス
aperitif	shokuzenshu	食前酒
appetiser	zensai	前菜
apples	ringo	リンゴ
apricot	apurikotto/anzu	アプリコット／あんず
artichoke	ātichōku	アーティチョーク
ashtray	haizara	灰皿
asparagus	asuparagasu	アスパラガス
aubergine	nasu	ナス
automatic teller (ATM)	genkin-jidō-shiharai-ki/ (ētīemu)	現金自動支払機 (ATM)
autumn	aki	秋
avocado	abogado	アボガド
awful	hidoi/mazui	ひどい／まずい
azuki bean	azuki	小豆

B

B & W (film)	shirokuro (firumu)	白黒（フィルム）
baby corn	bebīkōn	ベビーコーン
baby food	rinyūshoku	離乳食
bacon	bēkon	ベーコン
to bake	(ōbun de) yakimasu	（オーブンで）焼きます
baking soda	jūsō	重ソウ
bamboo shoot	take-no-ko	タケノコ
banana	banana	バナナ
bank	ginkō	銀行
banquet	enkai	宴会
a bar	bā	バー
barbecue	bābekyū	バーベキュー
barley	ōmugi	大麦
barracuda	kamasu	カマス
bass	suzuki/basu	すずき／バス

batter	batā	バター
bay	gekkeiju	月桂樹
bean sprout	moyashi	モヤシ
beef	gyūniku/bīfu	牛肉／ビーフ
beef jerky	bīfu-jākī	ビーフジャーキー
beefsteak	bīfu-sutēki	ビーフステーキ
beer	bīru	ビール
beetroot	bītorūto	ビートルート
berries	kinomi/berī	木の実／ベリー
betel	kinma	キンマ
bill	(o-) kanjō	（お）勘定
bird	tori	鳥
bitter	nigai	苦い
bitters	bitāzu	ビターズ
black bean	kuro-mame	黒豆
black olive	kuro-orību	黒オリーブ
black pudding	burakku pudingu	ブラックプディング
blackberry	burakkuberī	ブラックベリー
blender	burendā/mikisā	ブレンダー／ミキサー
blueberry	burūberī	ブルーベリー
to boil (something with hot water)	yudemasu	ゆでます
to boil (something with soup or sauce)	nimasu	煮ます
to boil (water)	wakashimasu	沸かします
bok choy	chingensai	チンゲンサイ
bottle	bin/botoru	ビン／ボトル
–opener	sennuki	栓抜き
bourbon	bābon	バーボン
bowl	bōru	ボール
to braise	nikomimasu	煮込みます
bran	nuka/fusuma	糠／ふすま
brandy	burandē	ブランデー
bread	pan	パン
breakfast	chōshoku/asa-gohan	朝食／朝ご飯
bream	tai	タイ
breast	mune	胸
brill	hirame	ヒラメ
brilliant	subarashii	すばらしい
to bring	motte kimasu	持ってきます
brisket	muneniku	胸肉
broad bean	sora-mame	そら豆
broccoli	burokkorī	ブロッコリー
broil	nimasu	煮ます
broth	dashi-jiru	だし汁
brown rice	genmai	玄米
Brussels sprouts	mekyabetsu	芽キャベツ

bubble	awa	泡
buckwheat	soba	そば
burnet	waremokō	ワレモコウ
butter	batā	バター
buttermilk	batā-miruku	バターミルク
butterscotch	batā-sukocchi	バタースコッチ

C

cabbage	kyabetsu	キャベツ
cafe	kafe/kissaten	カフェ／喫茶店
cakes	kēki	ケーキ
can	kan	缶
–opener	kankiri	缶切り
cancel (noun)	kyanseru/torikeshi	キャンセル／取り消し
to cancel	kyanseru shimasu/ torikeshimasu	キャンセルします／ 取り消します
candle	rōsoku	ろうそく
candy	kyandī	キャンディー
cantaloupe	kantarōpu meron	カンタロープメロン
capon	hiikudori	肥育鶏
capsicum	pīman	ピーマン
caramel (baked sugar)	karameru	カラメル
caramel (lolly)	kyarameru	キャラメル
caraway seed	kyarauē	キャラウェー
cardamom	karudamon	カルダモン
cardoon	karudon	カルドン
carp	koi	コイ
carrot	ninjin	にんじん
cash	genkin	現金
cash register	reji	レジ
cashew	kashūnattsu	カシューナッツ
cashier	reji-gakari	レジ係
cauliflower	karifurawā	カリフラワー
caviare	kyabia	キャビア
cayenne	tōgarashi	唐辛子
celery	serori	セロリ
ceramic	tōjiki/seramikku	陶磁器／セラミック
cereal	seriaru	セリアル（朝食用のコーン フレークなどの穀物食品）
chair	isu	椅子
Champagne	shanpen	シャンペン
change	o-tsuri	おつり
chanterelle	anzu-take	アンズタケ
chayote	hayatouri	ハヤトウリ
cheap (restaurant)	yasui (resutoran)	安い（レストラン）

cheese	chīzu	チーズ
blue	burū chīzu	ブルーチーズ
cottage	kotejji chīzu	コテッジチーズ
cream	kurīmu chīzu	クリームチーズ
goat's	yaginyū chīzu	山羊乳チーズ
hard	hādo chīzu	ハードチーズ
soft	sofuto chīzu	ソフトチーズ
chef	shefu/kokku	シェフ／コック
cheque	kogitte/chekku	小切手／チェック
cherry	sakuranbo/cherī	サクランボ／チェリー
cherry blossom	sakura	桜
cherry tomatoes	cherī-tomato/ hitokuchi-tomato	チェリートマト／ 一口トマト
chestnut	kuri	栗
chewing gum	chūingamu	チューインガム
chick pea	hiyoko-mame	ヒヨコマメ
chicken	toriniku/chikin	鶏肉／チキン
chicory	chikorī	チコリー
chilli	tōgarashi	唐辛子
china ware	setomono	瀬戸物
Chinese cabbage	hakusai	白菜
Chinese food	chūka-ryōri	中華料理
Chinese radish	daikon	大根
Chinese tea	chūgokucha	中国茶
chips	chippu	チップ
chive	chaibu	チャイブ
chocolate	chokorēto	チョコレート
chopping board	manaita	まな板
chops	choppu	チョップ
chopsticks	(o-) hashi	(お) 箸
chowder	chaudā	チャウダー
cider	saidā	サイダー
cigarettes	tabako	たばこ
cilantro	koendoro	コエンドロ
cinnamon	shinamon/nikkei/nikki	シナモン／肉桂／ニッキ
citrus	kankitsurui	柑橘類
clam	hamaguri/nimai-gai	ハマグリ／二枚貝
clean	kirei na/seiketsu na	きれいな／清潔な
to close	shimemasu	閉めます
closed	heiten	閉店
clove	kurōbu	クローブ
cockle	zaru-gai	ザルガイ
cocktails	kakuteru	カクテル
cocoa	kokoa	ココア
coconut	kokonatsu/yashi no mi	ココナツ／ヤシの実
cod	tara	たら

coffee	kōhī	コーヒー
–grinder	kōhī-hiki	コーヒー挽き
–machine	kōhī-mashin	コーヒーマシン
coin	koin	コイン
cold (object)	tsumetai	冷たい
cold (weather, room temperature)	samui	寒い
condiments	kōshinryō/yakumi	香辛料／薬味
conserves	satō-zuke	砂糖漬け
consomme	konsome	コンソメ
to cook	ryōri shimasu	料理します
cookies	kukkī	クッキー
coriander	korianda	コリアンダ
corn	tōmorokoshi	とうもろこし
corn flakes	kōn-fureku	コーンフレーク
cornmeal	kōn-mīru	コーンミール
counter	kauntā	カウンター
courgette	zukkīni	ズッキーニ
couscous	kusukusu	クスクス
cow	ushi	牛
crab	kani	かに
cracked wheat	hikiwari-mugi	挽き割り麦
cranberry	kuranberī	クランベリー
–sauce	kuranberī-sōsu	クランベリーソース
crayfish	ise-ebi	伊勢エビ
cream	kurīmu	クリーム
clotted	kokei-kurīmu	固形クリーム
dairy	nama-kurīmu	生クリーム
sour	sawā-kurīmu	サワークリーム
whipping	hoippingu-kurīmu	ホイッピングクリーム
credit card	kurejitto-kādo	クレジットカード
cress	kuresu/koshōsō	クレス／コショウソウ
croissant	kurowassan	クロワッサン
croquette	korokke	コロッケ
cucumber	kyūri	キュウリ
cuisine	ryōri	料理
cumin	kumin	クミン
cup	kappu	カップ
cupboard	shokkidana	食器棚
curd	gyōnyū	凝乳
to cure	hozonshimasu	保存します
currant	suguri	スグリ
curry	karē	カレー
–paste	karē-pēsuto	カレーペースト
–powder	karē-ko	カレー粉
cutlass fish	tachiuo	タチウオ
cutlets	katsu	カツ
cuttlefish	ika	イカ

D

dab	karei	カレイ
dairy products	nyūseihin	乳製品
dates	natsumeyashi	ナツメヤシ
to deep-fry	agemasu	揚げます
deer	shika	鹿
delicatessen	derikatessen	デリカテッセン
delicious	oishii	おいしい
dessert	dezāto	デザート
−spoon	dezāto supūn	デザートスプーン
diabetic	tōnyōbyō	糖尿病
to dice	sai-no-me ni kirimasu	さいの目に切ります
diced	sai-no-me	さいの目
dill	inondo	イノンド
dinner	yūshoku/bansan/dinā	夕食／晩餐／ディナー
dirty	kitanai	汚い
dried	kansō	乾燥
to drink	nomimasu	飲みます
drinks	nomimono	飲み物
drunk (to be)	yoimasu	酔います
dry (wine)	karakuchi	辛口
duck	ahiru/kamo	アヒル／鴨
dumplings	gyōza	ギョウザ

E

each	sorezore/kaku	それぞれ／各
to eat	tabemasu	食べます
eel	unagi	うなぎ
eggplant	nasu	なす
eggs	tamago	卵／玉子
endive	endaibu	エンダイブ
entree	zensai/antorē	前菜／アントレー
evening	ban/yūgure	晩／夕暮れ
excellent	subarashii	すばらしい
exchange rate	kawase-rēto	為替レート

F

fall (autumn)	aki	秋
family	kazoku/katei	家族／家庭
famous	yūmei na	有名な
fan (folding)	sensu	扇子
fan (machine)	senpūki	扇風機
farm	nōjō	農場
farmer	nōka/nōmin	農家／農民
fat	shibō	脂肪

favourite food	kōbutsu	好物
fennel	uikyō	ウイキョウ
–seed	uikyō no mi	ウイキョウの実
fenugreek	koroha	コロハ
ficld pea	endō	エンドウ
fig	ichijiku	イチジク
to fillet	kirimi ni shimasu	切り身にします
fillet	… hire/kirimi	… ヒレ/切り身
filling	gu	具
film (for camera)	firumu	フィルム
film (negative)	nega	ネガ
first course	fāsuto kōsu	ファーストコース
fish	sakana	魚
–paste	sakana no pēsuto	魚のペースト
–roe	sakana no tamago	魚の卵
–sauce	sakana no sōsu	魚のソース
flank	wakibaraniku	わき腹肉
flavour	aji/fūmi	味/風味
floor (storey)	kai	階
flounder	hirame/karei	ヒラメ/カレイ
flour	komugiko	小麦粉
corn	kōn-furawā	コーンフラワー
wholemeal	zenryū-komugiko	全粒小麦粉
flower	hana	花
flying fish	tobiuo	とびうお
folding screen	byōbu	屏風
food	tabemono	食べ物
food processor	fūdo-purosessā	フードプロセッサー
foreigner	gai (koku) jin	外 (国) 人
fork	fōku	フォーク
frankfurter	furankufuruto sōsēji	フランクフルトソーセージ
free-range	hanashigai	放し飼い
fresh	shinsen na	新鮮な
–juice	shinsen na jūsu	新鮮なジュース
Friday	kinyōbi	金曜日
fried	… itame/yaki …/	… 炒め/焼き … /
	… yaki	… 焼き
–noodles	yakisoba	焼きそば
–rice	chāhan/yaki-meshi	チャーハン/焼き飯
–vegetables	yasai-itame	野菜炒め
frog	kaeru	蛙
–legs	kaeru no ashi	蛙の足
frozen	reitō	冷凍
fruit	kudamono/furūtsu	果物/フルーツ
–cake	furūtsu kēki	フルーツケーキ
dried	dorai furūtsu	ドライフルーツ
–juice	furūtsu jūsu	フルーツジュース

–punch	furūtsu panchi	フルーツパンチ
–shop	kudamono-ya	果物屋
to fry	furai ni shimasu/agemasu	フライにします／揚げます
frying pan	furai-pan	フライパン
fugu	fugu	フグ
fun	tanoshii	楽しい

G

galangal	kōryōkyō	コウリョウキョウ
game	ryōchō/ryōjū	猟鳥／猟獣
garbage	gomi	ごみ
garfish	sayori	さより
garlic	ninniku/gārikku	にんにく／ガーリック
gelatin	zerachin	ゼラチン
ghee	gī	ギー
gherkin	kyūri no pikurusu	キュウリのピクルス
giblets	zōmotsu	臓物
gin	jin	ジン
ginger	shōga/jinjā	しょうが／ジンジャー
ginko nut	ginnan	ぎんなん
to give	agemasu	あげます
glass	gurasu/koppu	グラス／コップ
glutinous rice	mochi-gome	もち米
goat	yagi	ヤギ
good	ii/yoi	いい／よい
goose	gachō/gan	ガチョウ／ガン
gooseberry	suguri	スグリ
gram	guramu	グラム
grapefruit	gurēpufurūtsu	グレープフルーツ
grapes	budō/gurēpu	ブドウ／グレープ
grappa	gurappa	グラッパ
to grate	oroshimasu	おろします
grater	oroshigane	おろし金
gravy	nikujū	肉汁
grayling	kawahimemasu	カワヒメマス
grease	abura/yushi	油／油脂
great	idai na	偉大な
green capsicum (pepper)	pīman	ピーマン
green olive	gurīn-orību	グリーンオリーブ
green split pea	hoshiendō	干しエンドウ
greengrocer	yao-ya	八百屋
greens	yasai	野菜
grilled	... yaki	... 焼き
grouper	hata	ハタ
guava	guaba	グアヴァ

H

English	Romaji	Japanese
haddock	hadokku (tara no isshu)	ハドック（タラの一種）
haggis	hagisu	ハギス
hair	ke/kaminoke	毛／髪の毛
hake	heiku (merurūsa no isshu)	ヘイク（メルルーサの一種）
halibut	ohyō	オヒョウ
ham	hamu	ハム
hamburger	hanbāgā	ハンバーガー
hare	nousagi	野ウサギ
to have	... o motte imasu/	... を持っています／
	... ga arimasu	... があります
hazelnut	hēzerunattsu	ヘーゼルナッツ
heart	shinzō/hatsu	心臓／ハツ
herring	nishin	ニシン
high blood pressure	kōketsuatsu	高血圧
hominy	hikiwari tōmorokoshi	挽き割りトウモロコシ
honey	hachimitsu	蜂蜜
horseradish	wasabi	わさび
hot (object)	atsui	熱い
hot pot	nabe (mono)	鍋（もの）
hot (spicy)	karai	辛い
hot (weather, room)	atsui	暑い
hungry (to be)	onaka ga sukimasu	お腹がすきます
to hurry	isogimasu	急ぎます

I

ice	kōri/aisu	氷／アイス
ice cream	aisu-kurīmu	アイスクリーム
ice water	kōrimizu	氷水
icing sugar	konazatō	粉砂糖
indigestion	shōkafuryō	消化不良
ingredient	shokuzai/zairyō	食材／材料
inn	ryokan	旅館
inside	naka ni	中に

J

jalapeno chilli	harapenyo	ハラペニョ
jam	jamu	ジャム
Japan	nihon/nippon	日本
Japanese food	washoku/nihonshoku	和食／日本食
Japanese garden	nihonteien	日本庭園
Japanese (language)	nihongo/nippongo	日本語
Japanese (people)	nihonjin/nipponjin	日本人
Japanese tea	nihoncha	日本茶
jar	tsubo/jā	壷／ジャー
jelly	zerī	ゼリー

jellyfish	kurage	クラゲ
Jerusalem artichoke	kikuimo	キクイモ
John Dory	matōdai	マトウダイ
juice	jūsu	ジュース
juicer	jūsu-shiboriki	ジュースしぼり器
juniper berry	toshōshiyu	杜松子油

K

karaoke	karaoke	カラオケ
kelp	konbu	昆布
kettle	yakan	やかん
kidney	jinzō	腎臓
kilogram	kiro (guramu)	キロ（グラム）
kiosk	baiten/kiyosuku	売店／キヨスク
kipper	kunseisake	燻製サケ
kitchen	daidokoro/kicchin	台所／キッチン
kitchen (restaurant)	chūbō	厨房
kiwi	kīui	キーウィ
knife	naifu/hōchō	ナイフ／包丁
boning	honetoriyō naifu	骨切り用小型ナイフ
bread	pankiri naifu	パン切りナイフ
butter	batā naifu	バターナイフ
carving	kirimoriyō naifu	切り盛り用ナイフ
paring	kawamuki naifu	皮むきナイフ
knuckle	hizaniku	ひざ肉
kumquat	kinkan	キンカン

L

lacquer ware	shikki/urushi-nuri	漆器／漆塗り
ladle	hishaku/o-tama	ひしゃく／お玉
lager	ragā-bīru	ラガービール
lamb	ramu/kohitsuji	ラム／子羊
language	kotoba/gengo	言葉／言語
lard	rādo	ラード
large	ōkii	大きい
last	saigo no	最後の
last month	sengetsu	先月
last night	yūbe	ゆうべ
last week	senshū	先週
last year	kyonen	去年
late	osoi	遅い
laxatives	benpiyaku	便秘薬
leaf	ha/happa	葉／葉っぱ
to learn	naraimasu/ benkyō shimasu	習います／ 　勉強します
leatherfish	kawa-hagi	かわはぎ

leek	rīki/niranegi	リーキ/ニラネギ
left (not right)	hidari	左
leg	ashi	脚
lemon	remon	レモン
lemonade	remonēdo	レモネード
lentil	renzu-mame	レンズマメ
lettuce	retasu	レタス
to like	suki ni narimasu	好きになります
lime	raimu	ライム
liqueur	rikyūru	リキュール
liquorice	kanzō	カンゾウ
little (small)	chiisai	小さい
liver	kanzō/rebā	肝臓/レバー
loaf	pangata	パン型
lobster	robusutā	ロブスター
local	chihō no/chiiki no/ tochi no	地方の/地域の/ 土地の
loin	koshiniku	腰肉
loose change	kozeni	小銭
loquat	biwa	びわ
lotus root	renkon	れんこん
lounge	raunji	ラウンジ
lunch	chūshoku/hiru-gohan/ ranchi	昼食/昼ご飯/ ランチ
luxury	gōka na	豪華な
lychee	reishi	レイシ

M

macadamia	makadamia	マカダミア
mace	mēsu (natsumegu no kawa)	メース（ナツメグの 皮）
mackerel	saba	さば
main course	mēn-kōsu	メーンコース
mallard	magamo	マガモ
man (human)	hito/ningen	人/人間
man (male)	otoko (no hito)	男（の人）
mandarin orange	mikan	みかん
mango	mangō	マンゴー
many	takusan no	たくさんの
marinades	marine	マリネ
to marinate	marine ni shimasu	マリネにします
market	ichiba/māketto	市場/マーケット
marmalade	māmarēdo	マーマレード
marrow	kotsuzui	骨髄
marvellous	subarashii	すばらしい
mayonnaise	mayonēzu	マヨネーズ

meal	shokuji	食事
meat	niku	肉
medium (cooked)	midiamu	ミディアム
melon	meron	メロン
menu	menyū	メニュー
meringue	merenge	メレンゲ
milk	gyūnyū/miruku	牛乳／ミルク
condensed	kondensu miruku	コンデンスミルク
powdered	kona miruku	粉ミルク
skimmed	sukimu miruku	スキムミルク
soy	tōnyū	豆乳
millet	zakkoku	雑穀
mince	komagire	細切れ
mincer	nikubikiki	肉挽き機
mineral water	mineraru-uōtā	ミネラルウォーター
mini bar	mini-bā	ミニバー
mint	minto/hakka	ミント／ハッカ
to mix	mazemasu	混ぜます
mixing bowl	bouru	ボウル
Monday	getsuyōbi	月曜日
money	o-kane	お金
morel	amigasatake	アミガサタケ
mortar	surubachi	すり鉢
MSG	gurutaminsan-sōda	グルタミン酸ソーダ
muesli	mūzurī	ミューズリー
mulberry	kuwa-no-mi	くわの実
mullet	bora	ボラ
mung bean	yaenari	ヤエナリ
mushroom	kinoko	きのこ
mussel	mūru-gai/i-gai	ムール貝／イガイ
mustard	karashi/masutādo	からし／マスタード
mutton	maton	マトン

N

napkin	napukin	ナプキン
nausea	hakike	吐き気
near	chikai	近い
nearby (restaurant)	chikaku no (resutoran)	近くの（レストラン）
neck	kubi	首
next	tsugi no	次の
next month	raigetsu	来月
next to	tonari	となり
next week	raishū	来週
next year	rainen	来年
nice	suteki na	素敵な
night	yoru	夜

noisy	urusai	うるさい
noodles	men/nudoru	麺／ヌードル
nougat	nugā	ヌガー
nutcracker	kurumiwari	クルミ割り
nutmeg	natsumegu/nikuzuku	ナツメグ／ニクズク

O

oatmeal	ōtomīru	オートミール
ocean	umi	海
octopus	tako	タコ
offal	zōmotsu/motsu	臓物／モツ
often	yoku	よく
oil	abura	油
olive	orībuyu	オリーブ油
peanut	pīnattsuyu	ピーナッツ油
sesame	goma-abura	ごま油
sunflower	himawariyu	ヒマワリ油
vegetable	shokubutsuyu	植物油
OK	ōkē	OK
okra	okura	オクラ
omelette	omuretsu	オムレツ
onion	tama-negi	たまねぎ
on sale	yasu-uri	安売り
to open	hirakimasu/akemasu	開きます／開けます
opened	kaiten	開店
orange	orenji	オレンジ
to order	chūmon shimasu/ ōdā shimasu	注文します／オーダーします
order (noun)	chūmon/ōdā	注文／オーダー
ordinary	futsū no	普通の
oregano	oregano	オレガノ
organic	yūki	有機
oven	ōbun	オーブン
oxtail	ushi no o	牛の尾
oyster	kaki	カキ
oyster mushroom	hiratake	ヒラタケ

P

pan	nabe	鍋
papaya	papaiya	パパイヤ
paprika	papurika	パプリカ
parasol	parasoru	パラソル
parsley	paseri	パセリ
parsnip	pāsunippu	パースニップ
passionfruit	passhon furūtsu	パッションフルーツ

pasta	pasuta	パスタ
pastrami	pasutorami	パストラミ
pastry	pesutorī	ペストリー
peach	momo	桃
peanut	pīnattsu/rakkasei	ピーナッツ／落花生
pear	yōnashi	洋梨
Japanese pear	nashi	梨
pecan	pekan	ペカン
peeler	kawamukiki	皮むき器
pepper	koshō	胡椒
peppermint	pepāminto/hakka	ペパーミント／ハッカ
pepperoni	peparōni	ペパローニ
perch	suzuki/pāchi	スズキ／パーチ
persimmon	kaki	柿
pestle	surikogi	すりこ木
pheasant	kiji	雉
pickles	tsukemono	漬物
to pickle	tsukemasu	漬けます
pickling onion	tama-negi no suzuke	たまねぎの酢漬け
picnic	pikunikku	ピクニック
pie	pai	パイ
pig	buta	豚
pigeon	hato	鳩
pike	kawakamasu	カワカマス
pine nut	matsu-no-mi	松の実
pineapple	painappuru	パイナップル
pinto bean	buchi ingen-mame	ぶちインゲンマメ
pistachio	pisutashio	ピスタシオ
plaice	tsunogarei/akagarei/ hirame	ツノガレイ／アカガレイ／ ヒラメ
plain flour	komugiko	小麦粉
plate	o-sara	（お）皿
plum	sumomo	スモモ
plum tomatoes	puramu-tomato/ cherī-tomato/ hitokuchi-tomato	プラムトマト／ チェリートマト／ 一口トマト
to poach	yudemasu	ゆでます
polenta	porenta	ポレンタ
pomegranate	zakuro	ざくろ
popcorn	poppukōn	ポップコーン
poppy	keshi	ケシ
pork	butaniku/pōku	豚肉／ポーク
–sausages	pōku sōsēji	ポークソーセージ
porridge	o-kayu	おかゆ
port	pōto-wain	ポートワイン
pot (ceramic)	nabe/potto/tsubo/kame	鍋／ポット／壷／甕
potatoes	jaga-imo/poteto	ジャガイモ／ポテト

baked	bēkudo poteto	ベークドポテト
fried	poteto furai	ポテトフライ
mashed	masshu poteto	マッシュポテト
–masher	jaga-imo tsubushiki	ジャガイモつぶし器
poultry	toriniku	鳥肉
prawn	ebi	エビ
to prefer	konomimasu	好みます
preservative	hozonryō	保存料
pressure cooker	atsuryokunabe	圧力鍋
pretty	utsukushii/kirei na	美しい／きれいな
price	nedan	値段
prune	hoshisumomo	干しスモモ
puffball	hokoritake	ホコリタケ
pumpkin	kabocha	かぼちゃ

Q

quail	uzura	うずら
quality	hinshitsu	品質
quince	marumero	マルメロ

R

rabbit	usagi	うさぎ
radicchio	akachikorī	赤チコリー
radish	kabu	かぶ
raisin	rēzun/hoshibudō	レーズン／干しブドウ
rare (cooked)	rea	レア
raspberry	kiichigo	キイチゴ
ray	ei	エイ
receipt	reshīto/ryōshūsho	レシート／領収書
red cabbage	aka-kyabetsu	赤キャベツ
red capsicum (pepper)	aka-pīman	赤ピーマン
red kidney bean	aka-ingen	赤インゲン
red lentil	aka-renzu-mame	赤レンズマメ
red onion	aka-tama-negi	赤たまねぎ
redfish	kinme (dai)	きんめ（だい）
refrigerator	reizōko	冷蔵庫
relish	yakumi	薬味
reservation	yoyaku	予約
to reserve	yoyaku shimasu	予約します
restaurant	resutoran	レストラン
rhubarb	daiō	ダイオウ
ribs	abara	あばら
rice (cooked)	gohan	ご飯
rice (uncooked)	kome	米

basmati	bazumatimai	バズマティ米
brown	genmai	玄米
–cake	mochi	もち
–cracker	senbei	煎餅
glutinous	mochi-gome	もち米
jasmine	jasuminmai	ジャスミン米
short-grain	japonikamai	ジャポニカ米
wild	wairudo-raisu	ワイルドライス
rich (food)	kotteri shita (tabemono)	こってりした（食べ物）
ripe	juku shita/seijuku shita	熟した／成熟した
right (not left)	migi	右
river	kawa	川
roast	rōsuto/rōsu	ロースト／ロース
rocket	hana-daikon	ハナダイコン
rolled oats	rōrudo ōto	ロールドオート
rolling pin	menbō/nobebō	麺棒／延べ棒
rosemary	rōzumarī	ローズマリー
rum	ramushu	ラム酒
rump	shiriniku	尻肉
runner bean	benibana-ingen	ベニバナインゲン
rye whisky	rai-uisukī	ライウイスキー

S

saffron	safuran	サフラン
sage	sēji	セージ
sago	sago	サゴ
sake	o-sake	（お）酒
salad	sarada	サラダ
–bowl	sarada-bōru	サラダボール
salami	sarami	サラミ
salmon	sake/sāmon	鮭／サーモン
salt	shio	塩
salt & pepper mills	shio-koshōhiki	塩・コショウ挽き
salted pork	butaniku no shio-zuke	豚肉の塩漬け
salty	shoppai	しょっぱい
sardine	iwashi/maiwashi	イワシ／まいわし
Saturday	doyōbi	土曜日
sauce	sōsu/tare	ソース／たれ
saucepan	shichū-nabe	シチュー鍋
sausage	sōsēji	ソーセージ
sauté	sotē	ソテー
scad	aji	あじ
scales	uroko	うろこ
scallop	hotate	ホタテ
scampi	sukanpi/kuruma-ebi	スカンピ／クルマエビ
scissors	hasami	はさみ

sea	umi	海
sea urchin	uni	うに
sea vegetables	kaisō	海藻
seafood	kaisanbutsu/shīfūdo	海産物／シーフード
season	kisetsu	季節
seasoning	chōmiryō	調味料
seaweed	kaisō	海藻
kelp	konbu	昆布
nori	nori	海苔
wakame	wakame	ワカメ
self-service	scrufu-sābisu	セルフサービス
service (charge)	sābisu (ryū)	サービス（料）
sesame oil	goma-abura	ごま油
sesame seed	goma	ごま
shallot onion	wakegi	ワケギ
shallow-fry	itame	炒め
shandy	shandī	シャンディー
shank	suneniku	すね肉
sharpening stone	toishi	砥石
sharrot	wakegi	わけぎ
shellfish	kai	貝
sherry	sherī	シェリー
shiitake mushroom	shiitake	しいたけ
shopping	kaimono	買い物
short-grain rice	japonikamai	ジャポニカ米
shoulder	kata	肩
shrimp	ko-ebi	小エビ
to sieve	furui ni kakemasu	ふるいにかけます
sifter	furui	ふるい
sightseeing	kankō	観光
simmer	torobi de nimasu	とろ火で煮ます
sirloin	sāroin	サーロイン
to sit	suwarimasu	座ります
skewer	kushi	串
skipjack	katsuo	かつお
skirt	sukāto	スカート
to slice	usugiri ni shimasu/ suraisu shimasu	薄切りにします／ スライスします
slice	usugiri/suraisu	薄切り／スライス
a smell	nioi	におい
to smell	kagimasu	嗅ぎます
smelly	kusai	臭い
to smoke (cigarettes)	(tabako o) suimasu	（たばこを）吸います
to smoke (salmon)	(sake o) kunsei ni shimasu	（鮭を）燻製に します
smoked	kunsei	燻製
snacks	keishoku/sunakku	軽食／スナック

snapper	tai/madai/fuedai	タイ／マダイ／フエダイ
snow pea	sayaendō	サヤエンドウ
soap	sekken	石鹸
soda water	sōda	ソーダ
soft drink	sofuto-dorinku/ seiryōinryō	ソフトドリンク／ 清涼飲料
sole	shitabirame	シタビラメ
soup	shiru/sūpu	汁／スープ
soup spoon	sūpu supūn	スープスプーン
sour	suppai	酸っぱい
soy bean	daizu	大豆
soy milk	tōnyū	豆乳
soy sauce	shōyu	醤油
sparerib	supea-ribu	スペアリブ
sparkling wine	supākuringu-wain/ shanpen	スパークリングワイン／ シャンペン
spicy (hot)	karai	辛い
spinach	hōrensō	ほうれん草
spirits	jōryūshu	蒸留酒
spoon	supūn	スプーン
spring	haru	春
spring onions	negi	ねぎ
squash	sukasshu	スカッシュ
squid	ika	イカ
star anise	shikimi	シキミ
steak	sutēki	ステーキ
to steam	mushimasu	蒸します
steamer	mushiki	蒸し器
to steep	hitashimasu	浸します
stew	shichū	シチュー
stock	dashi/nidashi-jiru/sutokku	だし／煮出し汁／ストック
beef	bīfu-sutokku	ビーフストック
chicken	chikin-sutokku	チキンストック
fish	sakana no dashi	魚のだし
vegetable	yasai no dashi	野菜のだし
stout	kuro-bīru	黒ビール
straw	wara/mugiwara	わら／麦わら
strawberry	ichigo/sutoroberī	イチゴ／ストロベリー
stuffing	tsumemono	詰め物
sturgeon	chōzame	チョウザメ
sugar	satō/shugā	砂糖／シュガー
brown	kurozatō	黒砂糖
caster	kyasutatō	キャスター糖
icing	konazatō	粉砂糖
palm	pāmutō	パーム糖
summer	natsu	夏
Sunday	nichiyōbi	日曜日

sun-dried tomatoes	hiboshi-tomato/ sandorai-tomato	日干しトマト／ サンドライトマト
supermarket	sūpā	スーパー
supper	yashoku	夜食
sweet basil	mebōki/suwīto-bajiru	メボウキ／ スウィートバジル
sweet (lolly)	o-kashi	お菓子
sweet potato	satsuma-imo	サツマイモ
sweet (taste)	amai	甘い
sweet woodruff	kurumabasō	クルマバソウ
sweetcorn	suwīto-kōn	スウィートコーン

T

table	tēburu/shokutaku	テーブル／食卓
tablecloth	tēburu-kake	テーブル掛け
tap water	suidōsui	水道水
taro	satoimo/taroimo	サトイモ／タロイモ
tarragon	taragon	タラゴン
taste	aji	味
to taste	aji o mimasu	味を見ます
tasty	oishii	おいしい
tea	kōcha	紅茶
–ceremony	sadō	茶道
chamomile	kamirerucha	カミレル茶
decaffeinated	dekafe no kōcha	デカフェの紅茶
green	ocha/ryokucha	お茶／緑茶
herbal	hābutī	ハーブティー
Japanese	nihoncha	日本茶
lemon	remontī	レモンティー
milk	mirukutī	ミルクティー
peppermint	pepāmintotī	ペパーミントティー
–pot	kyūsu/tīpotto	急須／ティーポット
rose hip	bara no micha	バラの実茶
–spoon	chasaji/tī supūn	茶さじ／ティースプーン
–towel	fukin	ふきん
telephone	denwa	電話
to telephone	denwa shimasu	電話します
telephone number	denwa-bangō	電話番号
tequila	tekīra	テキーラ
to thank	kansha shimasu	感謝します
that	are/ano	あれ／あの
thirsty	nodo ga kawaite imasu	のどが乾いています
this	kore/kono	これ／この
this afternoon	kyō no gogo	今日の午後
this month	kongetsu	今月
this morning	kesa	今朝

GLOSSARY

this week	konshū	今週
this year	kotoshi	今年
Thursday	mokuyōbi	木曜日
thyme	taimu	タイム
time	jikan	時間
tin	kan	缶
tin opener	kan-kiri	缶切り
tip	chippu	チップ
tissues	tisshu	ティッシュ
toast	tōsuto	トースト
toaster	tosutā	トースター
tobacco	tabako	たばこ
tofu	tōfu	豆腐
tomatoes	tomato	トマト
tomorrow	ashita	明日
tomorrow afternoon	ashita no gogo	明日の午後
tomorrow evening	ashita no ban	明日の晩
tomorrow morning	ashita no asa	明日の朝
tonic water	tonikku	トニック
tonight	konban	今晩
tongs	hasami	はさみ
tongue	shita/tan	舌／タン
topping	toppingu	トッピング
tray	o-bon	（お）盆
trepang	namako	なまこ
tripe	toraipu	トライプ
trout	masu	マス
truffle	toryufu	トリュフ
to try	tameshimasu	試します
Tuesday	kayōbi	火曜日
tuna	maguro/tsuna	マグロ／ツナ
turbot	darumakarei/hirame	ダルマカレイ／ヒラメ
turkey	shichimenchō	七面鳥
turmeric	ukon	ウコン
turnip	kabu	かぶ

V

vanilla	banira	バニラ
veal	koushi no niku	仔牛の肉
vegetable	yasai	野菜
–oil	shokubutsuyu	植物油
vegetarian	bejitarian/saishoku (shugi) sha	ベジタリアン／菜食 （主義）者
venison	shikaniku	鹿肉
vermicelli	harusame	はるさめ
very	totemo/taihen	とても／たいへん

vinegar	su/binegā	酢／ビネガー
balsamic	barusamikku-binegā	バルサミックビネガー
cider	saidā-binegā	サイダービネガー
malt	bakugasu	麦芽酢
rice	yonezu	米酢
wine	wain-binegā	ワインビネガー
vineyard	budōbatake	ブドウ畑
vodka	uokka	ウォッカ

W

waiter	ueitā	ウェイター
waitress	uētoresu	ウェートレス
walnut	kurumi	クルミ
warm	atatakai	暖かい／温かい
to warm up	atatamemasu	暖めます／温めます
water	mizu	水
bottled	bin-iri no mizu	ビン入りの水
fresh	tansui	淡水
mineral	mineraru-uōtā	ミネラルウォーター
tap	suidōsui	水道水
watercress	kureson	クレソン
watermelon	suika	すいか
Wednesday	suiyōbi	水曜日
week	shū	週
weekend	shūmatsu	週末
whelk	sazae	さざえ
well done (cooked)	ueru-dan	ウエルダン
western food	seiyō-ryōri	西洋料理
wet (wine)	amakuchi	甘口
whale	kujira	くじら
wheat	komugi	小麦
–germ	komugibakuga	小麦麦芽
wheelchair	kuruma-isu	車椅子
whisk	awadateki	泡だて器
whisky	uisukī	ウィスキー
white cabbage	kyabetsu	キャベツ
white poppy seed	shirokeshi no mi	白ケシのみ
white pudding	howaito pudingu	ホワイトプディング
whitebait	shirasu	シラス
whiting	kisu	きす
wholewheat	zenryū-komugi	全粒小麦
–flour	zenryū-komugiko	全粒小麦粉
wild	yasei	野生
–boar	inoshishi/nobuta	いのしし／野豚
–greens	yasō	野草
–rice	wairudo-raisu	ワイルドライス

window	mado	窓
window seat	mado-giwa-seki	窓際席
wine	wain	ワイン
–glass	wain-gurasu	ワイングラス
Japanese	o-sake	（お）酒
–list	wain-risuto	ワインリスト
red	aka-wain	赤ワイン
sparkling	supākuringu-wain/ shanpen	スパークリングワイン／ シャンペン
white	shiro-wain	白ワイン
winery	wainarī	ワイナリー
winter	fuyu	冬
wok	chūka-nabe	中華鍋
woman	onna (no hito)	女（の人）
wonderful	subarashii	すばらしい
wooden spatula	hera/supachura	へら／スパチュラ
Worcester sauce	usutāsōsu	ウスターソース

Y

yam	yama-imo	山芋
yellow capsicum (pepper)	kipīman	黄ピーマン
yellow split pea	kiendō	黄エンドウ
yellowfin tuna	kihada	きはだ
yellowtail	buri/hamachi	ぶり／はまち
yesterday	kinō	きのう
yet	mada	まだ
yoghurt	yōguruto	ヨーグルト

Z

| zest | (tsuyoi) fūmi | （強い）風味 |
| zucchini | zukkīni | ズッキーニ |

Japanese Culinary Dictionary

All verbs listed in the following section are noted in the -masu form, as this form is most often used in everyday conversation. Please note that standard dictionaries do not list verbs in this way.

A

abekawa-mochi　　　安倍川餅
rice cakes covered with kinako and sugar (Shizuoka Prefecture)

abura　　　油
oil

abura age　　　油揚げ
deep-fried, thinly sliced tōfu

adzuki　　　小豆
see azuki

... ae　　　... 和え
dishes dressed with ..., eg, goma-ae

aemono　　　和え物
'harmonised things'; cooked and cooled vegetables, poultry or fish, 'harmonised' (blended) with a dressing that is often based on tōfu, sesame or miso paste

... age　　　... 揚げ
fried ..., eg, tatsuta-age

agedashi-dōfu　　　揚げだし豆腐
deep-fried tōfu in fish stock

agemono　　　揚げ物
deep-fried food

aigamo　　　合鴨
Japanese duck, cross between wild Mallard and duck

ainame　　　あいなめ
green ling/ling cod. Best eaten from spring to early summer. Used in sashimi and also served grilled, stewed and deep-fried.

aji　　　あじ
scad/horse mackerel

aka-amadai　　　赤あまだい
red amadai

aka-gai　　　赤貝
bearded clam/red clam/ark shell

aka-jiso　　　赤じそ
red shiso, used in pickling and in a summer juice

aka-zake　　　赤酒
reddish wine made of rice, barley and/or wheat, to which wood ash is added (Kumamoto Prefecture)

akiaji　　　秋味
(see aramaki-zake)

akita-gai　　　あきた貝
North Japan term for scallop

amadai　　　あまだい
tilefish / blanquillo / ocean whitefish. Highly prized and priced fish best eaten between late autumn and early spring. Also known as guji.

ama-ebi　　　甘エビ
sweet prawn

ama-nattō　　　甘納豆
sugar-coated beans boiled in syrup

ama-zake　　　甘酒
sweet, warm sake

amazu　　　甘酢
vinegar sweetened by adding sugar

ame　　　飴
lolly/candy

ami-yaki　　　網焼き
cooked on a griddle

an　　　あん
sweet bean paste

ana-kyū　　　アナキュウ
nori-rolled sushi with conger eel and cucumber

anago　　　あなご
conger eel

anbai　　　塩梅
'salt-plum', meaning 'balance'. A term used by the older generation in reference to food.

ankake　　　あんかけ
dishes topped with a sauce thickened with cornstarch

anko 餡子
azuki beans boiled with sugar

ankō あんこう
goosefish/angler/monkfish. Best in winter and good eaten in hotpot (*ankūnabe*).

ankoro-mochi あんころ餅
rice cake filled with sweetened azuki beans

anmitsu あんみつ
a dessert made from fruit, boiled red peas, diced Japanese gelatine and anko with syrup on top.

anpan アンパン
baked bun filled with anko

anzu あんず
apricot

ao-jiso 青じそ
green beefsteak plant. Also known as ao-shiso.

ao-nori あおのり
a strong green type of nori seaweed, produced in flake form. Sprinkled on okonomi-yaki and yakisoba.

ao-shiso 青じそ
see ao-jiso

aoto あおと
green peppers

aoyagi あおやぎ
trough shell/sunray surf clam. Also known as baka-gai.

aoyu あおゆ
green yuzu

ara あら
left-over fish head, bones and offal. Good for hotpot, clear soups and to make stock.

ara あら
type of sea bass/grouper/rock cod that reaches up to 1m in length. Used for hotpot and is best eaten in winter (Hakata, Kyūshū).

arai あらい
a style of sashimi where raw, white-fleshed fish is thinly sliced and washed in cold water to keep the meat firm

aramaki-zake 新巻鮭
salted whole salmon. Speciality of Hokkaidō where it is known as akiaji or tokishirazu.

ara-nabe あら鍋
hotpot made with sea bass (Kyūshū)

arare あられ
baked cracker made from mochi. Also known as kaki-mochi.

asa-gohan あさごはん
breakfast

asa-no-mi 麻の実
hemp seed

asari あさり
baby clam

asatsuki あさつき
very thin spring onion

asa-zuke 浅漬け
lightly salted pickles

assari あっさり
general term for light (not greasy). Often used to describe rāmen stock. *See also* kotteri.

atama-ryōri 頭料理
'head cuisine' using seafish entrails, from Taketa city

atsu-age 厚揚げ
fried tōfu

awa アワ
Italian millet/foxtail millet (rice substitute)

awabi あわび
abalone

awabi no kasu-zuke あわびの粕漬け
abalone pickled in sakekasu (Iwate Prefecture)

awamori 泡盛
an alcoholic spirit made from rice (Okinawa Prefecture)

ayu アユ
sweetfish/smelt

ayu-ryōri アユ料理
sweetfish cuisine

azuki 小豆
adzuki/red bean. Ingredient for the sweet paste used as a filling in many Japanese cakes and confections.

B

bai-gai   ばい貝
bloody clam

baka-gai   バカ貝
(see aoyagi)

banana   バナナ
banana

bancha   番茶
everyday tea. Tea made from the second tea harvest.

ban-gohan   ばんごはん
dinner

baniku   馬肉
horse meat

basashi   馬刺し
sashimi made from horse meat (Nagano Prefecture)

battera-zushi   バッテラ寿司
vinegared fish on pressed sushi

beni-shōga   紅しょうが
red pickled ginger

benitade   紅たで
water pepper, a dark red peppery garnish

(o-) bentō   （お）弁当
lunch box. Sold at small kiosks at stations and convenience stores. It normally contains rice with different vegetables, meat, fish and sometimes fruit. Some local train stations are famous for their special bentō varieties.

bera   べら
wrasse. A type of fish.

bettara-zuke   べったらづけ
pickled daikon

bīfu   ビーフ
beef

bīfu-katsu   ビーフカツ
beef cutlet

bīfu-sutēki   ビーフステーキ
beefsteak

binnaga   ビンナガ
albacore. A kind of tuna.

bīru   ビール
beer

biwa   びわ
loquat

bora   ボラ
mullet (see also karasumi and ina-manjū). This fish has many names depending on its size and age.

bota-mochi   牡丹餅
rice cake made from half sticky rice and half nonglutinous rice. Also known as o-hagi.

budō   ブドウ
grapes

buna-shimeji   ぶなしめじ
a small, yellow mushroom variety

buri   ぶり
yellowtail/amberjack. Best in winter. A specialty of Toyama Prefecture, where it is salted and dried then rolled in straw (waramaki-buri). Young fish are commonly known as hamachi.

buriko   ぶりこ
eggs of hata-hata (Akita Prefecture)

burokkorī   ブロッコリー
broccoli

buta no shōga-yaki   豚の生姜焼き
pork sauteed in ginger and shōyu

butaniku   豚肉
pork

butsu-ji   仏事
Buddhist funerary cuisine

C

chāhan   チャーハン
fried rice. Also known as yakimeshi.

cha-kaiseki   茶懐石
tea kaiseki

chanko-nabe   ちゃんこ鍋
sumō wrestler's mixed stew of meat and vegetables served in a pot

chanpon   チャンポン
noodle soup

cha-no-yu   茶の湯
tea ceremony

chāshū-men   チャーシュー麺
rāmen topped with sliced roast pork

cha-sōmen　　　　　茶そうめん
noodles containing green tea

chawan-mushi　　　　茶碗蒸
savoury steamed custard containing fish stock, chicken and gingko nuts

chidai　　　　　　　チダイ
'blood tai' fish, smaller than the madai

chikin　　　　　　　チキン
chicken

chikuwa　　　　　　ちくわ
sausage-shaped, minced fish meat. Used in stewed food and hotpot.

chikuzenni　　　　　筑前煮
chicken, taro, carrots, gobō, lotus root, konnyaku, dried shiitake mushroom and snow peas stewed in a stock made of sugar, shōyu and mirin.

chimaki　　　　　　ちまき
nonglutinous-rice cake wrapped in large leaves and steamed. Originally from China.

chinpi　　　　　　　陳皮
citrus zest

chirashi-zushi　　　ちらし寿司
sushi-meshi topped with raw fish, abura-age and vegetables

chiri-nabe　　　　ちり（鍋）
hotpot with white fish and vegetables. Eaten with a shōyu and ponzu sauce.

chīzu　　　　　　　チーズ
cheese

chōji　　　　　　　チョウジ
clove

chōmiryō　　　　　調味料
seasoning

chūgokucha　　　　中国茶
Chinese tea

chūhai　　　　　チュウハイ
shōchū served with various non-alcoholic mixers

chūka-soba　　　　中華そば
an old-fashioned term for rāmen; now suggests rāmen in a lighter, predominantly shōyu-based dashi

D

dagashi　　　　　　駄菓子
'no good' sweets

daifuku-mochi　　　大福餅
rice cake with anko inside

dai-ginjōshu　　　　大吟醸酒
highest grade sake made from rice ground to half its weight. Fruitier than ginjōshu.

daikon　　　　　　大根
giant white radish

daikon-oroshi　　　大根おろし
grated giant white radish

daitokuji-nattō　　大徳寺納豆
soy beans fermented with yeast

daizu　　　　　　　大豆
soy bean

dango　　　　　　　だんご
round balls made from rice and flour

danshaku-imo　　　男爵芋
type of potato, especially found in Hokkaidō

dashi　　　　　　　だし
stock, usually made from katsuobushi or konbu

datemaki　　　　　だて巻
sweetened, rolled omelette. Often served at New Year (osechi-ryōri).

debera　　　　　　でべら
dried cinnamon flounder (Hiroshima Prefecture)

denbu　　　　　　　でんぶ
boiled and roasted snapper or cod flavoured with sugar and shōyu. Made into pink flakes used in sushi rolls.

dengaku　　　　　　田楽
dishes where grilled fish, vegetables and tōfu are topped with miso sauce

dojō　　　　　　　ドジョウ
loach/oriental weatherfish

... don　　　　　　　… 丼
rice with savoury topping, eg, oyakodon, katsudon and unadon

dorai-bīru　　　　ドライビール
dry beer. Developed in Japan, it has a higher alcohol content and is more aerated than standard beer.

dora-yaki　　　　　　　どら焼き
sweet azuki bean paste sandwiched between two pancakes

dote-nabe　　　　　　　土手鍋
hotpot with miso paste stock, to which vegetables and seafood are added. Oyster hotpot with miso stock (*kaki no dote-nabe*) is famous.

E

ebi　　　　　　　　　　エビ
general term for prawn, shrimp, lobster and crayfish

ebi-furai　　　　　　　エビフライ
battered prawn

ebi-sōmen　　　　　　エビそうめん
shrimp sōmen

eda-mame　　　　　　　枝豆
young soy bean. Boiled and lightly salted eda-mame is a favourite accompaniment for beer in summer.

edo-miso　　　　　　　江戸味噌
dark, fiery red and slightly sweet miso from Tokyo

ei-hire　　　　　　　　エイヒレ
dried stingray fin. Served grilled as a snack for sake drinkers.

eki-ben　　　　　　　　駅弁
station lunchbox

endō　　　　　　　　　エンドウ
type of green pea

engawa　　　　　　　　えんがわ
base of the dorsal fin of flounder and sole. Considered the tastiest part of these fish when eaten as sashimi.

enoki-dake　　　　　　えのきだけ
velvet shank mushroom/winter mushroom

era　　　　　　　　　　えら
gill

F

fenneru　　　　　　　　フェンネル
fennel. Also known as uikyō.

fu　　　　　　　　　　　麩
shapes made from gluten flour used in clear soup

fucha-ryōri　　　　　　普茶料理
Chinese Zen cuisine

fugu　　　　　　　　　フグ
puffer/globefish. Famous fish that contains the deadly nerve *toxin tetrodotoxin*. The toxin varies in strength according to the season and is found in different parts of the body depending on the species. Fugu flesh is thinly sliced and eaten raw as usuzukuri or used in hot fugu-chiri. The milt is regarded as a delicacy and is served with ponzu.

fugu-chiri　　　　　　ふぐチリ
hotpot with fugu fish

fugu-shirako　　　　　ふぐ白子
milt of the fugu

fukagawa-nabe　　　　深川鍋
hotpot with baby clam and spring onion. Popular traditional food in downtown Tokyo.

fuka-hire　　　　　　　ふかひれ
shark fin

fuki　　　　　　　　　フキ
Japanese butterbur (vegetable). Often used in stewed food.

fuki-no-tō　　　　　　フキノトウ
bud of fuki plant. Food symbolising the beginning of spring.

fukuro-take　　　　　ふくろたけ
paddy straw mushroom

funa　　　　　　　　　フナ
crucian carp. Boiled with shōyu, mirin, and sugar (kanroni or tsukudani). Often eaten raw (arai) in Kyoto, Osaka and Kanazawa.

funa-zushi　　　　　　フナずし
female crucian carp with eggs that are salted then pickled whole in fermented cooked rice (Shiga Prefecture)

furai　　　　　　　　　フライ
deep-fried

furikake　　　　　　　ふりかけ
dried topping for rice

futo-maki　　　　　　太巻き
various ingredients rolled in nori seaweed (large sushi rolls)

G

gai-mai 外米
foreign-produced rice

ganmodoki がんもどき
minced tōfu, fried with finely chopped vegetables and seaweed. Used in hotpots, eg, oden.

gari がり
pickled, pinkish-red ginger. Usually served as an accompaniment for sushi.

genmai-cha 玄米茶
roasted tea with roasted and popped rice

geso げそ
squid tentacles

ginjōshu 吟醸酒
a type of sake with a clean, fruity taste. Made of rice ground back to 60% of its original weight.

ginnan ぎんなん
gingko nut

gobō ごぼう
burdock root

gobuzuki 五分づき
50% white, 50% brown rice

gohan ご飯
cooked rice. Also means meal, eg, asa-gohan, hiru-gohan and ban-gohan.

gohanmono ご飯もの
rice dishes

goma ごま
sesame seeds

goma-ae ごま和え
dishes mixed with a sauce made of sesame, salt and sugar

goma-dare ごまだれ
sesame sauce (often served with hotpot)

goma-dōfu ごま豆腐
tōfu-like food made of ground white sesame and starch

gomame ごまめ
a small sardine cooked in shōyu and sugar, typically served at New Year

gomoku-soba 五目そば
rāmen noodles topped with assorted vegetables, seafood and meat

gu 具
filling, topping

guji ぐじ
see amadai

gyokuro 玉露
highest-quality Japanese green tea

gyōza ギョウザ
Chinese-style dumplings. Normally made from minced pork, cabbage, garlic, ginger and garlic chives.

gyūdon 牛丼
thinly sliced beef simmered in sweetened shōyu and served on rice

gyūniku 牛肉
beef

gyūnyū 牛乳
milk

gyūtan 牛タン
beef tongue

H

hakumai 白米
plain, white rice

hakusai 白菜
Chinese cabbage

hamachi はまち
yellowtail/amberjack (see buri)

hamaguri はまぐり
hard clam

hamo ハモ
dagger-tooth/conger-eel. Highly sought-after fish in the Kansai region, especially Kyoto. Used in tempura, teriyaki, sunomono, chiri-nabe and suimono.

hana-mame 花豆
flower bean

hanasaki-gani 花咲がに
1. type of king crab 2. 'flower opening' crab, where a crab opens up when dipped into hot water

hanbāgā ハンバーガー
hamburger

hanpen はんぺん
sponge-like fish cake made of ground shark meat mixed with grated yam and rice flour. Used in stew and clear soup.

happōsai 八宝菜
stirfry with assorted vegetables, meat and seafood, thickened with Chinese-style sauce

harawata はらわた
gizzards/offal. Also known as wata.

harusame はるさめ
bean-starch vermicelli

hasami はさみ
crab claws. Also known as kani-basami.

(o-) hashi （お）箸
chopsticks

hata ハタ
grouper

hata-hata ハタハタ
sailfin sandfish. Used to make fermented fish sauce called shottsuru in Akita Prefecture. The eggs are called buriko and are prized in Akita.

hata-hata-zushi はたはた寿司
pickled hata-hata

hatchō-miso 八丁味噌
a dark miso originally created in Okazaki, Aichi Prefecture

hayashi-raisu ハヤシライス
stewed meat and vegetables with rice

haze ハゼ
goby fish

henpai 返杯
a drinking custom where someone offers to fill your glass, then you reciprocate

hidara 干だら
dried cod

higashi 干菓子
dried sweets, famous in Kyoto, eaten in the tea ceremony

hijiki ひじき
a type of seaweed

hijiki no nimono ひじきの煮物
hijiki simmered with shōyu, sugar, fried tōfu and boiled soy beans

hime-masu ヒメマス
see kawa-masu

himono 干物
dried fish

hiraki ひらき
fully open matsutake mushroom

hiramasa ヒラマサ
yellowtail/amberjack/kingfish. Best in summer.

hirame ヒラメ
flatfish/bastard halibut. Best between winter and spring. Considered to be the tastier karei. Eaten raw as sashimi and sushi, as well as cooked.

hiratake ヒラタケ
oyster mushroom

hirekatsu ヒレカツ
fried pork fillet

hiru-gohan ひるごはん
lunch

hitsuji 羊
sheep/lamb

hiyamugi 冷麦
cold noodles dipped in cold sauce. Slightly thicker than sōmen noodles.

hiyashi-chūka 冷やし中華
cold noodles in sweet and sour soup with cucumber, chicken and egg on top

hiyashi-udon 冷やしうどん
simple cold udon

hiyayakko 冷奴
cold tōfu

hōbō ホウボウ
gurnard/bluefin/sea robin

hōjicha ほうじ茶
parched bancha

hokkaidō-ryōri 北海道料理
Hokkaidō cuisine

hokke ホッケ
atka mackerel

hokki-gai ほっき貝
hen clam. Also known as ubagai.

honjōzōshu 本醸造酒
Japanese rice wine, ground back to 70% of its original size, and blended with alcohol and water

hon-mirin　　　　　本みりん
good quality mirin

hon-shimeji　　　　本しめじ
type of mushroom

hōrensō　　　　　　ほうれん草
spinach

hoshi-gaki　　　　　干し柿
dried persimmon

hoso-maki　　　　　細まき
thin sushi roll

hotaru-ika　　　　　ホタルイカ
Boston pota or firefly squid

hotate-gai　　　　　ほたて貝
scallop

hotate-ryōri　　　　ほたて料理
scallop cuisine

hoya　　　　　　　ホヤ
sea squirt. Eaten raw, mixed with cucumber and vinegar.

hyakuhiro　　　　　百尋
boiled whale intestine (Hakata City)

ichigo　　　　　　　イチゴ
strawberry

ichijiku　　　　　　イチジク
fig

i-gai　　　　　　貽貝／ムール貝
mussel. Also known as mūru-gai.

ii-dako　　　　　　いいだこ
'rice octopus'

ika　　　　　　　　イカ
squid, cuttlefish

ikizukuri　　　　　活き作り
a method of presentation of fish and lobster, where the fish is served still alive

ikura　　　　　　　いくら
salted salmon eggs

ina-manjū　　　　　いな饅頭
cleaned mullet stuffed with miso paste (Nagoya Prefecture; see also bora)

inago　　　　　　　イナゴ
rice locust. Often eaten as tsukudani.

inaka-ryōri　　　　　田舎料理
rustic cuisine

inari-zushi　　　　　稲荷ずし
vinegared rice in fried tōfu pouch

ingen-mame　　　　インゲンマメ
kidney bean

inoshishi　　　　　いのしし
wild boar

iridori　　　　　　　煎り鳥
stirfried chicken, dried shiitake mushroom, gobō, taro, konnyaku, lotus root, carrots and bamboo shoots. These are then stewed in shōyu and mirin.

iriko　　　　　　　いりこ
dried trepang/sea cucumber or dried sardine

ise-ebi　　　　　　イセエビ
Japanese spiny lobster, crawfish

ishikari-nabe　　　　石狩鍋
Hokkaidō salmon and vegetable hotpot

isobe-maki　　　　　磯辺巻き
grilled rice cakes dipped in shōyu and wrapped in nori

... itame　　　　　　... 炒め
stirfried ...

itamemono　　　　　炒め物
stirfried dishes

itaya-gai　　　　　いたや貝
a small scallop. It is also known as shakushi-gai.

ito-konnyaku　　　　糸こんにゃく
thinly sliced konnyaku

ito-na　　　　　　　糸菜
a pot herb mustard, used as a leafy green vegetable

ito-sōmen　　　　　糸そうめん
thinnest type of sōmen

iwana　　　　　　　岩魚
char. A type of trout-like fish.

iwashi　　　　　　　いわし
pilchard/sardine

izakaya　　　　　　居酒屋
a traditional restaurant-cum-bar; an informal, cheap drinking place serving various small Japanese dishes and snacks

J

jaga-batā　　　　　ジャガバター
baked potatoes with butter

jaga-imo　　　　　ジャガイモ
potato

... jiru/... shiru　　　　　... 汁
... juice/... soup

jūbuzuki　　　　　十分づき
100% plain, white rice

junmaishu　　　　　純米酒
Japanese rice wine made by grinding
rice back to 70% of its original
weight

junsai　　　　　じゅんさい
water shield (small water plant)

K

kabayaki　　　　　蒲焼
grilled fish or eel dipped in shōyu-
based sauce, eg, unagi no kabayaki

kabocha　　　　　かぼちゃ
Japanese pumpkin

kabu　　　　　かぶ
turnip

kabu-nameko　　　　　かぶなめこ
wild, slightly larger variety of nameko
mushroom

kabutomushi　　　　　かぶと蒸し
steamed head of large fish varieties

kabutoni　　　　　かぶと煮
stewed head of large fish varieties

kairui　　　　　貝類
shellfish

kaiseki　　　　　懐石
shortened word for kaiseki-ryōri

kaiseki-ryōri　　　　　懐石料理
multicourse set meal including many
small dishes presented with attention to
the aesthetic and seasonal nature of
food and delicacy of flavour. This style
of cooking originated from the tea
ceremony.

kaisō　　　　　海藻
seaweed

kaiten-zushi　　　　　回転寿司
cheap sushi bar serving dishes on a
rotating conveyer

kaiware-daikon　　　　　貝割れ大根
spicy salad sprout from the mustard
family

kaizoku-ryōri　　　　　海賊料理
'pirate food' (Tokushima Prefecture)

kajika　　　　　カジカ
similar to goby. Freshwater fish up to
25cm long. Dishes using kajika are
called gori-ryōri and are a speciality of
Kanazawa Prefecture.

kajiki　　　　　かじき
marlin

kake-soba/-udon　かけそば／うどん
buckwheat/wheat flour noodles in
broth

kaki　　　　　柿
persimmon

kaki　　　　　カキ
oyster

kakiage　　　　　かき揚げ
finely chopped seafood and vegetables
fried in tempura batter

kaki-meshi　　　　　かき飯
oyster rice

kaki-mochi　　　　　かきもち
(see arare)

kaki-nabe　　　　　カキ鍋
oyster hotpot (Hiroshima Prefecture)

kamaboko　　　　　かまぼこ
minced white fish meat that is steamed
and sold in blocks

kamasu　　　　　カマス
barracuda/sea pike

kamo　　　　　鴨
duck

kani　　　　　かに
crab

kani-basami　　　　　かにばさみ
(see hasami)

kani-miso　　　　　かに味噌
crab reproductive organs, often eaten
as an hors d'oeuvre

kankoku-ryōri　　　　　韓国料理
Korean cuisine

kanpachi　　　　　カンパチ
amberjack. Best eaten in summer.

kanpyō かんぴょう
dried fruit of bottle gourd, flavoured with shōyu

kanpyō-maki かんぴょう巻き
sushi rolls made using kanpyō

kanroni 甘露煮
small fish boiled in, and sweetly flavoured with, shōyu and mirin. Also chestnuts boiled in syrup.

kantodaki かんと炊き
the name used for oden in the Kansai region

kappa-maki かっぱ巻き
cucumber sushi rolled in nori seaweed

kappō 割烹
a type of Japanese restaurant. Usually small but expensive.

kara 殻
shell

kara-age から揚げ
meat or fish dusted in flour and deep-fried

karami-mochi からみモチ
rice cake with grated daikon

karashi からし
mustard

karashina からし菜
brown mustard

karashi-zuke からし漬け
pickled vegetables flavoured with mustard

karasumi からすみ
dried mullet roe (Nagasaki, Kyūshū; see also bora)

karē カレー
curry

karei カレイ
dab/flatfish/flounder

karē-nanban カレー南蛮
buckwheat noodles with chicken or pork curry

karē-raisu カレーライス
Japanese-style curry and rice

karē-udon カレーうどん
udon noodles with curry roux sauce

karifurawā カリフラワー
cauliflower

karin かりん
Chinese quince

karintō かりんとう
traditional sweet made of flour and baking powder that is deep-fried and coated with brown sugar

karukan かるかん
a confection made from yama-imo, rice powder and sugar, from Kagoshima

kashiwa-mochi 柏餅
rice cake wrapped in oak leaf. Eaten on 5 May (Children's Day).

kasu 粕
lees from sake

kasujiru 粕汁
thick soup flavoured with lees from sake

kasutera カステラ
yellow sponge cake, Nagasaki

kasu-zuke 粕漬け
vegetables pickled in lees from sake

katakuchiiwashi カタクチイワシ
anchovy/Japanese anchovy

katakuriko 片栗粉
arrowroot flour

kata-yakisoba 固焼きそば
crunchy fried noodles topped with vegetables

katsudon カツ丼
fried pork cutlet and egg on rice

katsuo かつお
skipjack/bonito. Eaten raw as tataki and in teriyaki.

katsuobushi かつおぶし
dried bonito flakes. One of the most important ingredients for stocks.

kawa-hagi かわはぎ
leatherjacket/filefish. Best between February and May.

kawa-masu 川マス
fresh water red salmon. Also known as hime-masu or niji-masu.

kawa-zakana 川魚
river/lake fish

kazu-no-ko かずのこ
dried herring roe. Eaten at New Year (*see also* osechi-ryōri).

kechappu ケチャップ
ketchup

ke-gani 毛がに
bristly crab, horsehair crab. Best in winter.

keshi-no-mi ケシの実
poppy seed

kidai 黄だい
yellowish tai, a cheap fish served as shio-yaki

kihada きはだ
yellowfin tuna

kikuko きくこ
cod milt. Used in hotpot.

kikurage きくらげ
Jew's ear/Judas's ear/woody ear tree fungus

kimi-sōmen 黄身そうめん
noodles with egg yolk

kinako きなこ
soy bean flour

kinako-mochi きなこ餅
rice cake covered with sweetened soy bean flour

kinko きんこ
dried trepang (sea cucumber)

kinme (dai) きんめ（だい）
redfish/alfonsino

kinoko きのこ
mushroom

kinpira-gobō きんぴらごぼう
thinly cut gobō, normally eaten flavoured with shōyu

kintoki 金時
large red bean

kinugoshidōfu 絹ごし豆腐
smooth, soft tōfu (*see also* momen-dōfu)

kirimi 切り身
fish or meat fillet

kishimen きしめん
flat noodles (Nagoya)

kisu きす
whiting. Used in sushi, sashimi, tempura, and also eaten fried.

kitsune-soba/ -udon きつねそば／うどん
buckwheat/wheat flour noodles with fried tōfu

kiyuzu 黄ゆず
yellow yuzu

kōbe-gyū 神戸牛
beef where the cow that is fed beer and massaged with sake

kobucha 昆布茶
tea made of konbu seaweed. Also known as konbu-cha.

kobu-maki 昆布巻き
small fish or gobō wrapped in konbu and boiled. Eaten at New Year.

kōcha 紅茶
black tea

kochijan コチジャン
a Korean sweet, spicy, pepper-miso paste

kohada こはだ
threadfin shad/gizzard shad. Pickled in vinegar and used for making sushi. Also known as konoshiro.

kōhī コーヒー
coffee

koi コイ
carp/common carp. Used for miso soup or arai.

koicha 濃茶
thick tea

koikuchi-shōyu 濃い口醤油
dark shōyu

kōji-zuke 麹漬け
vegetables pickled in fermented rice

komatsuna 小松菜
mustard spinach, green leafy vegetable from the *campestris* family

(o-) kome （お）米
uncooked rice

kome-miso 米味噌
miso made from rice

komugi 小麦
wheat

kōnago こうなご
sand eel

konbu 昆布
kelp. Usually sold in dried form. Used to make basic stock. Also eaten in simmered dishes such as nimono and tsukudani.

konbu-cha 昆布茶
(see kobucha)

konbu-dashi 昆布だし
kelp stock

konnyaku こんにゃく
devil's tongue – a tuber used to make a gelatinous paste. The paste is used in hotpots and stewed foods. The root is mixed with water until it becomes a paste, then lime is added and it is boiled until it becomes gelatine-like in texture (Gunma, Tochigi and Fukushima Prefectures).

konoko このこ
dried trepang roe. Eaten as a snack accompaniment with sake (Ishikawa Prefecture).

kōnomono 香の物
pickled vegetables, served during the hassun course of the cha-kaiseki

konoshiro コノシロ
(see kohada)

konowata このわた
salted trepang intestine

konsai 根菜
root vegetables

kōri-dōfu 凍り豆腐
freeze-dried tōfu. Used in stewed dishes. Also known as kōya-dōfu.

koro ころ
young, fully closed matsutake

koromo 衣
coating of deep-fried food

koshō 胡椒
pepper

kotteri こってり
general term for rich or thick. Often used to describe rāmen stock. See also assari.

kōya-dōfu こうや豆腐
(see kōri-dōfu)

kuchiko くちこ
salted trepang roe

kudamono くだもの
fruit

kujira くじら
whale

kumiage-dōfu くみ上げ豆腐
freshly made tōfu

kurage クラゲ
jellyfish

kuri 栗
chestnut

kuri-jōchū 栗焼酎
shōchū made from chestnuts

kurikinton 栗きんとん
chestnuts boiled in syrup and covered with mashed, sweet potatoes

kuro-anago 黒穴子
black conger-eel

kurodai 黒鯛
black bream, or porgy, served as shio-yaki

kuro-goma 黒ごま
black sesame seed

kuro-maguro クロマグロ
bluefin tuna

kuro-mame 黒豆
black soy bean

kuruma-ebi 車えび
kuruma prawn/tiger prawn

kurumi クルミ
walnut

kusa-mochi 草もち
green rice cake mixed with mugwort

kusaya くさや
strong-smelling dried fish (Niijima, Izu archipelago). Before drying, the fish is dipped into fermented salt water kept especially for this process (sometimes for over 100 years).

kūsū 古酒（クースー）
aged awamori alcohol. Often several decades old.

kuwai クワイ
arrowhead (water plant)

kuzu 葛
kudzu vine. The starch extracted from the root of the vine. Yoshino in Nara Prefecture is renowned for having the finest kuzu.

kuzukiri 葛きり
thin, vermicelli-like noodles made from kuzu

kyabetsu キャベツ
cabbage

kyōdo-ryōri 郷土料理
regionalised speciality cuisine

kyōna 京菜
a pot-herb mustard plant, used as leafy green vegetable

kyōriki-ko 強力粉
strong wheat flour

kyō-ryōri 京料理
Kyoto specialist cuisine

kyoto shiro-miso 京都白味噌
a delicate, sweet white miso used in kyō-ryōri

kyūri キュウリ
cucumber

kyūri-momi キュウリもみ
thinly sliced cucumber mixed and softened with salt

kyūshū-ryōri 九州料理
cuisine of Kyūshū

kyūtei-ryōri 宮廷料理
palace cuisine

M

maaji マアジ
scad/horse mackerel/jack mackerel. Often used to make kusaya.

ma-anago 真穴子
conger-eel

madai マダイ
red sea bream/silver sea bream. Considered the king of fish and highly sought after in Japan. Used in sushi, sashimi and soups, and is also eaten grilled and steamed. Kabutomushi and kabutoni are particularly delicious. Best eaten in winter and spring.

magamo マガモ
mallard

maguro マグロ
tuna. Caught mostly outside Japan. The fattier the meat, the better quality and the tastier it is considered (see also toro).

maitake まいたけ
hen-of-the-woods mushroom

maiwashi まいわし
sardine/pilchard

maki-zushi 巻きずし
general term for nori-rolled sushi

mame 豆
bean, includes pea and soy bean

mame-miso 豆味噌
miso made from soy beans

mangō マンゴー
mango

manjū 饅頭
steamed, sweet bun made from leavened flour and filled with sweet azuki beans

masu マス
1. pink salmon 2. generic term for trout

matcha 抹茶
powdered green tea

matcha-aisu 抹茶アイス
green tea ice cream

matcha-shio 抹茶塩
salt and powdered green tea, used for dipping tempura

matodai マトウダイ
John Dory fish

matsukawa-zukuri 松皮づくり
a type of sashimi made from unskinned tai. The skin is tasty and looks like pine bark (matsukawa).

matsutake マツタケ
matsutake mushroom. Expensive and highly fragrant mushroom variety eaten in autumn and grown in pine forests. Used in clear soup and also served grilled.

mayonēzu マヨネーズ
mayonnaise

mebachi メバチ
bigeye tuna

mebaru メバル
brown rockfish

men 麺
noodles (*see also* hiyamugi, hōtō, kishimen, rāmen, sōmen and udon)

menchikatsu メンチカツ
crumbed and fried mince meat patties

menrui 麺類
generic term for noodles

(karashi) mentaiko （辛子）明太子
salted cod roe pickled in chilli (Kyūshū)

meron メロン
melon

mi 身
generic term for flesh (of fish and shellfish)

migaki-nishin 身欠きにしん
dried herring

mikan みかん
mandarin orange

minami-maguro ミナミマグロ
southern bluefin tuna

mirin みりん
sweet rice wine used for cooking

miru-gai みる貝
otter shell

miso 味噌
generally used to describe fermented soy bean paste, miso can also be made from rice or barley. A standard ingredient in many Japanese dishes.

misoni 味噌煮
fish simmered in miso stock

miso-rāmen 味噌ラーメン
rāmen with miso-flavoured broth

misoshiru 味噌汁
soup made from miso paste with fish stock. Often includes vegetables, tōfu and wakame.

miso-zuke 味噌漬
meat, fish and vegetables pickled in miso

mitsuba みつば
Japanese wild chervil, used to add flavour to hotpots, chawan-mushi and oyakodon

mitsu-mame みつ豆
Japanese dessert made from boiled red peas, diced Japanese gelatine (*agar-agar*) and fruit topped with syrup. Similar to anmitsu, but does not include anko.

mizu 水
water

mizuna ミズナ
a pot-herb mustard plant, used as leafy green vegetable

mizutaki 水炊き
hotpot with chicken and vegetables boiled in their own stock. Eaten with dipping sauce made from shōyu and ponzu.

mizu-yōkan 水羊羹
mild, sweet yōkan jelly

mochi もち
rice cake made from glutinous rice

mochi-gome もち米
glutinous rice, used to make mochi

modanyaki モダン焼き
Japanese-style savoury pancake with noodles

momen-dōfu 木綿豆腐
rough, firm tōfu (*see also* kinugoshi-dōfu)

momiji-oroshi もみじおろし
grated daikon and chilli. Used as a relish.

momo 桃
peach

monaka 最中
sweet made of anko inside a thin wafer shell

mori-soba もりそば
cold buckwheat noodles served in a bamboo steamer and dipped into a cold sauce before eating

motsu モツ
chicken, pork, or beef offal

motsu-nabe　　　　　モツ鍋
hotpot made of chicken, pork or beef offal

motsuni　　　　　　モツ煮
simmered chicken, pork or beef offal

moyashi　　　　　　モヤシ
bean sprouts

mozuku　　　　　　モズク
type of seaweed. Served mixed with vinegar.

mozuku-gani　　　　モズクガニ
small freshwater crab

mugi　　　　　　　麦
general term for wheat, oat, barley and rye

mugicha　　　　　　麦茶
cold tea made of roasted barley

mugi-jōchū　　　　　麦焼酎
shōchū distilled from wheat, made in the ōita Prefecture

mugi-miso　　　　　麦味噌
barley miso popular throughout Kyūshū

mugi-toro　　　　　麦とろ
cooked rice and wheat with grated yam on top

munieru　　　　　　ムニエル
meuniere. A dish that is fried lightly in butter.

mūru-gai　　　　　ムール貝
(see i-gai)

mushi-gyōza　　　　蒸しギョウザ
steamed gyōza dumpling

mushimono　　　　　蒸し物
steamed dishes

mutsugorō　　　　　ムツゴロウ
a kind of goby/mud skipper. Found in mud flats of the Ariake Sea in Kyūshū. Best in late spring and summer. Usually grilled and dipped in a shōyu-based sauce.

myōga　　　　　　　ミョウガ
Japanese ginger. Used as a relish and pickled in vinegar, or in tempura and salads.

N

na/nappa　　　　　菜／菜っ葉
leaf vegetables

... nabe　　　　　　... 鍋
hotpot made of .... Hotpot is a common winter dish.

nabemono　　　　　鍋物
general term for hotpot. The diner selects the raw ingredients and cooks them in the nabe pot.

nabeyaki-udon　　　鍋焼きうどん
udon noodles, seafood, meat, and vegetables cooked in a small pot

namagashi　　　　　生菓子
uncooked sweet paste confections filled with red an

namako　　　　　　なまこ
trepang (sea cucumber)

namasu　　　　　　なます
thinly cut, raw seafood or uncooked vegetables steeped in vinegar. Traditional Japanese dish.

nama-tamago　　　　生卵
raw egg

nama-zake　　　　　生酒
sake that has not been pasteurised

namazu　　　　　　なまず
catfish

nameko　　　　　　なめこ
a small, golden-brown mushroom with a gelatinous coating. Related to the matsutake.

nanban-zuke　　　　南蛮漬け
fried fish marinated in vinegar with sliced onions and chilli.

nanohana-zuke　　　菜の花漬け
rape shoot pickle from Kyoto

nare-zushi　　　　　なれずし
salted ayu pickled in vinegar and cooked rice

naruto-maki　　　　なると巻き
thinly sliced fish cake served in noodles, such as rāmen and udon. Same ingredients as kamaboko.

nashi　　　　　　　なし
Japanese pear

nasu　　　　　　　　なす
eggplant/aubergine

natane　　　　　　　菜種
rape seed

natane-fugu　　　　菜種ふぐ
end-of-season fugu, at it's tastiest and most poisonous

natsume　　　　　　なつめ
date

nattō　　　　　　　納豆
sticky, fermented soy beans. Known for their strong smell and stringy consistency, often eaten with hot rice.

negi　　　　　　　　ねぎ
spring onion, scallion, welsh onion

negima　　　　　　　ねぎま
1. tuna and spring onion stewed in a hotpot (Tokyo). 2. grilled spring onion and chicken meat on skewers. Served in yakitori restaurants.

niboshi　　　　　　煮干
dried anchovies. Used to make stock.

nigauri　　　　　　にがうり
balsam pear/bitter melon

nigiri-zushi　　　　にぎり寿司
hand-pressed sushi

nigori-zake　　　　にごり酒
cloudy sake

nihon-ryōri　　　　日本料理
Japanese cuisine

nihonshu　　　　　　日本酒
another word for sake

niji-masu　　　　　にじます
see kawa-masu

nikiri-mirin　　　　煮きりみりん
mirin with alcohol that is burned off prior to use

nikkorogashi　　　　煮っころがし
potatoes or taro stewed in shōyu-based stock

niku　　　　　　　　肉
meat

niku-dango　　　　　肉団子
meatball

niku-jaga　　　　　肉じゃが
potato and meat stew

nimono　　　　　　　煮物
simmered dishes

ninjin　　　　　　　にんじん
carrot

ninniku　　　　　　にんにく
garlic

nira　　　　　　　　にら
Chinese chives/garlic chives

nishin　　　　　　　にしん
Pacific herring/herring. Best in spring.

nitsuke　　　　　　　煮つけ
fish or vegetables simmered in savoury stock until almost all the liquid evaporates

niwatori　　　　　　にわとり
chicken

nomiya　　　　　　　飲み屋
Japanese-style bar

nori　　　　　　　　海苔
sea laver/type of seaweed formed into sheets and used to wrap sushi

nori-maki　　　　　海苔巻
sushi rolled in seaweed

noshi-ika　　　　　のしいか
dried, hand-rolled squid

nuka　　　　　　　　糠
rice bran

nuka-miso　　　　　糠味噌
fermented rice bran used as a base to make pickles

nuka-miso-zuke　　糠味噌漬け
pickles with fermented rice bran, left to mature

nuka-zuke　　　　　糠漬け
vegetables pickled in nuka-miso

nuta　　　　　　　　ぬた
clam or tuna with spring onion covered in vinegared miso

nyūmen　　　　　　にゅうめん
sōmen noodles in hot soup

O

o-age　　　　　　　おあげ
thinly sliced, especially thick tōfu traditionally fried in sesame oil

ocha　　　　　　　　お茶
Japanese green tea (see also bancha, matcha, ryokucha and sencha)

ochazuke　　　　　　お茶漬け
white rice with green tea poured onto it

oden　　　　　　　　おでん
hotpot with tōfu, konnyaku, fish-cake meatballs and potato stewed in stock. This food is called kantodaki in the Kansai region.

odori-gui　　　　　　おどり食い
shrimps or small fish, such as icefish and whiting, eaten live and dipped in vinegar or shōyu

ōgi gai　　　　　　　扇貝
'the fan shaped shellfish' – scallop

o-hagi　　　　　　　おはぎ
(see botamochi)

o-hitashi　　　　　　おひたし
lightly boiled, green-leaf vegetables served cold with light shōyu

okara　　　　　　　おから
lees from soy milk. Eaten mixed with finely chopped boiled vegetables. Also known as unohana.

o-kashi　　　　　　お菓子
general term for sweets

okashira-tsuki　　　　尾頭付き
fish dish when the whole fish is served, including the tail and head. Snapper or sea bream is often served this way on special occasions such as weddings and festivals.

o-kayu　　　　　　　おかゆ
rice porridge/congee

o-kazu　　　　　　　おかず
a (side) dish, accompanying rice, miso, soup and pickles

okonomi-yaki　　　　お好み焼き
Japanese-style savoury pancake

okura　　　　　　　オクラ
okra

omuraisu　　　　　　オムライス
omelette and rice

omuretsu　　　　　　オムレツ
omelette

onigarayaki　　　　　鬼殻焼き
prawns in the shell, grilled over hot coals

o nigiri　　　　　　おにぎり
rice ball

onsen-ryōri　　　　　温泉料理
hot-spa cuisine

onsen-tamago　　　　温泉たまご
spa-boiled egg

... oroshi　　　　　... おろし
grated ...

oroshi-shōga　　　　おろししょうが
grated ginger

osechi-ryōri　　　　おせち料理
various preserved dishes served at New Year festivals. Each dish has a special meaning such as health, wealth or happiness. Foods are served and stored in layered lacquer ware dishes over the New Year break.

o-shiruko　　　　　　お汁粉
grilled rice cake served with sweet, stewed azuki bean. Eaten during winter.

oshi-zushi　　　　　押しずし
pressed sushi. Vinegared rice is pressed into a square box and sushi ingredients layered on top (Kansai).

oyakodon　　　　　　親子丼
chicken and egg on rice

o-zōni　　　　　　　お雑煮
rice cake in soup. Eaten during winter, especially during New Year celebrations. Ingredients and flavours differ from region to region.

P

painappuru　　　　　パイナップル
pineapple

pan　　　　　　　　パン
bread/bread roll

panko　　　　　　　パン粉
breadcrumbs

papaiya　　　　　　パパイヤ
papaya

pīman　　　　　　　ピーマン
capsicum (usually green)

pōku　　　　　　　ポーク
pork (see also butaniku)

pōkusotē　　　　　　　ポークソテー
sauteed pork

ponkan　　　　　　　　ポンカン
a large type of citrus fruit

ponzu　　　　　　　　　ポン酢
originally the term for the juice from citrus fruits, it also refers to a mix of shoyū, dashi, citrus juices and sometimes vinegar. This mix is used as a dipping sauce for hotpots and in salad dressings.

potetofurai　　　　　　ポテトフライ
fried potato/french fries

R

rakkyō　　　　　　　　ラッキョウ
scallion/baker's garlic. Eaten pickled in vinegar.

rāmen　　　　　　　　　ラーメン
yellow wheat noodles, mostly served in hot broth

rebasashi　　　　　　　レバ刺し
liver sashimi

renkon　　　　　　　　　れんこん
lotus root

retasu　　　　　　　　　レタス
lettuce

ringo　　　　　　　　　りんご
apple

rōru-kyabetsu　　　　　ロールキャベツ
cabbage rolls

ryokan　　　　　　　　　旅館
Japanese style bed & breakfast (dinner also included)

ryokucha　　　　　　　緑茶
green tea

(...) ryōri　　　　　　　(...) 料理
(... style) cuisine

ryōtei　　　　　　　　　料亭
high-class Japanese restaurant

S

saba　　　　　　　　　　さば
chub mackerel/Pacific mackerel. Best in autumn. Eaten as shimesaba, saba no misoni, saba no nitsuke or fried (see also battera-zushi).

saba no misoni　　　　さばの味噌煮
chub mackerel simmered with miso

saba no nitsuke　　　　さばの煮付け
chub mackerel lightly pickled in vinegar

sadō　　　　　　　　　　茶道
tea ceremony

sakana　　　　　　　　　魚
fish

sake　　　　　　　　　　鮭
salmon/chum salmon/dog salmon. Also known as shake.

(o-) sake　　　　　　　（お）酒
known in the west as rice wine, sake is an alcohol made from a fermenting process that uses grain. Also a general term for alcoholic drinks.

sake-ate　　　　　　　　酒あて
accompaniments to sake and beer

sakekasu　　　　　　　　酒粕
lees from rice wine

sakura-masu　　　　　　桜マス
cherry salmon

sakura-mochi　　　　　　桜餅
pink rice cake wrapped in a cherry leaf

sakuranbo　　　　　　　さくらんぼ
cherry

sakura-niku　　　　　　さくら肉
horse meat

sanjin-ryōri　　　　　　山人料理
'mountain man food', from Fukushima, Tōhoku

sanma　　　　　　　　　さんま
pacific saury/saury pike. Best in October. Most often eaten grilled and occasionally raw.

sansai　　　　　　　　　山菜
edible, wild mountain vegetables

sansai-ryōri　　　　　　山菜料理
mountain vegetable cuisine

sanshō　　　　　　　　　山椒
Japanese prickly ash pod, Sichuan pepper

sarashi negi　　　　　　さらしねぎ
spring onion, soaked in water to reduce its sharpness, drained and thinly sliced

sasage　　　　　　　　さ さげ
black-eyed peas

sashimi　　　　　　　　刺身
raw fish or meat

satō　　　　　　　　　砂糖
sugar

satoimo　　　　　　　サトイモ
taro. Often used in stewed food
(Chiba, Miyazaki and Kagoshima
Prefectures).

satsuma-age　　　　さつま揚げ
minced fish meat mixed with finely
chopped vegetables, then fried in
sesame oil. Used in nimono and oden.

satsuma-imo　　　　サツマイモ
sweet potato

sawachi-ryōri　　　　皿鉢料理
celebratory cuisine with vegetables,
seafood, nimono and agemono piled
on one large platter, from Kōchi,
Shikoku

sawa-gani　　　　　　沢がに
freshwater crab, often served deep-
fried in kara-age

sawara　　　　　　　　さわら
spotted mackerel/Spanish mackerel

sayaendō　　　　　さやえんどう
snow pea

saya-ingen　　　　　サヤインゲン
string beans

sayori　　　　　　　　さより
garfish/halfbeak/snipe fish. Best in
spring and autumn.

sazae　　　　　　　　さざえ
whelk

sazae no　　　　　　さざえの
tsubo-yaki　　　　　つぼ焼き
whelk, grilled in the shell

seishu　　　　　　　　清酒
sake. Generic term for clear rice wine.

seki-han　　　　　　　赤飯
'red rice' with azuki beans, eaten
at times of celebration

senbei　　　　　　　　煎餅
rice cracker

sencha　　　　　　　　煎茶
a typical Japanese green tea

sendai-miso　　　　　仙台味噌
salty miso from Miyagi Prefecture

sengiri　　　　　　　　千切り
vegetables thinly sliced lengthways,
julienne

senmai-zuke　　　　　千枚漬け
large turnips pickled in sweet vinegar
(Kyoto)

seri　　　　　　　　　　せり
water dropwort. Used as vegetable in
sukiyaki, soups and salads.

serori　　　　　　　　セロリ
celery

shabu-shabu　　　しゃぶしゃぶ
thinly sliced beef dipped into a boiling
hotpot, then into sesame or ponzu
sauces

shako　　　　　　　　しゃこ
squilla/mantis shrimp. Boiled in salted
water for use in sushi.

shakushi-gai　　　　　杓子貝
(see itaya-gai)

shiba-ebi　　　　　　芝エビ
shiba shrimp/prawn

shichibuzuki　　　　　七分づき
70% white, 30% brown rice

shichimi-tōgarashi　　七味唐辛子
a blend of seven spices including
chilli. It is a popular condiment for
noodle dishes and nabemono.

shiitake　　　　　　　しいたけ
shiitake mushroom

shika-niku　　　　　　鹿肉
venison

shimaaji　　　　　　　しまあじ
crevalle jack. Highly sought-after fish
used in sashimi, sushi and also eaten
grilled.

shima-dōfu　　　　　しまどうふ
hard tōfu suited to frying, from
Okinawa

shimeji　　　　　　　　しめじ
a type of mushroom. Best in autumn.

shimesaba　　　　　　しめさば
vinegared mackerel

shimofuri (gyūniku) 霜降り（牛肉）
marbled (beef)

shinachiku シナチク
pickled Chinese bamboo sprouts

shincha 新茶
new-season green tea. Usually available in stores in early summer.

shinshū-miso 信州味噌
miso from Nagano Prefecture

shio 塩
salt

shio-boshi-wakame 塩干しワカメ
wakame washed in salt water, then dried.

shiokara 塩辛
seafood pickled with salt

shio-nuki-wakame 塩抜きワカメ
wakame washed in plain, unsalted water, and dried

shio-yaki 塩焼き
salted and grilled food

shio-zuke 塩漬け
vegetables, meat or seafood pickled in salt

shippoku-ryōri 卓袱料理
a refined banquet cuisine from Nagasaki, an amalgam of Japanese and Chinese dishes

shirako 白子
milt

shirashime-yu 白絞め油
salad oil, normally rape seed oil

shirasu-boshi しらす干し
boiled and dried young anchovies or pilchards

shirataki しらたき
konnyaku in noodle form

shirauo しらうお
icefish

shiroae 白和え
vegetables mixed with sauce made from tōfu

shiro-amadai 白あまだい
white amadai

shiro-gohan 白ご飯
white rice

shiro-goma 白ごま
white sesame seed

shiro-miso 白味噌
white miso

shiromi-zakana 白身魚
white-fleshed fish

shirouo しろうお
ice goby – a type of fish eaten live, a practice carried out in Fukuoka

shiro-zake 白酒
white, cloudy rice wine

... shiru/... jiru ... 汁
... soup/... juice

shishamo ししゃも
capelin/longfin smelt/night smelt (Hokkaidō). Usually dried and eaten grilled.

shiso しそ
beefsteak plant/perilla (a member of the mint family). Used as a condiment and colouring and as a flavouring for pickles.

shitabirame シタビラメ
sole

shōchū 焼酎
distilled spirit made from sweet potato, rice, millet or lees from rice wine. Alcoholic content is normally between 35% and 45%.

shōga しょうが
ginger

shōga-su しょうが酢
ginger vinegar

shōga-yaki しょうが焼き
grilled meat or fish flavoured with ginger and shōyu

shōga-yu しょうが湯
ginger and hot water – a traditional cure

shōjin-age 精進揚げ
vegetarian tempura

shōjin-ryōri 精進料理
traditional vegetarian food. Originally developed for vegetarian Buddhist monks.

shokudō 食堂
cheap restaurant or dining hall

shokupan 食パン
square-shaped loaf of bread

shottsuru　　　　　しょっつる
　fermented fish sauce made from
　hata-hata (Akita Prefecture)
shōyu　　　　　　　　醤油
　soy sauce. Made from fermented soy
　beans and wheat. Basic ingredient
　in Japanese dishes.
shōyu-yaki　　　　しょうゆ焼き
　grilled with shōyu
shōyu-zuke　　　　　醤油漬け
　vegetables pickled in shōyu
shūmai　　　　　　シュウマイ
　steamed, round Chinese dumplings
shungiku　　　　　　　春菊
　crown daisy/garland chrysanthemum.
　Eaten as o-hitashi, aemono and nabe.
shutō　　　　　　　　酒盗
　Salted and fermented katsuo intestine.
　Considered a good accompaniment for
　drinking sake.
soba　　　　　　　　　そば
　buckwheat; noodles made of
　buckwheat
soba-cha　　　　　　そば茶
　buckwheat tea
soba-gaki　　　　　　そばがき
　dough made of buckwheat flour mixed
　with boiled water
sōmen　　　　　　　そうめん
　fine wheat noodles. Usually eaten
　cold and dipped in sauce. In hot
　soup they are called nyūmen.
sora-mame　　　　　　そら豆
　broad bean
sōsu　　　　　　　　　ソース
　sauce
su　　　　　　　　　　　酢
　vinegar
sugata-mushi　　　　　姿蒸し
　steamed whole fish
suguki　　　　　　　　酢茎
　turnip pickle, from Kyoto
suika　　　　　　　　すいか
　watermelon
suikuchi　　　　　　吸い口
　topping for clear soup

suimono　　　　　　　吸い物
　clear Japanese soup made of fish
　stock. Also known as sumashi (jiru).
suiton　　　　　　　すいとん
　balls made of wheat flour, boiled with
　vegetables in soup. Associated with the
　economic depression of World War
　II.
suji　　　　　　　　　スジ
　sinew/tendon of pork or beef. Term
　used in yakitori restaurants.
sujiko　　　　　　　　すじこ
　salted salmon roe
sukiyaki　　　　　　すき焼き
　beef, tōfu, vegetables and shirataki
　cooked in an iron pan with shōyu,
　sugar and sake. Served with raw egg
　dip.
sumashi (jiru)　　　澄まし (汁)
　(see suimono)
su-meshi　　　　　　　酢飯
　vinegered rice used for sushi
sumibi-yaki　　　　　炭火焼き
　charcoal-grilled food
su-miso　　　　　　　酢味噌
　sauce made of vinegar and miso
sunomono　　　　　　酢の物
　vinegared food
suppon　　　　　　　スッポン
　snapping turtle
suppon-nabe　　　　すっぽん鍋
　hotpot of suppon
suppon-ryōri　　　スッポン料理
　snapping turtle served as nabemono,
　sashimi, or deep-fried
sūpu　　　　　　　　　スープ
　soup
surigoma　　　　　　すりごま
　ground sesame
surume　　　　　　　　スルメ
　dried squid
sushi　　　　　　　　　寿司
　any food, most likely raw fish and
　seafood (sometimes raw vegetables or
　cooked egg) served on or rolled in
　vinegared rice

sushi-dane 寿司種
sushi topping

sushi-meshi 寿司飯
vinegared rice for sushi

sushi-ya 寿司屋
sushi bar

suyaki 素焼き
plainly grilled without salt

su-zuke 酢漬け
vinegared pickles

suzuki スズキ
common sea bass/Japanese sea-perch. Eaten raw, grilled or fried.

suzuki no スズキの
hōsho-yaki 奉書焼き
grilled sea bass. Served wrapped in traditional Japanese paper (Matsue, Shimane Prefecture).

suzume すずめ
sparrow. Served at yakitori restaurants.

T

tachiuo タチウオ
cutlass fish/hairtail

tai たい
snapper/bream

taira-gai たいら貝／たいらぎ
fan shell, sea pen.

tai-ryōri 鯛料理
sea bream cuisine

taishō-ebi 大正エビ
fleshy prawn

takana 高菜
broad-leafed mustard

takana-zuke 高菜漬け
mustard leaf pickles

taka-no-tsume 鷹の爪
red-hot peppers

take-no-ko たけのこ
bamboo shoots

takikomi-gohan 炊き込み御飯
rice cooked together with various vegetables and seasonings

tako たこ
octopus

tako-yaki たこ焼き
balls made of flour with octopus inside (Osaka)

takuan たくあん
pickled daikon

tamago 卵
egg

tamago-toji 卵とじ
cooked vegetables or meat covered with whisked egg

tamago-yaki 卵焼き
Japanese-style fried egg/omelette

tama-negi たまねぎ
onion

tamari-dōfu たまりどうふ
tōfu infused with egg

tamari-jōyu たまり醤油
wheat-free shōyu

tara たら
cod/Pacific cod/grey cod. Cod meat and offal (eg, milt, kikuko) are used in hotpot, nimono, and also eaten dried. Best between January and February.

taraba-gani たらばがに
Alaskan crab/king crab

tarako たらこ
salted cod or collack roe

taranome たらのめ
angelica tree sprout. Eaten fried as tempura, o-hitashi or nitsuke. Available only in early spring.

tare たれ
sauce. Usually made from shōyu, mirin and sugar, boiled until thickened.

tataki たたき
1. raw fish flesh served minced. 2. meat or fish seared on the outside and served sliced, with the inside remaining rare.

tatsuta-age 竜田揚げ
meat or fish dipped in shōyu and seasoned flour then deep-fried

teishoku 定食
set menu

tekkadon 鉄火丼
tuna sashimi on a large bowl of steamed rice

tekka-maki 鉄火巻き
tuna sushi roll

temaki-zushi 手巻きずし
do-it-yourself sushi roll

tendon 天丼
battered prawn on rice

tempura てんぷら
the English term for seafood, meat and vegetables deep-fried in light batter. Eaten dipped in a light sauce with ginger and grated daikon. The Japanese term is tenpura.

tempura-soba/ てんぷらそば/
-udon うどん
buckwheat/wheat flour noodles in broth with tempura pieces on top

teriyaki 照り焼き
meat or fish, brushed with shōyu, mirin and sugar marinade, then grilled

tessa てっさ
fugu sashimi

teuchi-soba 手打ちそば
traditional, handmade soba

tobiuo とびうお
flying fish

tōfu とうふ
soy bean curd

tōgarashi とうがらし
red chilli pepper

tokishirazu ときしらず
(see aramaki-zake)

tomato トマト
tomato

tōmorokoshi とうもろこし
corn

tonkotsu とんこつ
pork broth

tonkotsu-rāmen とんこつラーメン
rāmen with white pork broth

tōnyū 豆乳
soy milk

tora-fugu とらふぐ
tiger fugu, used as sashimi and in nabemono

tora-mame とら豆
tiger beans

toriniku 鶏肉
chicken

toro とろ
the fattiest (and also considered the tastiest) meat of tuna fish maguro

tororo-jiru とろろ汁
grated yam mixed with stock, creating a slimy, thick, soup-like substance

tsubame uo ツバメ魚
swallow fish; a type of batfish

tsubo-yaki つぼ焼き
1. shellfish (normally whelks) grilled in its own shell. 2. pot-grilled

tsukeawase 付け合せ
garnish, relish

tsukemono 漬物
pickles

tsukimi-soba/ 月見そば/うどん
-udon buckwheat/wheat flour noodles in broth with a raw egg

tsukudani 佃煮
seafood or vegetables simmered in a thick sauce made from salt, sugar and shōyu until all moisture is reduced

tsukune つくね
minced fish or chicken balls eaten fried or boiled

tsukuri 造り
slices of raw fish, another term for sashimi

tsuma つま
garnish

tsumire つみれ
fish-cake balls. Used in oden and stew.

tsuyu つゆ
dipping sauce

U

uba-gai うば貝
hen clam. Also known as hokki-gai.

udo うど
mountain vegetable eaten fresh in salad, stewed or pickled

udon　　　　　　　　うどん
thick noodles made of wheat flour

uikyō　　　　　　　ウイキョウ
fennel. Also known as fenneru.

uirō　　　　　　　　ういろう
steamed sweet made of rice flour and arrowroot (Nagoya)

uisukī　　　　　　　ウィスキー
whisky

ukon　　　　　　　　ウコン
turmeric

umami　　　　　　　旨み
an element of taste that refers to how tasty the food is

ume　　　　　　　　梅
Japanese plum

umeboshi　　　　　　梅干
dried and pickled Japanese plum

ume-zu　　　　　　　梅酢
sour-plum vinegar

uminomono　　　　　海のもの
seafood

umi-zakana　　　　　海魚
seafish

una-don　　　　　　　うな丼
grilled eel on rice

unagi　　　　　　　うなぎ
eel

unagi no kabayaki　　うなぎの蒲焼
grilled eel flavoured with soy-based sauce

unajū　　　　　　　　うな重
grilled eel served on rice in a lacquered box

uni　　　　　　　　うに
sea urchin. Sea urchin roe is eaten fresh in sushi and also preserved in salt.

unohana　　　　　　卯の花
(see okara)

uroko　　　　　　　うろこ
fish scales

ūroncha　　　　　　烏龍茶
oolong tea

uruchimai　　　　　うるち米
nonglutinous rice

uruka　　　　　　　ウルカ
salted innards of ayu

urume-iwashi　　　ウルメイワシ
Japanese sardine

ushio-jiru　　　　　うしお汁
delicately flavoured clear soup made from fish and shellfish

usuaji　　　　　　　薄味
light-tasting, or lightly seasoned

usucha　　　　　　　薄茶
thinner tea than koicha

usukuchi-shōyu　　うす口醤油
light shōyu

usuzukuri　　　　　薄作り
raw, thinly sliced fugu flesh

uzura-tamago　　　うずらたまご
quail egg

W

wagashi　　　　　　和菓子
Japanese sweets

wagyū　　　　　　　和牛
Japanese beef

wain　　　　　　　ワイン
wine

wakame　　　　　　ワカメ
type of seaweed

wakasagi　　　　　わかさぎ
pond smelt. Freshwater fish caught in icy cold lakes.

wakegi　　　　　　わけぎ
shallots

wani　　　　　　　わに
shark meat. In modern Japanese wani refers to crocodile, but originally it was used in reference to shark. Speciality of the Chūgoku region. Shark meat is less popular in other areas of Japan.

wantan-men　　　ワンタン麺
rāmen noodles in broth, with meat dumplings

warabi　　　　　　わらび
a kind of fern. Tender, young shoots are eaten.

waramaki-buri　　藁巻きぶり
salted and dried buri, which is then rolled in straw (Toyama Prefecture)

warishita 割り下
sauce of shoyu, mirin and sugar, used in sukiyaki

wasabi ワサビ
Japanese horseradish. Very hot.

wasabi-maki ワサビ巻き
sushi roll containing wasabi

wasabi-zuke ワサビ漬け
vegetables pickled in a wasabi base

wata わた
see harawata

watari-gani わたりがに
blue swimmer crab

Y

... ya ... 屋
...shop/...restaurant, eg, sushi-ya, tōfu-ya

... yaki/yaki ... 焼き／焼き ...
food that is grilled, baked, barbecued or pan-fried

yaki-dōfu 焼き豆腐
grilled tōfu. Used in hotpots.

yaki-gyōza 焼きギョウザ
grilled gyōza dumpling

yaki-meshi 焼き飯
fried rice. Also known as chāhan.

yaki-mochi 焼き餅
toasted rice cake

yakimono 焼きもの
broiled, grilled or pan-fried dishes

yakinasu 焼きナス
grilled eggplant, eaten hot or cold with grated ginger and shōyu. Summer food.

yaki-niku 焼肉
cook-it-yourself, Korean-style barbecue

yaki-nori 焼き海苔
lightly toasted nori

yaki o-nigiri 焼きおにぎり
grilled rice ball

yakisoba 焼きそば
fried noodles with vegetables and meat

yakitori 焼きとり
grilled meat on skewers served with tare or salt

yaki-zakana 焼き魚
grilled fish

yakumi 薬味
condiment/relish/seasoning

yama-imo 山芋
see yamano-imo

yamakake 山かけ
grated yam with seasoning. Sometimes served on top of tuna sashimi (*see also* mugitoro).

yama-kujira 山鯨
'mountain whale' – the renamed inoshishi

yamame ヤマメ
freshwater salmon

yamano-imo ヤマノイモ
yam. Also known as yama-imo.

yamanomono 山のもの
mountain dishes

yanagawa-nabe 柳川鍋
loach or weatherfish boiled in a shallow pan and with whisked eggs on top

yasai 野菜
vegetable

yatsugashira 八ッ頭
most-sought after type of taro

yatsuhashi 八橋
sweet cinnamon-flavoured hard crackers (Kyoto)

yōkan 羊羹
sweet jelly made of ground azuki beans

yomogi ヨモギ
mugwort

yōnashi 洋ナシ
pear (*see also* nashi)

yose-nabe 寄せ鍋
hotpot with seafood, chicken, and vegetables in a light stock

yōshoku 洋食
Japanese versions of Western dishes, eg, tonkatsu, omuraisu and karē-raisu

yuba ゆば
thin layers of skin skimmed from boiled soy milk. Can be used fresh, or dried

yude-gyōza ゆでギョウザ
boiled gyōza dumpling

yude-tamago ゆでたまご
boiled eggs

yu-dōfu 湯豆腐
tōfu boiled in a weak konbu broth

yūgao ユウガオ
white-flower gourd/bottle gourd. Peeled into thin strips, dried then reconstituted and simmered in shōyu (*see* kanpyō).

yushi-dōfu ゆし豆腐
a soft variety of tōfu, from Okinawa

yuzu ゆず
a type of citrus fruit. The tangy juice is used in various hotpot dishes and the skin is sliced for use in soups, steamed foods and sweets.

Z

zaru-soba ざるそば
cold buckwheat noodles served with nori, spring onion and wasabi

zenmai ゼンマイ
osmund/royal fern (a type of mountain vegetable)

zenzai ぜんざい
sweet azuki bean soup with rice cakes added

zomeki-ryōri ぞめき料理
cuisine of local vegetables and seafood, from Tokushima Prefecture

zōsui 雑炊
rice gruel/soup with vegetables and seafood flavoured with miso or shōyu.

zuiki ずいき
taro stem

zuwai-gani ズワイガニ
red crab/snow crab

Recommended Reading

Barr, Pat *The Deer Cry Pavilion* Macmillan (1968)

Booth, Alan *The Roads to Sata: A 2000 Mile Walk Through Japan* Penguin Travel Library (1985)

Chamberlain, Basil Hall *Things Japanese* London (1891)

Cortazzi, Sir Hugh *Victorians in Japan* The Athlone Press (1987)

Dogen & Uchiyama, translation by Thomas Wright *Refining Your Life: From the Zen Kitchen To Enlightenment* Weatherhill (1983)

Durston, Diane *Old Kyoto: A Guide to Traditional Shops, Restaurants & Inns* Kodansha International (1986)

Harper, Phillip *The Insider's Guide to Sake* Kodansha International (1998)

Hosking, Prof Richard *A Dictionary of Japanese Food: Ingredients & Culture* Charles E. Tuttle (1996)

The Kodansha Encyclopaedia of Japan Kodansha International (1993)

Kosaki, Takayuki & Walter Wagner *The Food of Japan: Authentic Recipes from the Land of the Rising Sun* Periplus (1997)

Kyoto Journal published by Heian Bunka Centre

Nihon wo shiru hyaku sho: 100 Key Words for Understanding Japan (*Taiyo Magazine* special issue), published by Heibonsha (1993)

Omae, Kinjiro & Yuzuru Tachibana *The Book of Sushi* Kodansha International (1995)

Richie, Donald *A Taste of Japan* Kodansha International (1985)

Sarai Magazine published by Shogakkan

Shurtleff, William & Akiko Aoyagi *The Book of Tofu: Protein Source of the Future – Now!* Ballantyne Books (1979)

Shurtleff, William & Akiko Aoyagi *The Book of Miso: Food for Mankind* Ballantyne Books (1981)

Tanizaki, Junichiro, translation by Thomas J. Harper & Edward G. Seidensticker *In Praise of Shadows* Charles E. Tuttle (1977)

Tsujii, Shizuo *Japanese Cooking: A Simple Art* Kodansha International (1980)

Udesky, James *The Book of Soba* Kodansha International (1995)

Yoneda, Soei & Koei Hoshino *Zen Vegetarian Cooking* Kodansha International (1998)

Yoshida, Mitsukuni & Sesoko Tsune *Naorai: Communion of the Table* Mazda (1989)

Web sites

www.bento.com

www.kampo.co.jp/kyoto-journal

Recipes

Boxed Text

Maps

The Lonely Planet Story

Lonely Planet published its first book in 1973 in response to the numerous 'How did you do it?' questions Maureen and Tony Wheeler were asked after driving, bussing, hitching, sailing and railing their way from England to Australia. Written at a kitchen table and hand collated, trimmed and stapled, Across Asia on the Cheap became an instant local bestseller.

Eighteen months in South-East Asia resulted in their second guide, South-East Asia on a Shoestring, which they put together in a backstreet Chinese hotel in Singapore in 1975. The 'yellow bible', as it quickly became known to backpackers around the world, soon became the guide to the region. It has sold well over ¾ million copies and is now in its 10th edition, still retaining its familiar yellow cover.

Today there are over 400 titles, including travel guides, walking guides, language kits & phrasebooks, travel atlases & maps, diving guides, restaurant guides, first time travel guides, condensed guides, illustrated pictorials and travel literature. The company is the largest independent travel publisher in the world.

The emphasis continues to be on travel for independent travellers. Tony and Maureen still travel for several months of each year and play an active part in the writing, updating and quality control of Lonely Planet's guides.

They have been joined by over 120 authors and over 400 staff at our offices in Melbourne (Australia), Oakland (USA), London (UK) and Paris (France). Travellers themselves also make a valuable contribution to the guides through the feedback we receive in thousands of letters each year and on our web site.

The people at Lonely Planet strongly believe that travellers can make a positive contribution to the countries they visit, both through their appreciation of the countries' culture, wildlife and natural features, and through the money they spend. In addition, the company makes a direct contribution to the countries and regions it covers. Since 1986 a percentage of the income from each book has been donated to ventures such as famine relief in Africa; aid projects in India; agricultural projects in Central America; Greenpeace's efforts to halt French nuclear testing in the Pacific.

Lonely Planet Offices

Australia
90 Maribyrnong Street Footscray, Victoria, 3011
☎ 03 8379 8000
fax 03 8379 8111
email: talk2us@lonelyplanet.com.au

USA
150 Linden St, Oakland, CA 94607
☎ 510 893 8555 TOLL FREE: 800 275 8555
fax 510 893 8572
email: info@lonelyplanet.com

UK
10a Spring Place, London NW5 3BH
☎ 020 7428 4800
fax 020 7428 4828
email: go@lonelyplanet.co.uk

France
1 rue du Dahomey, 75011 Paris
☎ 01 55 25 33 00
fax 01 55 25 33 01
email: bip@lonelyplanet.fr